THE COURT OF
BLUE SHADOWS

Also by Maynard Allington

The Grey Wolf
The Fox in the Field

THE COURT OF BLUE SHADOWS

A Novel

MAYNARD ALLINGTON

BRASSEY'S
Washington • London

Library of Congress Cataloging-in-Publication Data

Allington, Maynard.
   The court of blue shadows: a novel/Maynard Allington.
      p.   cm.
   ISBN 0-02-881104-6
PS3551.L449C68   1994   94-20236
813'.54—dc20   CIP

10 9 8 7 6 5 4 3 2 1

Printed in the United States of America

The author gratefully acknowledges the help of Michael Tuchman, M.D., Fellow of the American Academy of Neurology, past president of the Florida Society of Neurology, and currently a practicing psychiatrist and neurologist in Palm Beach, Florida. Any errors relating to memory dysfunction, as depicted in this novel, are the fault of the author, not of Dr. Tuchman.

PART ONE

JOSEF NEUMANN

ONE

The spring welled up, cold and clear, and the man lay flat in the grass on the bank and drank from the pool. The black hair at his sunburnt neck needed cutting, and his shirt, patched and faded, was streaked with sweat where the harness straps of the haversack looped across his shoulders.

He pushed up on his hands, his face darkly emblazoned among the sky images on the water. A scar in the shape of a cuneiform wedge was indented high up on one flat cheek, and the broad mouth looked as if some defiant humor were about to break from it. But there was no humor in the eyes, only a cold resistance in the pupils, which were blue and pale as winter light.

The man was a refugee with no identity. Whole sectors of his mind were blacked out. American troops reaching Dachau in the last days of the war had found him covered with blood and excrement among several dozen corpses in a mass grave outside the camp. Flies swarmed over the bodies, already starting to bloat, and maggots fed on the sclera of sockets. Here and there the squirming larval tubes attacked a tongue in an open mouth. All the victims had been shot from behind above a trench, and the bodies heaped on each other. In their haste to retreat, the SS guards had not bothered to close the grave. Nor, in the case of the man who had no memory, had they executed prudent marksmanship. The bullet had only clipped the skull behind one ear.

For ten days he had remained in a coma. In the rush to save his life, no effort had been made to identify him. But the medics had noted one odd feature that set him apart from the others in the mass grave—the tattooed number had been surgically excised from his arm. Apparently the prisoners who had been shot and thrown into the trench carried some incriminating secret, and they might have disappeared without a trace except for the arrival of American units. As for the survivor—inmates still at the camp after liberation could not identify him, and officers theorized that he had been transported to Dachau from another camp only days, perhaps even hours, before the bungled murder.

Doctors at the refugee center, where he was sent to convalesce, could not fix the cause of his amnesia. Loss of memory could have occurred in the course of blunt trauma to the head, or it might be linked to a dissociative reaction triggered, possibly, by the mass execution.

The man was articulate, and the doctors were surprised to discover that he was fluent in several languages, including Greek. They estimated his age to be no more than a year or two past thirty. Apart from recurring headaches and the impaired memory, he showed no long-term disabling effects from his ordeal, and by midsummer he had recovered enough strength to leave the DP center. While there, he had been the subject of several interviews by an American major from Counterintelligence whose job was to gather information about war crimes.

This officer's name was Ward. He was short, compactly built, and below a rust-red pompadour his face was full of blunt edges, as if a planing tool had been used on it. He remained puzzled about the sphere of scar tissue where the tattooed number had been removed from the other man's forearm.

"Why would they bother to take it off if they were going to get rid of you anyway?"

"Maybe I did it myself."

"The sutures were still in. You couldn't very well have tied them yourself."

"Then maybe we were escaped prisoners."

"You were the only one missing a serial number. There has to be a reason."

"You won't get the answer from anyone in the trench."

"No," the major agreed, and asked what name the other man wanted on his release papers and identity card.

The man shrugged and replied, "Does it matter?"

Well," the officer remarked, "you're a new man."

So he had taken the surname *Neumann*, if only for its phonetic irony, and added *Josef* to it.

Major Ward handed over the papers and said, "Where will you go?"

"South."

"You won't find much work there—other than farm labor."

"It's not important."

"I can give you the name of an ex-Bürgermeister if you want to stay in the lake country. He works for us, now, and he knows the area."

Neumann thanked him.

The major said, "I wish you luck—Josef."

The man at the spring stirred the mirror surface with his hand, obliterating the face of Neumann, but it only came back, the resistance unbroken in it. Ten months on a farm in Bavaria had been served like a sentence at hard labor for an unspecified crime. The reflected image on the water was only a piece of circumstantial evidence to prove that the missing person had once existed.

The letter from Major Ward had come two days ago, and it had taken a moment to connect the name to the Intelligence officer who had looked into his case at the DP camp almost a year earlier. The American was now in Munich as a CIC liaison officer with the War Crimes Commission, and he had tracked Neumann through the ex-Bürgermeister to the farm in the lake country. New information had come to light that might identify him, the major wrote, and asked Neumann to contact him. The letter was cleverly short on details, like an incentive to curiosity rather than hope.

Neumann stood up, shifting the weight of the haversack on his wide shoulders, and gazed at the white dusty road beyond a line of poplars. It ran north, past the sunny glint of fields and dark patches of forest, toward Munich, and he set out along it, his blanket roll under his arm.

TWO

In Munich, Neumann went directly to the district headquarters of the War Crimes Office on the Ludwigstrasse. Major Ward had a cramped space on the second floor above a courtyard. The door was open, and Neumann had a glimpse of him at a littered desk. His head was bent over a document held in both square hands, one of which had a cigarette in the blunt grip of two fingers. The smoke trailed upward past the red pompadour, tightly waved, like the crimp of a marcel. The officer raised his head, saw Neumann in the hall, and a smile dispersed the lines of concentration in his face.

"Come in, Josef. Sit down. Would you like some coffee?"

They shook hands, and Neumann replied, "No, thank you."

"Cigarette?"

Neumann glanced at the pack. In the street, American cigarettes were a more stable currency than the German mark. But he did not smoke, and some stupid pride prevented him from taking a cigarette and slipping it into his pocket. Pride was an inflated psychological luxury. Unlike a cigarette, it could not be bartered on the black market.

"So you've been on a farm," Major Ward said, "all this time?"

Neumann had the feeling the officer had known exactly where he was all along. He said, "Better than a refugee camp," and glanced out the open casement window at the courtyard below. A few scrawny pigeons poked about in the shade of a dry stone fountain crowned by a statue of Eros, missing a wing. A dead tree cast its emaciated shadow across the sunny gleam of cobbles. Everything, these days, was dead or broken. Why should his memory be any exception?

They chatted for a bit, and Neumann said, "You have some news. . . ."

Major Ward crushed the stub of his cigarette in a side-to-side movement of his fingers.

"Alina Levin," he said, looking at Neumann. "Does the name mean anything?"

Neumann stared back through a reflective frown.

"No," he said finally. "Who is she?"

"A doctor. Jewish. She was at Auschwitz. As an inmate physician, she had certain privileges."

Neumann smiled coldly.

"Not to be gassed, you mean?"

"I suppose that was one of the benefits."

Major Ward opened a folder and thumbed through a sheaf of papers.

"After the Russians liberated the camp," he said, "Dr. Levin was able to smuggle out a few items. This, for instance."

The officer drew a snapshot from the file and laid it on the desk in front of Neumann. It was a group photo of prisoners in their striped rags. Some distance behind them, the tall stack of the crematorium trailed a black wisp into the mother-of-pearl sky.

"Taken at Auschwitz," Major Ward said.

Neumann only shrugged.

"What does it have to do with me?"

"Better look again," the American said. "One of them is you."

The clang of an iron gate in the courtyard alarmed the pigeons, and they fluttered past the window with a loud beating of wings. Neumann did not want to pick up the snapshot.

"Use this." The officer held out a magnifying glass.

The face—Neumann's—jumped out of the second rank of prisoners onto the lens. There it remained, like an exhibit of evidence to contradict his current existence—more genuine, somehow, than the person known as Josef Neumann who was only a forgery.

"Were you ever at Auschwitz?" Major Ward said.

"I don't know."

"It would seem that you were."

"How do you explain it?" Neumann said.

"You'll have to ask the man in the photograph."

Once more, Neumann steadied the glass over the snapshot. The features were stunningly accurate. There could be no mistaking the oblong slant of the eyes under the black diagonal brows, the flat cheeks, or the strong, planed shape of the mouth.

"Did he have a name?"

"Krenek," the major replied.

Since his first glimpse of the photo Neumann felt as though his head had been clamped into a vise. Now the steel threads of the lever were turning, squeezing the plates together until his skull began to pound.

"You don't recognize the name?" Major Ward asked.

"No." Neumann shook his head.

The American leaned back in his chair, his eyes quizzical over the plume of a new cigarette.

"That's not to say you won't."

"What happened to him?" Neumann said.

"Dr. Levin isn't sure. He may have been gassed at Auschwitz, or . . ."

"Or?" Neumann pressed him.

"Shot in the head outside Dachau."

Neumann's hand went involuntarily to the welt of infertile flesh in the scalp behind his ear.

"Will Dr. Levin talk to me?" he said.

"I can give her a call," Major Ward said. He smiled and added, "Which is to say, I can call the U.S. billet, two houses over. The CQ can send a runner to her place. She has no telephone."

They chatted for ten minutes, waiting for a return call. It came, and while the officer was on the phone, Neumann glanced down into the courtyard. Two GIs were in laughing conversation with a German secretary. The girl sat in the sun on the edge of the stone fountain, the soldiers slouching in front of her, while Eros presided. The taller GI offered her a cigarette. It went into her bodice, like a deposit into a vault. Major Ward hung up the phone.

"She'll see you," he said. "My sergeant can run you there in the jeep."

It was only a short drive past the shells of government buildings on the Maximilianstrasse to the residential district where the scavenged rubble lay in piles. The sergeant let him out before a house that looked to be fairly intact behind a partially collapsed stone wall.

The gate was missing, and Neumann went in past the charred, jagged stump of a tree to the front door. A bronze plaque, affixed to the outer wall, read: LEVIN GALLERY. The bell did not work. He knocked and waited.

The woman who opened the door was slim in a dark dress that had probably been elegant at one time. She looked to be in her mid-thirties, though her face was still unlined and the skin smooth over angular cheekbones. Cut not quite to shoulder length, her hair had the shine of silver, as if it had been struck in some instant of alchemy. The luxuriant gleam of youth still clung to it, despite the contradiction of its color. Above the straight, unsmiling mouth, the eyes were gray and desolate, a terrain of emotional scorched earth left behind after the retreat of feelings from it.

"Dr. Levin?" he asked.

"Herr Neumann?" she replied, and suddenly her eyes widened as the empty distances in them filled with confused disbelief. Shock paled itself into her cheeks and left her lips parted.

Finally he said, "Are you all right?"

She recovered her composure and said, "Please come in."

A hall paneled in dark wood stretched back from a stairwell, and he could make out several faces peering at him from doors that had been opened a crack in the unlit gloom. She led him upstairs to a sitting room, small and sparsely furnished.

"I keep only two rooms in the house, now. The rest are occupied by people who lost their homes in the bombing raids. There was some damage to this one in the rear, but we were able to close that portion off. My father was an art dealer before the war. The rooms downstairs were his gallery."

"You're lucky to have it back still standing."

"It was taken over by the Nazi official who denounced us to the Gestapo. He's disappeared, of course. My father was less lucky. He contracted typhus in one of the camps after only a few weeks."

"I'm sorry," Neumann murmured.

"Perhaps it was better to go quickly," she said. "The survivors died in a different way. It's a death they have to live with."

"Unless they've lost the memory of it," he said.

She gazed at him and said, "I am afraid you startled me, Herr Neumann. It is quite an extraordinary resemblance."

"To the man in Auschwitz?"

"Krenek was his name." She nodded. "Sit down, won't you?"

She took a chair opposite him, her crossed legs locked into a long elegant line. But it was the pale, slim hands, smoothing the dress over her knees, that drew his attention. Some economy of motion in them suggested a neglected skill.

"What can you tell me about him?" Neumann said.

"Not a great deal, unfortunately. Someone told me he was a painter. My father knew many artists before the war. They often came here to the gallery. I don't recall any mention of the name Krenek, and I can't say I'm familiar with any of his work."

"Couldn't it be listed in some old catalog?"

"It isn't."

"How do you know he was an artist?"

"I don't, actually."

"You never personally talked to him?"

"No," she replied. "But as a doctor I had access to certain medical data. I knew about experiments on prisoners. It's possible Herr Krenek may have been the subject of one."

"What sort of experiment?"

"A surgical intrusion into the prefrontal lobes of the cerebrum. Berlin was interested in neurological data that might be applied in the treatment of head wounds. The research had to do with the effect on behavior. In Herr Krenek's case, there was a specific interest in the effect of the procedure on artistic ability—whether or not the creative desire would be diminished."

"What happened after the surgery?"

"A period of evaluation."

"And then?"

"I assume the subjects were gassed. That was the usual pattern after the data had been collected. It wasn't done to conceal the crime, but to provide the posthumous data from the autopsy. Herr Krenek would have been no exception."

"But you don't know if any of it happened?"

"I didn't witness it," she said. "But a record was made of the project, and another doctor confirmed it."

"SS?"

"No. Jewish. A pathologist. He didn't survive. But before his death he gave me the photograph to hide."

"Did you ever see the man in the photograph?"

"Only once," she said. "From a distance."

The pain in Neumann's head had started again.

"And you think I could be him?"

Dr. Levin gazed at him for a long time, the gray eyes unblinking and clinical in their judgment.

"It's possible," she said, "but not if the surgery were performed the way it was described to me. There would be scar tissue at the site. You don't have a scar across your forehead."

"What else do you know about him?"

"I was told that he was transported east from the Belsen KZ early in 'forty-four. Beyond that, I haven't any facts."

"Belsen." Neumann frowned.

"Were you in Belsen?" she said.

"No, Dachau."

"Before Dachau, I mean."

"I've tried to remember," Neumann said, clenching his fists, "but it's a blank."

The pain in his head had a fine edge of panic, as if it had to break out of his skull. The figure of the woman on the chair went out of focus from the pressure, and even as his mind fought to keep control, he could feel himself falling.

A warm light flooded his consciousness like a balm. Neumann opened his eyes and stared up at the ceiling fixture. He lay on the floor, a cushion under his feet. Alina Levin was bending over him. He started to get up, but she pressed a hand against his shoulder.

"Lie still. Don't try to get up just yet. You blacked out a few moments ago. Has this sort of thing happened to you before?"

"I had a seizure of some kind a few months back," he said. "And I get headaches."

"Describe them to me."

"The pain comes on suddenly," he said. "Usually when I try to remember."

"It could be organically based, a complication from your head wound. You shouldn't try to force the past into the present. You'll remember when your mind is ready."

"When will that be? Ten years? Twenty?"

"I don't know."

"You're a doctor, aren't you?"

She glanced away, and he could sense some instant cool withdrawal in her.

"No," she murmured. "I don't practice medicine anymore."

"Sorry," he said. "I only meant . . ."

"It doesn't matter what you meant," she said quietly.

"I suppose nothing matters," he agreed, "when you get down to it. That's the joke, isn't it? In any case, I'm grateful for the information. It's getting late. I'll be off."

Neumann got to his feet. The blanket roll and haversack were on the floor beside the chair, and he clamped a hand around the shoulder straps and straightened, the pack dangling against his leg.

"Do you have a place to stay?" Alina asked.

"Not yet," Neumann said.

"You'll have trouble finding anything. The city's overrun with homeless. You're welcome to stay the night, if you like. You can have this sitting room if you don't mind sleeping on the floor. It's safer than the streets."

"I don't want to put you out," he said.

"It's nothing. There's only potato soup for the table, I'm afraid. Not much better than the camps."

* * *

That night, Neumann lay on his bedroll on the hardwood floor of the room, fingers laced behind his head. A crack of light seeped in under the sliding doors that closed off Alina's bedroom, and for a while he was aware of her shadow moving across it. Later, she blew out the lamp. The darkness came down like a weight on his eyes, and he closed them.

Asleep, he fell into an odd dream—odd because there was no one else in it, only sculpted figures on pedestals in a ruined colonnade that had the look of a Greek court bathed in blue shadows. Pillars slid up on a dark sky, and the crumbling mosaic of tile dislodged easily underfoot. A moon burned down, investing the landscape with a cold, brilliant purity and giving the statues a translucent sheen. Shadows devoured the empty sockets in the marble faces and exaggerated the blind fury of the stares that held fast to Neumann.

Then he saw that each of the figures had been deliberately maimed, a nose or an ear lopped off, a nipple gouged from a breast, fingers snapped from a hand. Neumann began to walk faster. There seemed no end to the sterile terrain of the dream that stretched for miles in his mind. In his panic to get away, he blundered into one of the busts and knocked it from the pedestal. It toppled over, crashing silently. The armless torso lay, helpless, on the decaying tile. Not far away was the severed head, the mouth screaming at Neumann without moving or making a sound. He stepped over it and rushed on.

From time to time, he thought he heard children's voices. The sound drifted from a distance, a muffled whimpering, like the children of Hamelin trapped in the darkness of their mountain. But each time he stopped to listen, he heard nothing. The blue shadows of the court deepened, spilling in somber pools. With every few steps, now, came the splintering crunch from bits of broken sculpture underfoot. More figures accumulated, like street beggars surrounding a prosperous stranger, and finally it was no longer possible to move. The rage on the marble faces had intensified. "Give us Josef Neumann!" they seemed to shout. His leg brushed against the polished stump of a hand. Terrified, he jerked away from the cold touch. An oily sheen of sweat clung to his body, and the air had turned to chalky powder like quarry dust so that each intake of breath grew shallower and shallower. He opened his mouth to shout, but the shout was only a moan.

He woke with it still constricted in the cords of his throat, and the fear had condensed itself into a slick of moisture in his clenched fists.

Alina Levin was kneeling beside him in the glow of a paraffin lamp. An older woman in a man's robe with the sleeves rolled back stood in the doorway.

"It's all right," Alina said to Neumann. "You've had a nightmare, that's all." She glanced at the woman in the doorway. "Hilda, bring me a damp cloth, please."

"A dream," Neumann said hoarsely.

"You were crying out quite loudly in your sleep."

He heard the water running in the bathroom sink across the hall. The old woman in the man's robe that fell nearly to the floor came with the wet cloth.

"Go back to sleep, Hilda," Alina said. "It's very late."

Neumann and Alina were alone in the low flicker of the paraffin lamp. She used the cloth to wipe the perspiration from his face.

"Have you ever had the dream before?" she asked.

"No," he murmured. "They say if you die in a dream, then you really die." He gave a low, bitter laugh. "I thought I was dying."

"It's nothing to laugh about," she said.

"Isn't it?" Neumann asked.

She gazed down at him. The cool touch of her fingers lingered for a moment on his forehead.

"I have them too," she said. "The dreams. It's not uncommon for anyone who was in the camps. Try to go back to sleep."

She was gone, closed from view by the sliding doors. He lay staring up into the dark, but he did not go back to sleep.

THREE

In the morning they had tea and black bread at a table under a white birch near the garden wall.

"You say the man in the picture would have had a scar across his forehead," Neumann said. "Couldn't it have been removed by plastic surgery?"

"It's possible," Alina said. "But rather doubtful, I should think. On the other hand, you have a small cicatrix on your left cheekbone. If you look through a magnifying lens at the face in the photograph, you'll see something similar. It could have been a speck on the camera lens—or a small scar from a blow or an accident." Out of professional habit, her fingers grazed the scar high on his cheek as she examined it. "How did you get that?"

"Who knows?" Neumann shrugged.

"It's definitely scar tissue. Probably a cut that should have been stitched."

"How do you account for the resemblance?"

"It may have been just a fantastic coincidence, two people remarkably alike . . . or a twin. That's another possibility. But you have no memory of family or friends?"

"I don't even know what happened at Dachau. They say I was shot and left for dead in a mass grave."

"Do you have any memories at all that might predate that experience?"

"A few. But they don't connect to anything."

"Just vague images?"

"There's a hillside of flowers. Like wildflowers in summer. I can see them blowing and swaying in sunlight. That's all there is. . . ."

"Herr Neumann," she said, "I'll speak as a physician. As far as can be determined, the onset of your amnesia was coincidental with a bullet fired into the back of your head. The bullet itself creased the skull, apparently with enough force to fracture it, but didn't inflict any appreciable damage on the brain. That opens several possibilities. First, the impact from even a glancing shot could have caused enough microscopic intercranial trauma to precipitate memory dysfunction. A second hypothesis is that loss of memory occurred as a direct result of a severe emotional disturbance. It would be somewhat rare to find both of these causal factors operating at the same time, but it's not unheard of. What seems a bit unusual is that you still can't recall your name. That's not typical in view of the fact that you've retained a few shadowy memories, like the hill of wildflowers. A person's name is a repetitive memory that doesn't vanish easily. It makes me wonder if something else is involved."

"Such as what?"

"You spoke of having had a seizure a few months ago. Yesterday, when you blacked out, you exhibited some mild convulsive behavior. It's possible that you sustained a contusion to a frontal or temporal lobe. That type of injury could even have occurred from your fall into the pit. Swelling and bleeding inside the skull can produce postepileptic fits that impair memory. That might account for the fact that you can't recall your name. Or it could be linked to what we call a dissociative reaction. Maybe you don't want to recall it."

"Will I keep having seizures?"

"No, they should subside as the condition resolves. As for the headaches—they could relate either to the cerebral assault that I've described or to a dissociative behavior. You've been doing manual labor on a farm for nearly a year. Why did you choose that?"

"The American doctor at the camp thought I needed physical activity and no stress. He thought I'd have a better chance of getting my memory back."

"But it hasn't happened," she said. "Your mind is still hiding from the past."

"It's not what I want," he insisted.

"Perhaps not," she said. "But your subconscious has a different view of things. You shouldn't treat it as an adversary. It knows what's best for you. It can even throw up headaches like a protective barrier."

"Or kill you in a dream?" A smile dragged faintly at his mouth.

"But it didn't," she said. "You woke up out of your—what did you call it? *Court of shadows?* Quite often dreams are just scenarios of frustration."

"You sound like a psychiatrist," Neumann remarked.

She looked away and said, "I *was* a psychiatrist."

They fell silent under the motionless leaves of the white birch. Finally Neumann raised his head.

"You said the man in the photograph came to Auschwitz from the KZ at Belsen—in the British zone?"

"That was my understanding."

"Then I suppose Belsen is the place to start. I'll see Major Ward about a travel permit. Maybe the British can tell me something."

"Perhaps," she said. "But I would not be too optimistic."

They finished their tea. A bird sang overhead in the sunlit leaves. Then it flew off across the high slate roof of the house, like one of the darting shadows of unseen truth in his own mind.

"Thank you for your kindness, Fräulein Levin," he said.

"You should know that a return of memory can be spontaneous in cases of retrograde amnesia," she said. "That doesn't mean it will all come back at once. But the first step of the process could occur unexpectedly."

"Or not occur?" He shrugged.

She drew a card from the pocket of her dark dress. It was a faded business card for the Levin Gallery. "I've put my name on the back, and a number where I can be reached. It might be wise to keep the card on your person. In any event, I should like to know what develops in your case." She shook her head and added, "If only for the sake of the man in the photograph."

Neumann's haversack and blanket roll lay against the stone wall in the sun. He picked them up, and Alina walked to the gate with him.

"I hope you find the answers you're looking for."

"And you," he said. "Maybe you'll be treating patients again if the country gets back on its feet."

She stared at him gravely, and he saw the pain in her pupils that did not flinch in their gray emptiness.

"No," she murmured. "I shall never practice medicine again."

FOUR

Neumann reached the village of Bergen-Belsen on foot a week later and went directly to the British Military Authority. He was carrying typed credentials from Major Ward that identified him as a civilian investigator for the War Crimes Office of the U.S. Army CIC.

"It should open a few doors for you that might be closed otherwise," the American had told him. "When you get back, you can give us any bits of information you picked up."

At Belsen, a British sergeant of bantam-cock size sat in charge. The area CO, he said, was in Hannover and would not be back for two days. Neumann inquired about a place to stay.

"No digs here," the sergeant replied. "You're more likely to find something in Celle. We've a supply lorry going in. Give you a ride. Best we can do."

So he had ridden into Celle in the bed of the lorry, the sun hot on the canvas above his head, the country streaming away in the plume of white dust behind the tailgate. The driver dropped him at the square. It was an old town with high-roofed houses, narrow streets, and a castle overlooking a river. A bulletin board had been put up in the square. Tacked to it were offers to barter goods for other goods. In a nearby alley children sifted through refuse bins. Two of them began to argue over a prize.

Neumann had the address of a lodging the sergeant in Bergen-Belsen had written down for him, along with directions to reach it, and he set off. It was a room behind a sawmill on the river, and in the morning the *choof-choof-choof* of the donkey engine and high-pitched whine of the round-saw woke him.

A piece of dry pastry, washed down with black ersatz, made up breakfast. Afterward he walked out onto the bridge over the river, leaned on the handrail, and watched the boats chugging upstream. The sun flashed on the water, and birds slanted on warm drafts of air below the span, but the scene would not lock into any memory of itself.

Lunch was a bowl of watery soup. In his room he read a week-old newspaper, then tried to nap, but the buzz saw in the mill kept him awake. Later, he took a walk through the town. Many shops were empty, their broken windows boarded, and, once, he passed a work crew digging up rubble and piling it into a horse-drawn cart. The sound of their picks grew faint against the distant hoot of small craft on the river.

The street climbed to the square, and he paused in front of a consignment shop that looked open. The items on display in the window were useless in the starving economy of a country ravaged by war, but they were up for sale anyway. There was a bust of Beethoven, an accordion box, and a set of silver goblets tarnishing for lack of polish. To the left of these was a large painting that had been set up for viewing on a cut-off easel.

It was the painting that drew his stare. Almost at once the ether of some odd anxiety was loose in his nerves, and his heart began to pound. The canvas could have been an illustration of his nightmare at Alina Levin's—an empty landscape, like a Grecian ruin, its columns toppling on a dark sky, its marble figures broken and maimed. Even the shadows stretching across the surreal distances had a blue tinge. Beyond a striking impression of decay, there was in the faces a mixture of rage and horrified panic, as if they were trying to shout from the inert silence of the sculpture.

The painting streamed across his own face on the glass, and the two images merged like a double exposure. The pain swelled in his head to an unbearable pressure, then burst like a psychological abscess from within. Whole pieces of memory floated up, disconnected, out of some dark, interior recess.

From somewhere across the desolate reaches of the painting, it came to him: *Your name is Krenek. . . .*

PART TWO

THE KRENEKS

ONE

From the window of the first-class compartment, Paul Krenek watched the buildings of Berlin surfacing on the horizon where the summer burnt its blue gleam into the day. The year was 1937 and he was twenty-three, a bit over six feet, slim-hipped, with good shoulders, and the face that the glass reflected back against the streaming landscape was unflawed and scorched dark by the Heidelberg sun.

He was returning home from the university after a regimen of postgraduate work in classical languages that had led to the Greek Prize. The award offered a year in residence at the University of Athens, with a chance to travel, but he had not yet made up his mind to accept or decline.

The buildings grew larger, no longer unfurling on thermal waves. Finally the train coasted into the switching yards, and the Bahnhof dome swung into sight.

Paul lifted his bags down from the rack and left the coach. Passengers swarmed over the platform. The engine blew steam from its boiler, the dark iron sweating onto the ballasted ties. Against the clank of a pressure valve, a girl called out his name.

"*Paul! Paul!*"

He glanced toward the gates and saw Leni and Georg in the crowd. Georg lifted a hand. Leni ran toward Paul, her legs flashing below the hem of her tan dress.

Before Paul could put down his bags, Leni flung her arms around his neck. Her warm mouth on his was breathless, the lips too full of excited laughter for a proper kiss. She threw back her head, the flush of pleasure dark on her cheeks beside the wildly affectionate smile.

"I can't believe you're back. I'm so happy!"

"And still the prettiest girl in Berlin," Paul said.

Georg came through the crowd. He was shorter than Paul, chunky, and the wire-rimmed glasses gave him a scholarly air. His features were almost too symmetrical, as if they had been measured with a micrometer to balance exactly in the face, and the fair cheeks had a perpetual bloom of color like the skin of a peach.

He gripped Paul's hand warmly in both his and said, "It's good to have you back."

"How's medical school?" Paul asked.

"The most cunning torture ever conceived by man."

Georg spoke in a clipped, precise way. He was not one to display emotion in public, though the air of reserve hid an underlying warmth, a need to be liked, at least where Paul was concerned. Growing up, Paul had defended his friend often enough with his fists, for Georg had been overweight, awkward at sports, and myopic. It had been his bad luck to be born brilliant, possessed of a photographic mind, and early on at school he had become the target of bullying by the other boys.

Paul glanced over the crowd, dwindling on the platform, and said, "Didn't Ernst get in from Florence?"

"Ernst went down to . . ." Leni hesitated. "To Zossen."

Zossen was the site of the convent school for retarded children where five-year-old Liesel Krenek was confined. Of course, Ernst would have gone to see her. She adored her twin brothers, who had tried to fill some void in her life after the death of their mother.

Georg took one of the bags and Paul carried the other. Leni walked beside Paul, clinging to his arm. Her blond hair was cut short in a crescent shape across her cheek, and her skin had a golden sheen.

In the terminal Georg excused himself to buy a packet of cigarettes at the kiosk.

Leni said, "Ernst brought back some of his paintings. They're quite modern. The lines are very spare and full of—I don't know—tension, I suppose."

"You don't think much of them?"

"It's hard to like something you don't understand." Leni shook her head and added, "Ernst has changed. I can't quite describe it, but he's different, somehow. You'll see."

Georg had turned from the kiosk with his cigarettes. He was staring at Paul and Leni. Something in his face, a sad flicker of resignation, caught Paul's eye. Coming back, Georg covered it with a smile.

"Is anything wrong?" Paul asked.

"Wrong? No, of course not."

The blaring of the public address system drowned further talk.

Outside, Georg hailed a taxi. The driver put Paul's bags into the boot. A veteran of the 1914 war sat on the sidewalk against a wall in the sun. His uniform was shiny, patched, the trousers pinned back over the stump of a missing leg. The soldier stared straight ahead. Paul hesitated, then reached into his pocket. He would have left several marks in the cloth cap on the pavement, but Georg gripped his arm.

"No, Paul. He's a Jew."

In the taxi, Leni pressed close to Paul and took his hand in both of hers. Georg sat a little apart, the flush still dark in his cheeks, like an emotion that would not be absorbed. Paul assumed it had to do with the Jew and the brief embarrassment in front of the station.

TWO

That evening Kurt Krenek hosted a party to celebrate the homecoming of his two sons. Laughter swelled through the brightly lit mansion, and servants bearing trays of hors d'oeuvres and champagne passed among the guests.

At six-foot-five, Kurt Krenek towered over most men and looked to be physically powerful despite the advancing years that had left a slack of loose flesh in the florid face. But his eyes still flashed with the competitive heat that had driven him to success in the chemical industry. He was a man who demanded perfection from life, and usually got it, and he was very proud of his sons, though Paul was his favorite. The twins drew their dark good looks from their mother, dead in childbirth at age forty-seven, five years ago—a loss Krenek still mourned.

Paul was the dominant twin, and perhaps for that reason had come under the influence of their father while Ernst had gravitated toward their mother. Ernst was the more serious and sensitive and early on had shown a gift for drawing that their mother strongly encouraged.

Paul was by nature more aggressive. His father taught him to ride and box, and every fall they had a week's skiing at Saint Moritz. Paul chose the dangerous slopes and took them too fast. The tight traverses on a near-vertical drop put a thrilling tension into his nerves, and the wind cutting his face around the goggles as his skis snaked downward in the racing whiteness of packed snow filled him with a wild silent enjoyment. There were times when it was not enough, and he would tuck the ski poles under both arms, his body bent low and forward, boots locked together, to gain more speed before braking at the bottom of his own hurtling descent. Then he would gaze back at the feathery plume settling on the slope, as if death had been left behind among the airborne crystals floating earthward like spangles. Their mother would not let Ernst do any of these things, worrying that he might injure his hands. So the boys had grown up with certain differences in personality.

But differences were hardly evident now as the twins stood side by side in matching white dinner jackets open on pleated dress shirts and black cummerbunds. Among the guests circling them were Georg and one of Georg's professor doctors at the university—Fritz von Stroelin.

Of medium height and bullish, von Stroelin was a practicing plastic surgeon, though he was perhaps better known outside the medical community as a former champion pistol shooter in international competition. His skill with a handgun had earned him an Olympic silver medal early in life, a press following, and the indictment of glamour. Scandals with several prominent women had followed, including one with a lady whose husband had shot himself, but von Stroelin wore this notoriety like another marksmanship medal. The years had begun now to mount their first assault on the blond good looks, leaving their skirmish lines entrenched under the false tan of sunlamps, though his smile remained quick and accessible and the force of his personality could hold an audience.

The talk had drifted to an odd topic—the euthanasia of mental defectives—and among the men listening to von Stroelin, only Ernst seemed to disagree in principle.

"Killing is killing, isn't it?" he protested.

Von Stroelin smiled and said, "Apart from the humane considerations in terminating useless life, these are difficult times. How can the economy support a system of custodial care that may span a lifetime?"

"I was thinking about the morality," Ernst said, "not the economics—"

"Exactly," von Stroelin interrupted. "And I contend that a waste of resources on life devoid of value is immoral. It becomes immoral when it deprives the more deserving cases of care."

"Who would make the final decision?" Ernst asked.

Von Stroelin's gaze, above his smile, had a cold force of conviction.

"Let's say a team of three experts. That way, no single judgment would prevail."

"In other words," Ernst said, "the patient wouldn't have anything to say about it?"

"The patients we are talking about would be quite beyond deciding such things for themselves. If I were to take you into the children's ward at the Charité right now, you would find a deformed infant boy lying on his belly on a special rack. The first thing you'd see is an external cystic tumor protruding from the small of the back. Because the spinal cord lies in the cyst wall, there is a slow but constant excretion of urine and feces. The body wastes can only be drained into a bedpan, and so there is a problem with painful excoriations around the perineum. The case is complicated by leakage of cerebrospinal fluid into the cranial region. The boy's head is massively swollen and soft, like an overripe melon." Von Stroelin gazed directly at Ernst. "My question is—are we doing him a kindness, or a disservice, in prolonging his life?"

"That's hard to say," Ernst replied.

"The prognosis is very poor," von Stroelin went on. "The little fellow's legs are already paralyzed. I should guess that death will occur from progressive malnutrition or some intercurrent infection. If by some miracle the infant were to survive, he would require institutional care for the rest of his life. Well?" The physician looked around for support. "Tell me what I should do about this patient. Let's be compassionate. But wait! Maybe there are some people who have the wrong idea about compassion. It attaches to some obsolete morality that places value on the continuation of life above the quality of life. What a few of us are trying to say is that it's time for a new morality—a different perspective. . . ."

There was a fine edge of impatience behind von Stroelin's smile that kept dragging at one side of his mouth as if pulled by a concealed wire.

"But suppose the patient were a member of your own family?" Ernst frowned.

"All the more reason I wouldn't want him to suffer," the physician replied. He saw that the group was with him, and his tone took on a patronizing air. "I'm surprised that you don't see the logic. You've studied philosophy, haven't you? I think if you would apply the Hegelian concept of abstract right to the question, you might reach the proper conclusion."

Paul had been listening to the debate with a derisive grin, as if the issue were absurd. But he suddenly felt an odd dislike for von Stroelin's air of exalted knowledge and intolerance of any viewpoint in conflict with his own. Clearly, there was a competitive edge to his nature that did not like to lose, whether it was target shooting, adultery, or an interpretation of ethics.

"The problem with Hegelian logic," Paul said to von Stroelin, "is that Hegel is a pompous shit. . . ."

Other heads in the room turned at the laughter. Von Stroelin laughed the loudest, but the back of his neck was red above the stiff collar, and afterward the smile went slack on his mouth, as if the wire had been cut. Only Paul saw the flash of anger, like the click of a hammer on an empty cylinder—the promise of a bullet next time.

Leni had arrived at the party and was crossing the room toward Ernst and Paul. The sleek cocktail dress of gold lamé took on a radiant glitter under the chandelier, and the short hem showed off her well-shaped legs. She gave each twin a kiss on the cheek and squeezed Paul's hand.

The dress left her shoulders bare except for two thin straps, and Paul saw that von Stroelin could not take his eyes off the bare swell of her bosom. Georg introduced him, and immediately the physician engaged her in a light, bantering dialogue, leaning close, his stare overpowering hers.

A trio of musicians started to play, and Georg said to Paul, "Shall we have a drink?"

Paul knew his friend well enough to realize Georg had something to tell him. They stepped over to the punch bowl with its berg of floating ice and ladled out two glasses.

Georg said, "Sorry the discussion got out of hand."

"What makes you think it did?" Paul was still amused.

"I could feel it."

Beyond the table, Leni smuggled Paul a quick smile past von Stroelin, who was still talking.

Paul said, "Better hope you never get him for your doctor if you're dangerously ill."

"You'd be lucky to have him," Georg said. "He's one of the finest in his field." He saw the wry skepticism in Paul's face and added, "He's been offered a very high post in the Health Ministry. They say Himmler himself is behind it."

Leni had broken away and was coming toward them. Von Stroelin stood holding his cocktail glass and staring after her in the crowd.

"I couldn't get away from him," she whispered to Paul as she came up. "He thinks he's something."

Georg shook his head and said, "I forgot to warn you that Fritz has a romantic reputation."

"And what an ego to go with it!"

"All great physicians have great egos," Georg said seriously. "In medicine, it's symptomatic of genius. A doctor gambles with the life of the patient, and if he cheats death consistently, he tends to get cocky. It's an arrogance to look for."

"Well, he needs deflating," Leni said, frowning. She brushed the hair from her cheek with the backs of her fingers and a slight, antagonistic toss of her head. She might have been tossing off the topic of von Stroelin as well. The smile on her mouth was suddenly gay and teasing. "Paul, aren't you going to dance with me?"

On the floor, he took her in his arms. Leni closed her eyes and put her cheek against his. Dancing, he had a glimpse of Georg staring at them.

Georg glanced away, but not before Paul observed the pain underlying the pink guilt. The expression matched exactly the look he remembered on his friend's face in the railway station. But this time the answer came in a lightning flash of comprehension, absurdly simple—Georg was in love. . . .

The musicians had left their instruments to take a break. At the big Steinway, one of the guests played Brahms amateurishly. The resonances of sound rose from the seasoned wood to the shimmering images in the cut glass of the chandelier, and fell away.

"Can't we go somewhere to talk?" Leni pleaded. "I haven't had any time alone with you since you got back."

Outside, Leni had his hand, pulling him down the wide steps that plunged to the garden. The sound of the Steinway and laughing voices from the brightly lit gallery grew faint. The two young people followed a path out to the summer pavilion, half hidden in the gloomy speckling of leaves. Only a little moonlight penetrated the foliage snarled in the latticework, and the floorboards creaked underfoot in the dark.

"Remember the games we played here?" Leni said.

"A lot of pretending."

"Don't you miss it?"

"Children grow up." He smiled.

"Do you think I'm grown up?"

Paul looked at her upturned face, the moonlit shadows blowing silently on it. They stirred hardly at all under his touch, as if the leaf-patterns would absorb the way she closed her eyes before he kissed her. The quick, thermal response of her own lips, under his, left some overheated emotion there as they broke apart.

"I thought you'd never come home," she murmured.

The night breathed again on the hanging clumps of foliage where a few blossoms gleamed. Paul stepped over to the circular bench and groped behind the backrest. At last he found it, still bundled in oilcloth. He broke the cords and unfolded the fabric on a child's treasure—two pfennigs and a toy soldier. The paint was flaking from the lead soldier, which had a leg snapped off.

"I used to pretend this fellow had been wounded on the western front. One day my father noticed the missing leg. He told me to throw the soldier away and he'd get me a new one. That's when I hid it."

Leni laughed and said, "But he didn't know that it was a special toy."

"I'm not sure it would have made any difference," Paul said, shaking his head. "I suppose distaste for anything imperfect is a peculiarly German attitude, isn't it?" The smile curling into his mouth was faintly cynical.

"You even find it among doctors."

The wind blew more torn-off laughter from the house and flung it, with a scrap of piano music, into the deeper silences of the night. Looking at the broken toy soldier made him think of the Jew outside the railway terminal, and it was almost as if the two were interchangeable.

3

The last guests were leaving when Paul walked Leni down the graveled drive under the trees to the silver Mercedes Benz. The driver touched two leather-gloved fingers to the brim of his chauffeur's cap, then opened the door.

"We're having tea tomorrow afternoon at the Esplanade," Leni said. "Don't forget."

"I won't," Paul promised, and brushed her cheek with a kiss.

She gave his hand a hard squeeze. The gold cocktail dress glittered in the moonlight as she climbed into the custom limousine, crossing her legs.

Paul stepped back as the Mercedes rolled off. He had a last glimpse of Leni turning to wave through the rear glass, and he lifted a hand. Walking back to the house, he thought again of the look on Georg's face and the quick flash of light on the wire-rimmed glasses as he averted his gaze. The bloom of guilt on his friend's cheeks left little doubt as to his feelings.

In the garden he caught sight of a lone figure standing in the summer pavilion. The gloom under the lattice roof touched out his upper body except for the chalk-white gleam of the dress shirt above the cummerbund, and the smoke from his cigarette hung in the moonlight that left a glaze on the leaves.

"Paul," Ernst's voice came from the dark foliage.

Paul went over, the crunch of gravel soft underfoot.

"What are you doing out here?" he asked.

"Waiting for you," Ernst said. "I wanted to have a talk."

"What about? It's late."

Ernst hesitated, as if not sure how to start.

"I saw Liesl today. She asked about you."

"I'll go down to Zossen tomorrow and see her. How is she?"

"A very sweet five-year-old. Claps her hands together when she laughs. Enchanting—and heartbreaking—all in one package. I would have brought her back to the party, but father. . . ."

"You know how he feels," Paul said. "He can't help it. When he sees Liesl it makes him remember Mother. It's too painful. She's better off at the convent school."

The familiar half smile on Ernst's mouth seemed to push, as always, to the edge of some wry knowledge.

"You don't think it has anything to do with the fact that she's mildly retarded?"

Deep down, Paul knew it was true. Liesl did not fit comfortably into their father's orderly world, where struggle and achievement were the virtues of the soul. It was not that he resented his daughter for her mental deficiency, but only that he was reluctant to confront it, for that would have meant acknowledging some degree of biological blame.

When Paul did not reply, Ernst said, "You heard Fritz von Stroelin tonight. He's an influential figure in his profession. How do you suppose he would feel about Liesl?"

"It was just talk," Paul scoffed.

"Was it?"

"Of course."

Two shadowy hollows formed below Ernst's high cheekbones as he drew unhurriedly on his cigarette, then blew another stream of smoke into the light, where it seemed to writhe painfully.

"I once made a promise not to tell you something," Ernst said. "But now I have to break it. You have a right to know, if only for Liesl's sake. What you do with the knowledge is your own business."

Paul gave a low laugh and said, "That sounds like a cheap mystery."

Ernst's own smile was heavily sad. He said, "Our mother was Jewish."

A nerve flinched in Paul's cheek as he gazed at his brother across a gulf of silence.

"What are you talking about?" he replied, his voice hoarse from the anger that had already worked its way into his throat and lodged in the cords standing out in his neck.

"It's true, Paul." Ernst shook his head. He looked down and added, "I didn't want to believe it either, at first. I think that hurt her worst of all."

Paul shoved past his brother and sat down on the circular bench in the deep shadows, his elbows on his knees, fists curled against his forehead. His eyes were squeezed shut, his jaw tightly clenched, as if every nerve and fiber were resisting the truth.

"So you see how it is," Ernst went on softly, "with Liesl, you and me. We're *Halbjuden*—whether we like it or not."

Halbjude! Half Jew. Paul might as well have been given the news that he was afflicted with cancer, or leprosy—except that a tumor could be cut out, and leprosy arrested. Jewishness was untreatable.

"How long have you known?" Paul said.

"Mother told me a few weeks before Liesl was born. She had a premonition that something might go wrong during childbirth. She'd gone back to her religion in secret. We had some long discussions about it."

"Why didn't you tell me before?"

"She made me promise never to mention it. Hitler had just become Reich chancellor. Most of the anti-Jewish feeling was still only talk. No one could have imagined then the things that have happened since. I thought about telling you after I saw Liesl today. When I heard what the doctor said tonight, I made up my mind that you should know. If something were to happen to me, and it somehow came to light that Liesl was half Jewish, I think she would be quite helpless." Ernst drew once more on his cigarette and stared at the smoke flexing away. "Are you going to marry Leni?"

Paul raised his head slowly, and the emotional heat in his pale stare was like a combustible force that needed only a spark to set it off. But it remained inert, and the silence circumscribed into the pupils was like an answer by default.

"That's the other reason I thought you had to know," Ernst murmured.

"I've never even seen the inside of a synagogue," Paul said in pained disgust.

"I have," Ernst said. "For almost a year, now. In Florence it's still possible to worship without the Gestapo watching. But that's not really the point, is it? Whether you're half Jew, quarter Jew, or have a drop of Jewish blood, you're still a Jew under the law. It's a question of racial purity. That's German eugenics. Ask Georg. He'll tell you."

Paul sprang from the bench into the patch of moonlight and slammed the heel of his fist against a support post. He stared at the starry night beyond the dark slump of foliage, as if the answer lay in the cosmic arrangement of that silver brilliance.

"I say *damn* all Jews," he said bitterly.

Ernst shrugged and replied coolly, "Maybe you'll get your wish."

Minutes later, Paul was alone with his father in the older man's study. Kurt Krenek's tough, seamed features were more florid than ever, like the shell of a crab plucked from a steam vat. But his anger, like Paul's, came out of his frustration and was directed at no one, least of all his son. He turned now to the large oil portrait of his late wife, and the moisture brimmed in his eyes but did not spill over into tears. Ropes of pearls banded the black hair piled atop her head, and the dark eyes had a liquid shine, as if some warm joy of life had been newly poured into them. Her mouth gave an impression of softness, if only for its fullness, and even without paint, it had the color of an unfurled rose.

"She was a woman of great beauty," Kurt Krenek said, "and it came from within."

"You knew she was Jewish," Paul said.

"That was never a source of conflict. She did not practice her religion. No one ever knew." The older man turned from the portrait to gaze at his son. "There is no reason that anyone should have to know about it, now. As you get older, you'll realize that the past dies a little more each day."

"So does the future," Paul said. "In the meantime, we're stuck in the present. There's nothing in Germany for a Jew. Suppose somebody finds out?"

"I have a certain amount of influence," his father said, "and some important friends, not to mention government contracts. Discretion can be bought, if necessary."

"The price of discretion goes up every day," Paul said.

"Listen to me. Don't you think I know what's happening? I've watched the situation for the last four years. The laws and decrees against the Jews are nothing more than a strategy to get them to leave Germany, like evicting a bad tenant. It's working, too. Look at the emigration figures. I believe the problem has already been solved. As the Jewish population shrinks, so will the conflict. Then this business will all be forgotten and life will go on as usual."

"And what happens if you're wrong?" Paul asked.

"The next twelve months should tell. I don't see any drastic change coming in the Reich's position on the Jewish problem. But in any case . . ." Kurt Krenek hesitated, and his gaze turned once more to the portrait on the wall. "It might be best if you took your year in Greece, and Ernst went back to Italy, while we see what happens here at home. It's what your mother would want."

"If it's so safe," Paul said, "why run away?"

"Because only a fool risks all his chips on one number," his father said shortly. "I've made certain arrangements in Geneva for you and Ernst. A large sum of money in two secret accounts. It's not to be used, except in the worst sort of emergency. Let's just call it insurance, eh? In case events take a wrong turn. And now—we've had our talk. I don't wish ever to speak of this again. The sooner you forget what you've learned tonight, the better."

In his room, Paul lay on top of his bedcovers in the dark, his forearm across his eyes. The French cuffs on the dress shirt were rolled back, and he had untied the bow tie and opened his collar, but he still wore the cummerbund and formal trousers. All in all, it had been quite a day. He had made an enemy of a prominent medical figure with connections in the Party, discovered that his best friend was in love with his girl, and that he himself was a half-Jew. As for the secret account in the Geneva bank—that was only racial insurance, and from now on the premiums would be paid in lies that would probably build up to a large equity in deceit.

FOUR

The next afternoon, Paul met Leni for tea in the gardens of the Hotel Esplanade. They took a table in the shade under the trees near the dance platform. A breeze stirred the leaves into a green glitter as the musicians in white shirts and bow ties struck a waltz. Leni's mood was light, and if she noticed some withdrawal in Paul, she did not let on.

"There's something I have to tell you," he said finally.

"It must be serious," she replied in a teasing tone, "from the look on your face."

"I've decided to use the Greek Prize and go abroad for a year."

Leni's smile faded and she looked down.

"But I thought you weren't going to accept it," she protested.

"I've changed my mind."

"Oh, Paul," she pleaded. "Why?"

"It's the sort of chance that only comes along once."

The distress mounting behind her composure was already evident.

"Does your father know?"

"He knows," Paul said, unable to keep the irony out of his tone.

"Last week he was talking about your coming into the chemical business."

"I can always do that. Right now, I'm not interested in the chemical business."

"Then what *are* you interested in?"

"Greek civilization." Paul smiled bitterly.

Leni shook her head and said, "I don't think that's very amusing."

"I didn't say it to be amusing."

She snatched her hand from under his.

"Don't touch me. Of course I'm angry. Why shouldn't I be? I think your decision is totally selfish."

"I agree with you." The wry pain spilled over into another half smile that his mouth threw away.

"Is that all you have to say?" The outburst of temper had left a faint rash of pink at her throat, inflaming the honey sheen of the skin. Her emotions, like Paul's, had always been close to the surface and undisciplined, for she was used to having her way. Now, he half expected the long painted nails to fly across the table and rake their anger across his face. Instead, they jerked sideways and overturned a water glass on the white tablecloth. The waiter hurried over and mopped the stain with his napkin. Leni sat, stiff and silent, until he withdrew. Even then, she did not speak, staring off into the distance where the leaves flung their dissolving shadow patterns onto the cropped green. But after a few moments, her eyes clouded.

"A year," she murmured. "It might as well be five. It's an eternity." She looked down. "Besides, I thought . . ."

Once more he put his hand over hers. This time she did not draw away. Her head remained bent so that he couldn't see her face, only the hair curving in a gold slash across her cheek.

"What is it?" he said, and felt a warm tear splash onto the back of his hand.

"Nothing," she said. "I thought we were going to be engaged, that's all."

"It's a bad time to think about marriage. Things are too uncertain. There's even talk that Germany might be at war in the next year or two."

The excuse sounded lame, even to Paul.

"Did you meet another girl at Heidelberg?" Leni's voice quavered.

"No."

"Then what's changed you?"

"Greece is important to me."

"Aren't I important to you?"

He took in a long breath and let it out slowly. The hurt glistening in her eyes was too much for him. He couldn't just break off the relationship like this. It would have to be done from Greece in the course of a separation.

"We can still be engaged when I come back," he said. Instantly, shame overtook the lie. It was exactly the sort of emotional compromise that would cause more pain in the long term than the truth now. But he was too ashamed of the truth to bring it out.

Leni had regained her composure sufficiently to raise her head and stare at him through her tears.

"When we were small," she said, "Ernst was the one who used to make castles out of clouds. You kept telling him they were just clouds. You were always the one who faced reality. Now it's you who's chasing some silly, romantic idea."

"Most people are chasing an idea," Paul said, "or running from one."

The musicians finished the waltz and laid their instruments down beside their music stands. The chatter at the other tables went on—a pleasant sound in the windblown shade in this fashionable corner of Berlin. Paul wasn't sure whom he despised the most—Jews, or himself for being one.

"When will you leave?" Leni forced a smile that did little to conceal her feelings of disappointment and anger.

"Not for another month. I promised Liesl a boat ride on the Rhine, but we'll only be away for a few days."

The smile stayed on her mouth with an effort while her gaze brimmed with more bright sadness.

"A few days," she said resentfully.

FIVE

Earlier that morning Paul had driven out to the convent school for retarded children near Zossen. Sister Clara, the mother superior, had met him in the gloomy hallway.

"You must be eager to see Liesl." The lined face under the starched white mantle of the habit had a look of severity. But the smile, scattering the creases, radiated an inner sweetness. "Come, please."

Paul followed her outdoors. A few children played in the yard. Sister Clara shielded her eyes from the sun and pointed toward a wooded knoll beyond the playground. On a footpath, a younger nun walked beside Liesl, holding her hand. The little girl wore knee stockings, and one small fist clutched several wildflowers.

"Liesl," Sister Clara called out. "Look who is here to see you!"

Liesl ran to Paul and threw her arms around his neck as he bent to pick her up.

"Look at you." Paul laughed. "Haven't you grown to be a big girl!"

Her face had not yet lost its chubbiness, and the smile made it even more round.

The younger nun said, "Aren't you going to give your brother his flowers?"

The little girl thrust the bouquet out and looked away shyly. Paul put her down and took the flowers.

"My favorite color." He grinned. "I've brought you a surprise, too."

He watched her tear off the brown paper. A flash of joy lit her eyes.

It was a rag doll with yellow mop strings for hair and a smile sewn into the face. Two ciphers of dyed cloth gave the cheeks a happy flush.

"What are you going to name her?" Paul said.

For a moment she gave him a blank stare. All at once she hugged the doll close to her cheek and cried, "Ilse."

They were standing close to the swing set, and Paul said, "Shall I give you a turn on the swing? Here, let's put Ilse down on the grass. She can hold the flowers you picked for me while she watches you."

Later, when Paul was saying good-bye, the little girl started to cry because he could not take her with him.

"Don't you want to stay here with all your friends?" he asked.

Liesl shook her head firmly, tears rolling down her cheeks.

"I've got a better idea." Paul was down on one knee, his hands on Liesl's shoulders. "How would you like to go for a nice boat ride?"

The sobs grew less intense, and at last she nodded.

"Well, then, if you'll stop being sad, I'll go see about it right now."

So Paul had arranged the cruise on the Rhine. They went by rail to Bonn and spent the night at a pension on the river. The sun rose early, bathing the roofs of the town in a lemon glow. After breakfast, Paul paid the bill and they walked down to the dock where the ferry steamer was tied. A few passengers were already boarding, and Paul took Liesl's hand on the gangplank. The upper deck was warm in the sun, and they stood aft at the railing and looked out at the cathedral spires lifting above the trees along the bank and Liesl pointed at the reflections on the water.

"The clouds like to look at themselves," Paul said. "So they use the river for a mirror."

The captain climbed aboard and went into the wheelhouse. He had a pitted face with a white mustache and stood, stiff and thick-necked and heavy-bellied, like a Prussian sergeant in his braided jacket behind the glass of the wheelhouse. At last he barked orders through a speaker horn. The engines throbbed, sending a shudder through the vessel. The crew cast off the mooring lines, and the ferry nudged away from the dock piles, the screws churning up a slash of bubbles in the stern.

"Look, Liesl, we're off! Aren't you excited?"

The little girl giggled nervously, clutching the railpost. The boat chugged upstream, and there was a last view of the town sliding away from them, the cathedral spires shrinking above the trees.

The river ran, sparkling, past many villages, and there were long river valleys and meadows, the grass shifting under drafts of wind, and wooded ridges stampeding into the horizon. The villages all looked old, the high-roofed houses crowding down on each other and dominated by the steeple of a church, and sometimes the gravestones of the cemetery showed beside a church wall in the sun.

Other traffic moved on the river, smaller craft chalking their wakes, and big barges sliding downstream on the current, and Liesl pointed each one out to Paul. The boat put in at several towns to take on passengers and unload cargo and, once, steaming away from a dock into the channel, the captain motioned Paul and Liesl to come into the wheelhouse. Perspiration beaded his cheeks above the white mustache. He lifted Liesl so that she could ring the ship's bell. The first clang of brass drew a delighted laugh from her. Again and again she rang it.

The warm afternoon waned pleasantly, as if it were in no hurry, lulled by the green sunlit distances and placid flow of the river. They tied up for the day at a town below Koblenz. A guide stacked luggage onto a cart and wheeled it across the road to the hotel. Paul signed the register and as soon as they were settled into their room he took Liesl out for a bite to eat.

The town nestled below a wooded hill crowned by a castle. They ate at an outdoor café on the cobbled square and listened to band music, and Paul drank a beer with his sausage. Shadows flooded the town, but the bluff behind the church still had sunlight. The slope in back of the church wall was smothered in wildflowers.

"Can we go pick some?" Liesl asked.

They walked back through the narrow streets, steeped in shadow, and climbed the hill into the sun behind the bell tower. Paul lay back with his fingers laced behind his head among the bright delicate ciphers that broke and swayed on each whisper of wind.

He smiled at Liesl and said, "Did you know that in Greece there is a field where fallen stars at night become flowers by day?"

"Do stars fall out of the sky?" Liesl asked.

"Sure they do," Paul said. "Maybe this is a field of fallen stars. Do you think it could be so?"

"Could we see them fall and turn into flowers?"

"Well, maybe we could watch some night, but they say it's very secret."

The sun was down when they started back, the castle walls bathed in rosy light on the hill above the river. At the hotel they sat on the covered porch in the dusk and watched the barges gliding past, lamps ablaze on the water.

Liesl began to yawn, and they went upstairs. Paul opened the windows that looked out over the town. The moon was up behind the castle, and they could see the steeple of the church and the bluff, the wildflowers pale in the radiant blaze. Suddenly a star skated down the sky and went out. Liesl saw it and gave Paul an excited, questioning look.

"Will it be a flower in the field tomorrow?"

"A pretty one, I should think."

Liesl climbed into bed with her doll. Paul bent down and brushed her cheek with a kiss. She held Ilse up to be kissed too. Paul blew out the lamp, undressed behind the paper screen, and turned back the coverlet of the other bed. Liesl was already fast asleep, her hair spread out on the pillow, the doll loosely cradled in her arm. It was hard to think of her as *Halbjude*. Her features were altogether Aryan. At least she would never have to know about her Jewishness. He wondered if she were dreaming about the flowers.

The next afternoon, the captain put in at Worms, where Paul and Liesl left the boat. They planned to spend a day sightseeing and then return to Berlin by train.

That night, Paul took Liesl to a carnival. Tents sloped skyward and pennants streamed aloft, the wire rigging strung across the blue dusk above the teeming grounds. The canvas looked old and dark, speckled with mold spores, and there was a smell of rot in hidden places.

On the midway, Paul helped Liesl roll a wooden ball toward some standing pins. Two pins toppled and the little girl laughed and clapped her hands. For a prize she chose a paper bird attached by a string to a rod and Paul showed her how to make it fly.

Later, they paused before a tent where a tall, cadaverous magician, wearing a swastika on his cloth armband, stood on a platform lit by flares. The crowd was laughing at his jokes about Jews. A high varnished hat exaggerated the gauntness of his face, powdered white, the lips painted.

On the stage behind him stood a brown-haired girl in shorts, a robe draped over her thin shoulders. She stared out over the faces in the audience as if they did not exist, her mouth sullen. Next to her, on a stool, sat a dwarf dressed like a jester. Above the medieval patches of his collar, his face was swollen and ugly, and his misshapen legs dangled above the stage. Each time he squirmed on the stool the bells sewn into his dirty costume jingled.

A canvas poster showed the girl in a cabinet skewered with pokers and dripping blood. It was a chamber of horrors, and in a gutteral voice the magician described what would be seen inside.

Now, in the flicker of the torches, he drew a scarf from his hat and began to pull it deftly through his hands. The colored silk streamed out each time like a puff of smoke, but at last he gave a tug and there was nothing. Paul stood, holding Liesl in his arms, in the front rank of the crowd.

The magician leaned down, grinning at Liesl, his eyes burning.

"*Ist es möglich?*" He turned his hands to show they were empty. "Is it possible? But yes! I can even make little girls disappear—like a piece of silk!"

Liesl's arms tightened around Paul's neck. She buried her face against him and began to whimper. Someone stepped on the paper bird, crunching it.

Paul turned away and moved through the crowd. A ripple of nervous laughter went up, and he had a glimpse, over his shoulder, of the powdered face still grinning in the glint of the flares. His own heart was beating fast, and it took him a moment to realize that it had to do with being a Jew.

SIX

On his last evening in Berlin, Paul had dinner with Leni and Georg at the Adlon. Georg was the host, and after dessert and coffee they squeezed into the front seat of his coupe and drove out to the cabaret district.

"Where shall we go?" Leni asked.

"They say there's a hot act at the Pink Cat," Georg replied.

It was a warm evening on the Kurfürstendamm, the boulevard looking somehow naked without its parade of prostitutes, homosexuals, and transvestites. Hitler had swept them from the streets. In the new Reich, there would be no deviation from the party line, not even sexual.

They parked the car and went on foot into a lane where a flashing neon tube, twisted into a feline shape, marked the entrance to the Pink Cat. It was a basement cabaret, and the music drifted up as they went down the stone steps. There was a crowd, and smoke hung over the tables. A waiter brought drinks, and Paul asked Georg if he had decided what he would do after medical school.

"I've always wanted to get into research." Georg's thick glasses held his clear gaze like a specimen on a slide. Even the flicker of enthusiasm had a microscopic clarity. "Fritz said he'd find the right spot for me."

"Von Stroelin," Leni said. "That egoist."

Georg said, "Would you be surprised if I told you Fritz spent a year doing reconstructive surgery at a free clinic in a slum in Brazil? The patients were mostly children with congenital deformities. He never took a pfennig for his work."

"He's still an egoist," Leni said. Suddenly she stared past Paul and gasped, "My God, there he is!"

The bullish figure was advancing in the crowd at the tables. He came up, smiling, took Leni's hand as if it were already a possession and brushed the back of it with a kiss.

"You are very chic tonight, Fräulein Reibel." He held her hand until she drew it away.

"Fritz," Georg said with obvious pleasure. "What are you doing here?"

"I'm with a group of criminally boring people. It would be an immense relief to join you for a drink."

For the first time, the physician glanced at Paul and said, "Is it Ernst, or Paul? I can't tell the difference."

"Whichever one doesn't bore you," Paul said with a half smile.

"So it's Paul, then." Von Stroelin smiled too.

"Are you sure?" Leni said. "How do you know?"

"Because Paul is more competitive." The physician looked at her. "About everything."

"Even marksmanship," Georg said. "Paul's a crack shot, too. Not in the international class, of course, but very good."

"We shall have to find out sometime," von Stroelin said, "on the range."

"I don't like guns," Leni said. "Besides, I don't see any connection between shooting and medicine."

"But you're wrong, my dear," von Stroelin insisted. "A pistol is as much a tool as a scalpel. Both are an extension of the will. When you fire a pistol, the target is only of secondary importance. The act of concentration is wholly within yourself. You have to imagine that your hand is made out of steel and part of the weapon. You create a vision that the ligaments in your arm are steel wires. From your pupil, through your brain, down your shoulder, arm, and hand to the iron sights of the pistol, everything is a single working mechanism. Those are the metaphysics of shooting. It requires absolute precision. There's no room for error. In that respect, the mental discipline is not so different from a complex surgery."

"Fritz has even taught Himmler some tricks," Georg said.

"Actually," von Stroelin said, "the Reichsführer is not a bad shot in his own right."

"He can always practice on Jews," Paul said, "if paper targets run short."

"Do you think so?" The physician frowned.

The band finished its number, and the MC stepped to the microphone to introduce the act. A chubby blonde in tight shorts, leather suspenders, and high-heeled boots came out to sing. The painted bow of her mouth glistened in the spotlight, which also picked out the shine of cocaine on her eyes, outrageously bordered in blue crayon. While the girl sang, a drunk lurched out of the crowd and squeezed her breast. Still gripping the microphone, she shoved him away.

The drunk turned out to be part of the act. He tried next to pat the singer's backside. The crowd hooted as she slapped his face, sending him into a pratfall to the roll of drums. A few voices shouted encouragement as the drunk approached her from behind. A deft move of his hand unzipped the shorts that opened down the front, like a boy's, exposing part of a brassy pelt. Another slap sent him sprawling.

At first Paul wondered how the show had slipped by the censors. The answer became clear as the dialogue turned anti-Semitic. The Reich would tolerate a touch of prurience as long as it could be cloaked in Jew-baiting humor. There was much laughter from the tables, and the blond singer's own laugh made a harsh sound each time her lips parted in an angry arch that bared her white teeth. The racial bantering seemed only to heighten some vicious erotic allure.

Von Stroelin's booming laugh led the others. Paul's stomach tightened into a sick knot. A few weeks ago, he might have been laughing with the rest. Now, every joke came up like a gorge in the throat that had to be swallowed back while he sat and listened.

Finally it was over and the lights came up. While the applause went on, von Stroelin put a hand over Leni's wrist on the table and said, "Look over there."

Two tables away, Paul caught sight of a transvestite. The lights, dimming again, conspired with the excessive rouge and powder to hide all but a few of the crow's-feet around his eyes. A cigarette boy holding a tray passed by and called out: "*Zigarren? Zigaretten?*" The thin lips of the transvestite were painted purple, and the smile he flashed to the boy showed dingy, neglected teeth. His fingers toyed with his colored scarf in an effeminate way so that the folds billowed, and Paul saw an oily drop of sweat squeeze past the headband of his wig and trickle down his temple.

"You don't see many of them around, these days," Georg said.

"Naturally," Paul said. "The Führer has them shot. It's the surest road to spiritual reformation."

"Don't you agree with it?" von Stroelin asked pleasantly. On the other side of the smile was a challenge that struck Paul as less a contest of ideas than a competition for Leni.

"Why shouldn't I agree?" Paul shrugged. "I'm not the one who's getting shot."

"But you think the measure is too severe," von Stroelin pressed him.

"Hegel would love it," Paul said.

"Only as a moral imperative."

"What do morals have to do with politics?" Paul smiled.

"I could explain it," von Stroelin said, "but you might not like the answer."

Paul glanced at the transvestite and said, "Explain it to him. He might even be a Jew in the bargain. One bullet would serve the concept of Hegelian efficiency."

Georg interrupted in a joking fashion, "Only if you assume a Jew is worth a bullet."

Paul looked at his friend and could remember him crouched in a corner of the schoolyard, his face buried in his hands while sobs wrenched his body. Perhaps it was the certainty he would not fight back that had made him the victim of constant bullying. The next time it started, Paul blackened the eye of the ringleader. He wondered what Georg would think if he knew he had been defended by a half-Jew.

"I'm sick of talk about Jews," Leni said. "That's all you hear these days. I know they're subhuman and vile, but do we have to dwell on the problem? I want to have fun!"

The band had come back to the platform, and the players were taking up their instruments. Von Stroelin asked Leni if she would dance.

"I promised this one to Paul," she said.

On the dance floor, they turned to each other. For most of the evening, Leni had concealed her sadness behind animated talk and impulsive laughter. Now, close to the band, it was too noisy for talk and she put both arms around his neck, their bodies tight in the crowd. It was as if she were clinging desperately to these few minutes of being alone together. The heat left them perspiring as they came back to the table. Von Stroelin's chair was empty.

"You and Fritz don't get along," Georg said to Paul. "That's clear."

"It's not a crisis for civilization," Paul said.

"I don't understand it, that's all."

Paul shrugged and said, "Most things in the world are beyond comprehension, these days."

Later, coming out of the men's room into the cramped hallway, Paul ran into the transvestite. The rouged features were caked with sweat, and in the light of the harsh ceiling bulb the face itself seemed to be disintegrating in cracks and seams under the makeup. The purple lips wavered in a half smile, expectant and hopeless at the same time, as he fled past Paul into the ladies' room. Not far behind came two plainclothes police. They shouldered past Paul, pounded on the door of the ladies' room, and burst in. On the other side of the partition their voices rose, and Paul heard a gasp of pain that could have come from a fist to a kidney.

At the table, Georg said, "The waiter just told us that the police are here to arrest that pervert."

"They already have," Paul said.

Georg shook his head, smiling. "Well, I wouldn't want to be in his shoes."

"You're not," Paul said.

As they left the cabaret, Paul had a glimpse of von Stroelin watching them from the group at his table. Von Stroelin lifted a hand. Only Georg waved back.

On the drive out of the district, they blundered into a police cordon. Near the mouth of a narrow alley the headlights picked out a black-shirted SS man who waved his arms furiously.

"Get those fucking lights off," he yelled at Georg. "How did you get past the barricade?"

"What barricade?" Georg had his head out the side window.

Paul reached across the dashboard to cut the lights. He was out of the car before Georg could get the gears into reverse.

"What's going on?" His tone was a bit too openly impertinent. To cover it, he added, "Do you need help?"

The offer of help seemed to appease the blackshirt, who was beefy and big and had a crushed nose in a concave face.

"Just stay back," he said. "The Gestapo are making an arrest. A dozen Bolshevik Jews. . . ." He pointed to an attic apartment beyond a bench and lamppost in the cobbled square. "Up there."

In the confusion of shouted orders and screams, someone smashed out a window, and the falling glass shattered on the pavement. Paul could see uniformed SS moving in the lighted apartment, and Gestapo in plain-clothes.

A pair of SS dragged a struggling youth downstairs into the square. They beat him with their truncheons until he went down. There was a darting movement on the high slate roof, and two figures slipped across the skyline of chimneys and drain spouts. The blackshirt next to Paul spotted them and called to the others standing over the boy on the cobbles by the bench.

"They're going out over the roof!"

The two SS bolted into the side street to cut off the retreat. Upstairs, the uniformed figures with the blood-red brassards on their sleeves were smashing furniture and flinging articles down into the street. From the windows of darkened apartments, faces peered out like blanks of flesh above hands clamped into the lace of curtains.

The boy who had been beaten still lay near the bench where the street lamp picked up the grimy shine of cobbles. Now he pushed to his feet and ran, staggering, toward the lane where Paul and the others were. Paul wanted to shout at him to go back, but already it was too late. A jackboot came out of the shadows, taking the fugitive off his feet.

"I'll teach you to play Jew games," the blackshirt snarled.

The splat of the truncheon across the upturned face drew a cry from Leni in the coupe. The boy let out a grunt as a boot went into his ribs. He squirmed in the gutter, one hand over his crotch and the other across his face as the blackshirt kicked at him and swore.

"You're killing him," Paul said.

"Then I'm doing him a favor," the other replied, breathing hard.

All evening, the anger had been gathering in Paul's fists. It had started with the jokes of the two performers in the cabaret, and the bantering air of von Stroelin had only made it worse. Now some last shred of control snapped in him, though his voice retained an odd calm.

"One favor deserves another."

Paul swung at the midsection. The wind went out of the blackshirt with a sound of sick surprise on the slack mouth below the mashed nose. Before he could recover, half a dozen short quick punches, coming out of nowhere on a boxer's clipped rhythm, sent him reeling backward. It was von Stroelin's blood-smeared face in front of Paul, but all at once he realized it was not the other man that he was hitting. It was the pent-up bitterness of the last few weeks over his own Jewishness. The legs went out from under the blackshirt and his skull cracked against the curb. He rolled limply and did not move.

The boy, who looked about sixteen, groaned as Paul propped him up against the wall. Streamers of blood ran down his neck from his split cheek. Several teeth had been knocked loose and one hung by a thread. He started to sink to the pavement but Paul caught him, drew out a handkerchief, and pressed it to the flow of blood.

Leni was tugging at Paul's arm.

"Let's get away from here!"

In the deeper shadows, Georg was bent over the blackshirt. He used a thumb to lift an eyelid, and let it drop. Then he groped for the carotid.

"This one's badly hurt," he whispered anxiously. "Severe concussion would be my guess."

"To hell with him," Paul snapped.

"Oh, let's get away from here while we can," Leni pleaded again.

"Hold the handkerchief in place," Paul said to the boy. "Can you walk?"

The youth opened his mouth and a glut of black blood and saliva spilled down his chin.

"Jew?" Paul said.

"*Nein . . .*" The boy shot him a terrified look. Then his gaze fell away in guilt and he nodded.

"Then you'd better get out of here fast," Paul said, "and keep out of sight."

Another gob of blood spilled from the boy's mouth down his chin.

"*Danke,*" he gasped.

Paul watched him stumble into the shadows, a bent figure holding his ribs with one hand, the handkerchief still clamped to his cheek with the other.

In the car, no one spoke. Leni was shaking, her leg pressed against Paul's. The steering wheel looked ready to fly apart in Georg's white-knuckled grip. In their silence they seemed to be asking why. *Why* had he attacked a blackshirt to save a Jew? Paul had a momentary urge to tell them. It would have ended everything in one clean stroke—his relationship with Leni, his friendship with Georg. But the situation was not that simple. The truth would involve Liesl and Ernst, and even their father.

"I hope that handkerchief didn't have a monogram on it," Georg said finally.

"Better switch on your lights," Paul replied, "unless you want to be stopped."

The paving stones melted away under the moving brightness. Soon the lamplit boulevard swung its reflection onto the windshield. Hitler might clean up the Kurfürstendamm, but evil would only change its form like the silk in the hands of the magician at Worms, a cheap carnival trick. The powdered face and painted lips in the torchlit darkness seemed, now, less a flesh-and-blood memory than a specter beckoning with a pitchman's leer to all of Germany. Paul was almost glad to be leaving Berlin for Greece.

SEVEN

For a year, in Athens, Paul lived in a room above a taverna on a hill in the old quarter. He had little time to think about Leni. His regimen at the university kept him busy during the day. In the evening, after an early meal, he would study or read for a couple of hours, then blow out the lamp and go down into the courtyard to drink a glass of retsina, talk to the patrons, or play chess.

Ernst wrote from Florence that some of his pictures were now on display in a gallery on the Piazza della Signoria and were selling, about one a month, for a good price. He planned a walking trip, in the spring, across Tuscany and would do some painting.

Leni wrote often, telling Paul the news of Berlin, and how much she missed him. Georg expected to graduate early from medical school, would intern at the Charité, and hoped to go on to a post in biomedical research. Paul's own letters were less frequent and made no mention of coming home. Still, he could not bring himself to break off the relationship.

That spring he spent six weeks in the monasteries of Mount Athos. The trip by mule from Daphne to Karyes had been arranged through the university, and he had a cell to himself and access to the hand-copied manuscripts in the library. The isolated site, high above the sea, made a good excuse not to write.

The hot weather had set in by the time he got back to Athens. At the taverna, the first person he saw as he climbed the stairs was the proprietor's sixteen-year-old daughter. She was on her knees scrubbing the floor, the skirt tight across the curve of her flanks, and perspiration streaked her blouse at the small of her back.

"You're always working, Lila," he called out to her from the landing, his hand on the railing.

She turned on her knees, brushing the wings of black hair away from her eyes, and a smile lit her face. She ran down the hall to collect the mail she had saved for him.

In his room Paul opened the shutters to let in light and read the mail. A card from Ernst said only that he had set out on his hike across Tuscany and was putting up for a week at a pension near Siena. There was a letter with a Geneva postmark from his father. For the first time, Kurt Krenek spoke freely of the situation in Berlin. Decrees had been posted requiring Jews to register their assets, and making it a crime to camouflage Jewish industries. All Jews previously convicted of minor offenses, including traffic violations, were being sent off to camps. "It might be wise," he advised in closing, "to extend your stay in Greece for a few months until things settle down. All of this has happened so fast. It's bound to change."

Paul wrote to Leni that he had the offer of a part-time teaching post and would stay on in Athens. A month went by before he heard from her. She wrote that she would be traveling with her mother to Greece at the end of August and planned to spend a week in Athens.

EIGHT

Paul was waiting in the crowd the day the liner bringing Leni and her mother to Greece tied up at the dock. The two women had traveled by rail through Italy and sailed from Trieste down the Adriatic coast. It was noisy on the pier with the creak of cargo cranes, the hooting of tugs, and the screech of gulls, and Paul caught sight of Leni among the passengers near the top of the gangplank. She saw him and waved, and he lifted a hand. Later, she ran to him in the throng and her warm mouth, under his, clung to the kiss for a long time and broke away, breathless and laughing.

"*Oh, Paul!*" She squeezed his fingers.

Paul kissed her again, then turned to greet Frau Reibel. The older woman gave him a stiff embrace, and he wondered if he only imagined the cool reserve that she projected.

"Did you have a pleasant voyage, Frau Reibel?"

"Long voyages are never pleasant," she said pointedly, "only tiring."

"Then we'd better get you to your hotel. I'll see you through Customs and find a taxi."

On the drive into the city they spoke of friends and family, and Paul asked about Georg.

"I wrote you about his appointment at the Charité," Leni said. A touch of color came to her cheeks and she gazed out the window. "He's doing splendidly. The SS wants him, but I don't think he'll go into uniform unless there's a war."

"Georg has a brilliant future," Frau Reibel remarked with a glance toward Leni. "Quite a catch for some girl."

Paul had reserved a suite for them at one of the new hotels off the main square. A porter carried the bags in from the street. The clock above the desk showed a few minutes after four. Paul said he would come back in two hours and take them to dinner.

At six Paul was in the lobby when the elevator descended. Leni was alone with the operator in the scalloped iron of the sinking cage. She had bathed and changed into a dress of creamy silk, a wide-brimmed hat, and matching gloves.

"Where's your mother?"

"Still resting. Besides, she thought we might prefer to be by ourselves the first evening."

Leni insisted on seeing where he lived, and they took a horse-cab into the *Plaka*. It was a pleasant ride in the open carriage, the canopy folded back, the sun-warmed stucco of walls and houses drifting by in the clop of hooves. The driver pulled up in the lane below the taverna. Paul paid the fare, and they climbed the stone steps and went in through the courtyard. He presented Leni to the proprietor, asking the old man's permission before taking her upstairs. In his room, she gave the flaking plaster a glance.

"Come over to the window," Paul said. "You can see the whole *Plaka*."

Beyond the plane tree in the courtyard the roofs of the quarter sank away in shadow. There were shouts of children playing and the sound of a dog barking. On a distant rooftop restaurant, a man unstacked chairs from the tops of tables. Paul pointed to the limestone crown of Lykabettos lifting above pine woods.

"The Greeks believe it was dropped there by Athena on her way from Pentelicon."

There was a sound in the hall, and the proprietor's daughter appeared at the door with his laundry. Paul introduced them, speaking in Greek and German. Lila nodded but did not smile. Then she looked at Paul, and her expression softened. She put the armful of clothing down on his bed, glanced once more at him, and went out.

"Lila's shy," he said, "but sweet, once she knows you."

"*Und tüchtig*," Leni said, smiling. "Capable, too."

Downstairs, in the courtyard, they sat under the plane tree, where a lantern, slung in its brass cradle, lit the leaves, and the proprietor brought out his best wine.

"So this is where you've hidden away from the world for the last year," Leni said.

"Most people are hiding from something." Paul shrugged. "This is as good a place as any to do it."

"With a pretty girl to look after you," Leni added.

"Lila? She's a child."

"Hasn't it occurred to you that she's in love with you? In the room, when she looked at you, it was written all over her face."

"Don't be silly."

The smile stayed on her mouth like a bit of camouflage, but the faint rash of angry pink at her throat compromised the emotion behind it.

"Just tell me if it has anything to do with your wanting to stay in Greece," Leni said. On the other side of her tolerant amusement lay a jealous anger, uncompromising and childishly possessive.

"No." Paul gazed at her.

"I almost wish it had." Leni shook her head.

"Why?"

"Because I could always take you away from another woman." The half smile on her mouth had a careless assurance. "Tell me what we're going to do this week."

"Tomorrow I'll show you the city. I've hired a car for the day after. We'll take your mother to the monastery on Hymettus. There's a nice garden with honeysuckle and you can drink from Ovid's fountain. From there we could drive down into Attica."

"Wonderful." Leni was leaning forward, her hands folded under her chin.

"After that, I thought the three of us might take one of the short cruises down to Hydra. You haven't really seen Greece until you've seen the islands . . ."

They spent a pleasant three days in and around the city and on the fourth boarded a small cruise ship, much to Frau Reibel's misgivings, and from the stern watched Piraeus recede on the morning skyline. They steamed south past the steep pine slopes of Poros and down the coast where lemon orchards gleamed in the sun, and the ship dropped anchor in the bay off the island of Hydra. The vessel was too large to put in at the dock. Small boats, each manned by a single oarsman, came out to unload passengers and the cargo—baskets of tomatoes and cucumbers, sacks of grain and flour, and drums of oil for the lamps of the island.

A young boatman rowed them into the harbor, the muscle pack on both forearms jumping each time he dipped the oars and pulled. He tied up at the quay and held the boat steady as they climbed out. Smiling, he carried their bags up to the hotel. It was a small hotel, the pastel front sun-baked and faded, and they had two nice rooms that looked out on the bay.

There were no vehicles on the island, not even a bicycle, and no roads, but only trails where pack mules carried food and supplies inland. Along the quay were cafés, and shops selling vegetables, and stalls with sponges harvested by the fishermen of Hydra, and stands where artists worked.

While Frau Reibel rested in her room, Paul and Leni climbed the hill behind the hotel. It was a steep climb past the whitewashed houses, the bay sinking behind them with every step. At the top of the hill they followed a footpath to a ridge where a line of windmills stood against the sky. The thatched towers were abandoned and the canvas sails hung, torn and rotting, on the poles that served as vanes.

Perspiring, they sat down in the shade and listened to the canvas thumping in the hot wind. Leni leaned back on her elbows and closed her eyes. There was something outrageously attractive in the long arch of her neck and the thrust of her breasts against the cotton blouse. Paul bent to kiss her, and the response of her lips, stirring lazily under his, went deep to some male center of hardening desire. The world seemed pleasantly shrunk to the windy silence of the moment, only the canvas snapping overhead like wings beating to release the straining maleness within him. When he finally drew back, she gave him a stare that was impossibly tender and direct in its assent.

"Let's look for a place to swim, shall we?" Paul said.

"All right." The smile on her mouth had a trace of secret amusement, as if she knew something he did not.

They took the path that looped along the cliff above the sea. There were inlets notched into the island where the water ran, flashing, over rocky shoals. Schools of tiny fish darted in the depths, changing direction in the current with a flicker of movement.

Paul found a cove deep enough for swimming, and they climbed down from the cliff rim to the rocks above the pool and stripped to their bathing costumes. The water, clear as a spring, made it hard to judge the depth where the sandy bottom wavered. Paul dove first and found it to be nearly two fathoms. Surfacing, he looked up to see Leni poised to dive from a flat ledge, her body sculpted into the blue afternoon. The horizon swung against her arms as she pushed off with her toes. Her figure hung for an instant on space before the sky arched away from it. The sun sparkled against her silhouette, and then she plunged down in a diagonal plane of pointed flight against the vertical sheet of rock into the sea pool. Her feet dislodged a cloudy swirl of sand, and Paul watched her golden figure melting upward through the blinding parcels of marine light that rippled in bands about her head.

They laughed and swam in the crystalline water, drying afterward on a sun-warmed ledge, and tramped back to the hotel with their clothing bundled under their arms.

Later, at an outdoor café on the quay, they dined with Frau Reibel on squid and salad greens. Fishing boats chugged into the bay, dragging their wakes like smoke that vanished among the reflections emblazoned on the water. On the mainland of Peloponnesus the mountains formed dark blue ridges, one behind the other, which faded in the dusk.

The boatman who had rowed them ashore came up to their table and smiled in the lamplight. Paul invited him to sit down for a glass of wine, but the youth replied that he was on his way home. He asked if they had seen much of the island, and Paul said, "We took a hike today and found a place to swim."

"But there are no beaches on Hydra," the young man said. "If you want a sandy beach for swimming, I could row you across to Molos tomorrow and come back for you."

Paul translated for Leni, who nodded approval. They set a time to meet. The young Greek smiled again, bowed to the ladies and moved off.

At the next café, under a string of colored bulbs, someone strummed a mandolin. Several men linked arms and danced while the crowd at the tables clapped in rhythm.

It was a warm evening and Leni told Paul she wanted to climb the hill and see the bay at night. Frau Reibel told them to go ahead. She would finish her coffee and go back to the hotel.

Paul and Leni set off, the grade pulling at their legs. There was a breeze on the top of the cliff and a view of the promenade, stretching below in a crescent, the lights swimming on the water.

Stars burned overhead and the moon was at full intensity, rolling the night back from the landscape. They followed the footpath out along the cliff, and Leni said, "Look, there's the pool where we swam."

Paul looked down at the water, which had the shine of phosphorus.

"It's so warm." Leni squeezed his hand. "Paul, let's go for another swim, shall we?"

He laughed and replied, "Without bathing suits?"

"We don't need them. It's dark."

Paul hesitated, thinking of Frau Reibel.

"What would your mother say?"

"Oh, don't be so old-fashioned. Besides, do you think I'd tell her?"

He had only to say no, but the heat from the core of aroused feeling earlier that day, went all the way through him like a paralyzing agent.

"Somebody might come." His voice was thick, like a stranger's.

"There's nobody," Leni whispered, giving his fingers an insistent tug. In another moment they were picking their way down the rocky incline.

Paul left her to shed his clothing. Even before he finished he heard a sound of loose rocks falling, turned, and had a glimpse of Leni on the ledge from which she had dived that afternoon. Her head was thrown back toward the sky and her bare breasts were tilted and wide apart, the tips pointed and gleaming.

Then she dove, her body arching across the bank of summer clouds where the moon left the immaculate blaze of its candlepower. Paul saw the erupting chain of bubbles as she plunged below the surface that was clear and dark like the celluloid of a film negative. The bands of refracted moonlight around her nude figure drifting upward had the shimmer of quicksilver. She swam toward the shadow below the ledge of stratified rock on the side of the cove untouched by the moon.

The sight swept away the last restraints that he had built over the last year like a dam around their relationship. The whole torrent of feeling came loose in a flash flood that was unstoppable, a rampage of need in the nerves and glands. Carried away in it were the cold cerebral resolve of many months, the fear of consequences, the possibility of regret.

It was a scenario Leni herself had created, hoping Paul would react as he had. Her mind had been locked into that purpose even as she dove toward the melting light of the stars, surfaced, and swam into the shadowy side of the cove where a couple making love would not be seen from above. No sooner had she reached it, clinging to the rock, than she felt the hydrostatic lift of the water against her shoulders as Paul swam after her. A shiver of dark excitement passed through her—part anticipation, part fear.

Turning, she saw the gleam of his shoulders in the water before he passed into the bank of shadow. One hand grasped the rim beside her head. The other encircled her waist. No words came from the mouth that kept its cold hard shape as if the silence had been carved into it. There was no need to explain or ask. The planes of his face were hardened too, and his eyes had a dark brilliance in the pooled shadows of the sockets. The resistance of the water against their bodies exaggerated the sense of slow motion. She let herself be swept against him, her arms locked about his neck, and her mouth surrendered its own surprising lust in the long heat of a kiss.

Even as her legs drifted about him in the weightless density of the pool she heard herself gasp at the first shock of entry. His muscles were swollen, his body taut and steel hard in some pent-up sexual force.

Another long gasp was torn from her throat, and another, as his penetration went to some unexplored zone of pain and pleasure. The water ran down their faces past their mouths, still locked together, and long before seed broke from him she felt the deep seismic quiver begin in her and become one with the thrusting hardness.

Even after he withdrew from her she still clung to him, her eyes closed, trying to hold the sensation of shattering, rapturous pleasure. Already it was falling back, somewhere out of reach within her. But that was unimportant. Only the explosion of life-bearing matter in her had importance now, and she smiled blissfully.

NINE

At breakfast Paul wondered if Frau Reibel suspected they had been intimate. Leni's face shone. Paul's own guilt burned into a dark flush each time he looked at the older woman. But if she knew about them, she did not show it.

At noon they met the boatman, Dimitrios, on the waterfront, and he rowed them across the channel to Molos. Leni wore shorts and halter, and Paul had on white bathing trunks and a cotton shirt open down the front. They sat at the thwart in the stern, and once, when their bare legs touched, Paul could feel a circuit open on some voltage of excitement. Behind Dimitrios's grin lay a sense of complicity. He made a point of beaching the boat at an obscure sandy inlet and gave Paul a knowing wink.

Paul helped him launch the craft into the surf, then waded out of the water to Leni. They watched the young Greek straining at the oars. In a few minutes he was beyond the swells, his figure shrinking. The sand scorched their feet as Paul drew her to the shade of the dunes lifting back under scalp locks of grass.

They gazed out to sea once more to make sure Dimitrios was gone from view. Smiling at Paul, Leni put both hands behind her back to unfasten her halter. When their clothing was shed, they stood naked before each other, the sun glinting off their bodies.

Almost shyly, Leni touched his bare chest, her fingers spread, and Paul kissed her. Her lips opened under his, and he felt the hand on his chest trail downward, like a caress. Even as the fingers drew hardness from him, their bodies sank into the heavy dune grass. She sucked on his tongue, and after a moment he felt the freshets of a different wetness where she forced herself onto the thickness in her grasp in a slow impaling movement that sought the burning release of that white-hot seminal core, and later he was only half aware of the sounds coming from her, her eyes squeezed shut, as the deep sliding contractions enclosing his own male part quickened all at once and became a quivering flow.

For a long time, neither stirred. He could see tiny beads of perspiration around her eyelids before she opened them and gazed at him, the pleasure still rounded into her pupils. The tips of her breasts were swollen hard against him, and he did not want to move away from the languor of the moment. He brushed her cheek with a kiss while the sun burned down on his neck and shoulders.

They bathed in the sea to cool off, then sat on the beach, their ankles in the water. In the aftermath of lovemaking, Paul was silently withdrawn, preoccupied with the conflict of his Jewishness, as if it could be transmitted like a venereal disease. It seemed to him now that sexual intimacy would exact an exorbitant price in guilt, which would be paid each time like blackmail.

Leni leaned back in the sand, one knee uplifted, and closed her eyes in the sun. She began suddenly to talk of their future and spoke of his returning to Berlin as if it were already a fact.

Paul shook his head and said, "I'm not coming back to Berlin—not for a while."

The words had the effect of a slap. Leni sat upright, looking away. Finally she said in a gently reproachful tone, "But, Paul, surely you still don't want to stay here—after . . ." She did not finish.

"It's not a question of what I want."

"Then why would you do it?"

"People do what they have to do," he said. "It isn't always convenient, or easy."

"Or honorable?" There was a note of accusation at the center of her disappointment.

Paul stared at the curve of her back, sun warmed and tawny. From now on, the need for each other would only intensify each time the opportunity was there.

"Or honorable," he agreed.

Leni turned on him antagonistically.

"Well it's clear, isn't it? You don't care anything about me. You don't want to be married, and staying in Greece is the perfect excuse!"

The hot drafts of wind tore at the silence, as if trying to ransack the truth from it. Finally Paul let out a long breath and closed his eyes.

"We can't marry." He might have been confessing to a capital crime. "My mother was a Jew. I didn't know about it until a year ago. Ernst knew. He told me that night at the party. That's why I came here. I thought a separation might change things. You'd meet someone else, and that would solve the problem."

Leni did not move, her gaze fixed on the far-off sparkle of the sea, as if the promise of their future had been suddenly lost among the spangles of sunlight. At last she bent her head and slowly scooped up a puff of foam from the shallows and let the wind take it from her hand. Paul watched it blow away in pieces. When he glanced at her again she was in tears with both hands over her face. Crying, she made no sound, and her shoulders did not shake. But the moment Paul pulled her hands from her face, she broke down.

"I don't care!" she sobbed. "I don't care what you are!"

"You once said Jews were subhuman and vile." He shook his head. "Maybe you're right."

"It was just a stupid remark," she protested. "It didn't mean anything."

"Listen to me," Paul said sadly. "You know what the penalties are for breaking the law. If it ever came out that I was a half-Jew, we'd both be in a concentration camp."

"If we were married—"

"It would only be worse," Paul cut off her protest. "The marriage would be invalid. If there were children, they'd be taken away, too. You have to think about the consequences. I don't care about the risk to me, but when it involves you, and other people, that's different."

"How would they find out? You didn't even know about it yourself all these years."

"Somebody else is bound to know. Suppose they don't keep their mouth shut? All it would take would be one phone call to the Gestapo."

"Then why haven't they made it?"

"That kind of information is like money in an account. You don't draw it out until you need it."

"But I love you!" Her fingernails dug into his wrist. "There's never been anyone else for me but you. Even when we were growing up, I knew it. I know I'm not perfect. I'm self-centered, and I've got a temper, and I've always had my way even when I shouldn't have. But I'm perfect for *you*. No woman will ever love you as much as I do. Physically or otherwise, you'll never find anyone who can give you what I can give you. You know it's true!"

"That's not the point," Paul said.

She flung his wrist away. The tide was out now, the water unfurling onto the beach in a few lazy scrolls. It was only the emotional tide in Leni that had risen to flood stage.

"What you're saying is that we're *never* going to be together." The remark had a ring of finality, like a pronouncement of death. "You knew it last night—and again today. . . ."

"Don't you see? That's why it has to stop. The whole thing's impossible."

"You know it'll happen again." Her tone had an edge of taunting contempt. "Somewhere—sometime."

"Not if we're separated," Paul said.

Her head dropped, and she dug her knuckles into her red-rimmed eyes, trying to hold back the tears. When Paul touched her bare shoulder she sprang up, her body only half perceived like an afterimage in the sun's blinding incandescence. Even as he raised a hand to shield his eyes, she was gone in a flashing erotic curve of naked movement against the solar blaze. He did not turn to watch her hurrying across to the dunes where her shorts and halter lay.

By the time Dimitrios appeared, skimming in on the blue swells, Leni was coldly composed. But the tension below the surface was evident. As they set out toward Hydra, the young Greek soon sensed that something had gone wrong. After a few exchanges, he fell silent and pulled harder on the oars.

On their last afternoon together in Athens, Paul and Leni took a walk in the pine woods below Mount Lykabettos. The day was drawing to an end as they climbed the looping path out of the trees to the top of the hill. Paul went with her into the stone chapel of Saint George and waited while she knelt and said a prayer in the cool, dust-lit silence, and then they stepped out and stood by the wall, still warm in the lemon light pouring off the horizon.

"When will you come home to Germany?" Leni said.

"After things settle down," he replied.

"That's not a very definite answer."

"Nothing's definite these days, is it?"

Her eyes stared straight into his, and the smile on her mouth was impossibly sad, as if the debris of a happier emotion from an earlier time had washed up on it.

"I never thought it was possible," she said coldly, "to love and hate someone at the same time."

"Are you sure that's how you feel?" Paul asked.

"I'm sure of the pain," Leni said. "Someday I'll make you feel it, too. That's a promise."

Paul shook his head and said, "Don't you think I already feel it?"

THE COURT OF BLUE SHADOWS

"I want you to know something else," she said. "Georg asked me to marry him."

After a long silence, Paul said, "What did you tell him?"

"That I couldn't give him an answer."

"Are you going to?"

"I don't know."

Paul nodded. He knew she had seen a great deal of Georg in the last year. Her letters made no secret of it. Why should it be surprising that Georg, who had remained silent so long about his feelings, would finally reveal them? Still, Paul felt betrayed by his friend.

"Would it make any difference to you if I did?" Leni said.

They were speaking of their own relationship, Paul thought, as if it were a terminally ill patient. He might have been a doctor injecting a bubble of air into a vein.

"Not if you believe it would make you happy," he said.

Both were now staring into the east, where the long purple shadow of Mount Hymettus soared up out of the plain.

"I suppose," Leni replied, "that I just wanted to hear you say it."

TEN

Leni and Georg were married in November. The news reached Paul while he was in Corinth, and he sent a jade figurine as a wedding gift.

When he got back to Athens, late in December, there was a card of acknowledgment, along with a clipping of the newlyweds on the steps of the Protestant Cathedral behind the royal palace. Leni wore a garland of flowers in her hair and held her bridal train draped over one arm. Georg was handsomely turned out in tails, varnished top hat, and silk gloves. To his left in the crowd stood Fritz von Stroelin, who had served as best man. They had honeymooned, Leni wrote, in Interlaken, done some skiing around the Jungfrau, and come home. Georg now had an important new post under von Stroelin in the Health Ministry.

At Christmas, a letter came from his father: "There was some trouble with the Jews last month, but most of the unrest has died out. The Jews are frightened. They seem to be learning their lesson and know better than to make a fuss." The code Kurt Krenek now used in writing to his sons simply involved telling the truth, but always from a Nazi viewpoint. Paul read the words and smiled bitterly. He had seen the accounts in the British press of the burning of synagogues, the smashing of Jewish shops and looting of homes. After a night of terror, thousands had been carted off to concentration camps, and more than a few had committed suicide.

Paul's second year in Greece was slipping away faster than the first. His work kept him busy. The winter had hardened into cold clear days. To keep fit, he boxed at the gymnasium, swam, and hiked in the pine woods above the monastery on the slopes of Pentelicon. He no longer brooded about being a half-Jew. It was something he did not want to think about or confront, like a disease in remission.

He had moved into rooms behind the university, but still visited the taverna to see his friends. Lila would soon be eighteen, robust and over-ripe in her long peasant skirts and high-necked blouses that seemed now a bit tight for her figure. One of the patrons told Paul that a marriage was being arranged for her.

Ernst wrote that he would spend part of the summer in Capri and would send Paul an address when he had one. The letters from his father were less frequent, but had the same tone of disguised caution about the situation in Berlin. About once a month, Paul corresponded with Sister Clara in Zossen for news of Liesl. He heard nothing about Leni and Georg and did not mention them in his own letters.

Lila's wedding took place in August. Family and friends, including Paul, packed the stone church in the quarter. In a bridal gown of brocaded satin, Lila stood before the altar, the glow of the gilded liturgical candles dancing on her skin. A bearded priest, sweating in his vestments, recited from a holy book and blessed the union. The groom, tall and hollow-cheeked, fidgeted in his rented formal clothes, the stiff, old-fashioned collar too small for his neck.

There was a celebration at the taverna. Wedding guests crammed the courtyard, lamp stained in the blue evening, and there was much laughter and loud talk and drinking of wine drawn from casks. A fiddler sat on a stool and played a dance tune, tapping his foot. Watching, Paul felt an odd sort of detachment, as if his own life had been stranded on a side track, and the switchman holding the lever was a mad corporal who would let all the other trains pass.

It was a balmy night, and after he had kissed Lila on the cheek and wished her much happiness, he took a horse-cab out of the quarter. The wedding made him think of Leni, and watching the unhurried drift of the star-burnt sky beyond the rim of the canopy, he could not put her out of his mind. When he got back to the pension there was a cable from Berlin informing him of his father's death from a stroke.

ELEVEN

Kurt Krenek's funeral drew a crowd to the cathedral, and many followed the hearse out to the cemetery, where the sprays and garlands were heaped over the freshly dug dirt of the open grave like a quilt of flowers turned back and waiting to be spread over the deceased in that last long night of sleep. After the graveside service Paul and Ernst, wearing black armbands on their sleeves, stood in the shade under the canvas shelter and shook hands with mourners and friends. Georg and Leni were there, and when she pressed Paul's hand and gazed at him, he could almost read the message on the sad silence of her eyes—*So you've finally come back....*

Georg embraced him and said, "Please come by, Paul—you and Ernst—when you feel up to it."

A few minutes later Paul watched the mound of flowers receding among the cenotaphs and marble tablets that left their chalky brilliance on the curtained window of the moving limousine. It was hard for him to imagine his father in the company of the dead, as if a contract had been violated before its date of expiration.

The limousine dropped them at the house, empty now except for the maid, Frau Kleist, heavyset and matronly in her dark dress and lace apron. Serving them tea in the garden pavilion, she suddenly burst into tears. Ernst tried to comfort her.

"You needn't stay today, Frau Kleist."

"*Nein, nein,* Herr Krenek," she fussed. "Who would look after the both of you?"

After she had left, Paul said, "What about the chemical works?"

Ernst crossed his legs and lit a cigarette.

"He expected you to step in for him one day and run it. There's no reason why you shouldn't."

"We're joint owners."

"I prefer to be an inactive partner," Ernst said. "You make the decisions. We can draw up a legal paper to that effect."

Beyond the latticework of the pavilion, the blue looked to have been burnished into the sky, as if the day had to be gleaming for Kurt Krenek's departure from the world.

"Liesl will have to be told sometime," Paul said.

"I've got to make a trip to Vienna to see an art dealer," Ernst said. "I thought I might take Liesl along. I could break the news to her at the right time."

"Is there ever a right time?"

"Face it," Ernst said. "Her father was never close to her. I don't think the news will be such a shock. But she ought to be told now, while she's young enough to accept it."

Paul took a sip of tea, gazing moodily over the cup cradled in both hands.

"We'll have to keep Frau Kleist on."

"Yes." Ernst nodded. "But I'd feel a bit easier if she weren't so enamored with her beloved Führer."

"Isn't everybody?" Paul shrugged.

"Not the Jews."

"The quickest way to get caught is to start thinking like a Jew," Paul said. "Sooner or later you'll get careless and say or do something to tip off the Gestapo."

"How do you stop thinking like a Jew?"

"By thinking like a good German who despises them."

"And acting like one?"

"What's the point of sticking your neck out," Paul asked, "when someone's waiting to chop it off?"

"I forgot to tell you," Ernst said. "The Customs police lifted my passport the other day when the plane I was on touched down at Tempelhof."

"Did they give you a reason?" Paul frowned.

"They don't have to give you a reason."

"There's probably a simple explanation."

"They didn't pick yours up, did they?"

"No."

"Then I must be under official scrutiny."

"Now you're making guesses before you know the facts."

"Am I?" Ernst smiled around the cigarette. "I'm not sure it matters, anyway. Has it occurred to you that if war breaks out with Poland, we'll be trapped in Germany? Suppose the Poles don't give in to Hitler on this Danzig business?"

"They will," Paul said.

"But if they don't?"

"Then we'll shift to war production at the chemical works and sign more government contracts."

"And if we're found out," Ernst said, "the chemical works will be expropriated by the Reich, and we'll sit out the war in a concentration camp, if we're lucky, or a cemetery, if we're not—the only two communities left that don't exclude Jews. More are moving in every day."

"I told you," Paul said, "we're safe enough as long as you forget that you're a Jew. Go on with your life the way it was before you knew. We're only responsible now to ourselves and Liesl. That makes it easier if anything should go wrong."

"If anything should go wrong . . ." Ernst repeated the words as if they were somehow prophetic.

Ernst and Liesl arrived in Vienna on the afternoon of the twenty-eighth. They stayed at a hotel near the Hofburg palace in the Ringstrasse, dined that evening on rabbit stewed in vinegar and pepper, and for dessert had spice cake. The next three days were warm and pleasant. Ernst took her to see the museums, and they walked in the Prater, and one afternoon they went for a stroll along the Danube.

"Did I tell you, Liesl," he said casually, "that your father has gone away to be with your mother?"

"Where?" Liesl gave him a blank stare.

"*Sehr weit,*" Ernst murmured. "Very far."

Across the river, a light shower of rain misted down from a cloud like a widow's veil, and a rainbow arched across it.

"Where the rainbow is?" She pointed.

"Yes." Ernst nodded. "Where it strikes the gold."

"Why did they go *there?*"

"So you wouldn't forget them. Every time you see a rainbow, you'll know they're thinking about you."

"Look." She frowned, holding his hand. "It's going away."

"Then I'll have to paint you a nice picture of one," Ernst said, "to keep all the time."

On the fourth day, when they came down for breakfast, the dining room buzzed with nervous talk. It seemed an interminable time before a waiter appeared, his cheeks flushed, and Ernst inquired about the stir.

"Haven't you heard, sir? We're at war with Poland."

"No!"

"There was a provocation. Our units crossed the frontier during the night. The bulletins have been coming over the radio. They say we're counterattacking."

The waiter brought coffee and a saucer of pastries, and Ernst sent him out for a newspaper. From the table, he watched him through the window in the press of people at the kiosk across the street.

"Is it a game?" Liesl said.

Ernst looked at the little girl across the table. They had made up so many games these last few days. Now, he thought, they would have to cut short their holiday and take the train back to Berlin. By evening the railroads would be crowded. In a few days, travel might be impossible.

"Yes." He watched the waiter darting back through the traffic, the paper folded in one hand. "It's a game."

TWELVE

Ernst did not get in from Vienna until the afternoon of the third. He had dropped Liesl at the convent in Zossen before coming on to Berlin by bus. Paul met him at the Bahnhofplatz.

"I suppose you've heard," Ernst said, "that Britain and France have come into it."

Paul nodded and said, "I was in the Wilhelmplatz at noon when it came over the loudspeakers."

"I hear we've gone to ration cards, too," Ernst said.

"Food and soap," Paul said, "and a blackout in the bargain."

"No Polish bombers?"

"The air raid sirens went off the first night, but no enemy planes."

"I wouldn't mind bombs falling," Ernst said, "if Germany's savior could manage to be under one when it came down."

"Be careful," Paul warned.

"Now who's thinking like a Jew?" Ernst smiled.

"Let's go home," Paul said. "I've got something to show you."

Traffic was heavy on the boulevards, and there were many military trucks hauling troops and supplies, antiaircraft batteries ringed with sandbags, searchlights, and a few shopkeepers were piling sandbags around store windows.

"It's a madhouse," Ernst murmured.

"Don't worry," Paul said. "We've all been certified."

The sun was going down when they left the car in the drive and went into the house. Frau Kleist was in the kitchen cooking stew in an iron pot. Paul called out to her that they were home, then said to Ernst, "Come upstairs."

They climbed the stairs to Kurt Krenek's study, shut the door, and Paul asked, "Do you find anything odd about the way Father died?"

"Strokes aren't uncommon at his age."

"That's not what I mean. I've been asking a few questions. Some of the answers are missing."

"What are you getting at?"

"The evening he had his stroke, he'd come back to the chemical works with two men in street clothes. The receptionist and clerks were gone home, but the plant manager saw them go into his office. They were alone in there for about thirty minutes. Nobody seems to know who the two were. It wasn't a scheduled meeting. There weren't any names on the appointment calendar. The two men left, and then the ambulance came. The dispatcher said the man on the line identified himself as Kurt Krenek and complained about dizziness and blurred vision and a numbness in his extremities. Then he broke off, as if the stroke had hit him. The ambulance crew found him dead at his desk." Paul stared hard at Ernst. "How do we know it was a stroke that killed him?"

"The autopsy confirmed it."

"One of von Stroelin's pathologists," Paul said, "from the Ministry of Health."

"But what makes you think it could have been anything else?" Ernst frowned.

"Did you know he had an appointment set up the next day with a foreign correspondent—a Britisher? They were going to meet here at the house."

"How did you find out?"

"Frau Kleist. The Britisher called here and identified himself. His German wasn't very good, and she was upset anyway, and didn't write down his name. There's no way to check, now. The British and French journalists have all been expelled."

"What do you suppose it was about?"

Paul was unlocking a drawer in the massive oak desk near the window.

"While you were gone, I went through Father's personal effects and papers. I found this locked up in his private files."

He handed an unmarked folder to Ernst, who sat down in the leather armchair. There were two documents, one a blueprint, the other a memorandum of understanding. The memorandum was a tentative agreement between the Ministry of Interior and Krenek Chemicals for the ongoing delivery of carbon monoxide in large quantities to six state hospitals. Dated in July, the document bore several signatures—including that of Fritz von Stroelin, who had signed for the secretary of health. In the left margin, Kurt Krenek had scrawled: "T-4 PROGRAM."

Paul was sitting on the edge of the desk, his arms folded.

"Those are mental institutions," he said. "What use would they have for canisters of carbon monoxide?"

"It's odd, all right."

"Look at the blueprint. What do you make of it?"

For several moments Ernst stared at the scale drawing on the graph paper while a puzzled frown worked itself into his face.

"I'm not sure. It almost looks like a shower facility. See the shower heads on those pipes across the ceiling?"

"Take a closer look," Paul said. "It's a gas chamber. The door has an airtight seal. The intake for the gas is on the wall outside the peephole and controlled by a cock valve. The ventilation unit sucks out the gas and pumps in air."

"Yes." Ernst began to nod. "I see what you mean."

"When I saw von Stroelin's name on it, I took a second look. Remember the talk at the party about putting mental defectives and severely disabled cases out of their misery?"

"Did you speak with anyone at the chemical works?"

"I asked the plant manager. He knows everything that's going on in production. He never heard of the T-4 program or a requirement for carbon monoxide."

The first stain of twilight lay across the window pane, like a blood smear on a slide.

"What do you suppose the 'T-4' means?" asked Ernst.

"Georg ought to know. I asked him to meet me for lunch tomorrow. If he doesn't know, he should be able to find out from von Stroelin."

Ernst held out the folder, and Paul put it back into the drawer and turned the key in the lock.

"Has it occurred to you," Ernst said, "that if the war goes on for any period of time we could be called up?"

"It won't happen right away. Our industry is critical to the war. Besides, Poland won't last more than six weeks. Then we can negotiate a cease-fire with the French and British. They don't want to fight any more than we do."

"I was thinking about Liesl," Ernst said. "If anything were to happen to us, she'd have no one to look after her. This business of doing away with mental defectives—if it's true . . ."

"She'd stay on at the convent. Her trust fund would take care of it. I think she'd be safe as long as she didn't become a burden on the state."

"That's not what I mean," Ernst said. "Don't forget she's a half-Jew."

There was a knock at the door, and Ernst jerked forward in the chair, gripping the armrests.

Paul said, "Come in."

The door opened and Frau Kleist poked her head inside and said, "Dinner, *meine Herren*. Shall I serve it or wait?"

"We were just coming down," Paul said.

"*Ja, Herr Krenek.*" Her dark eyes went shrewdly from one to the other above a smile that seemed artificial, though perhaps it had to do with the unnatural whiteness of the teeth that were false. Then she was gone.

"Do you think she heard anything?" Ernst asked.

"That would depend on how long she was outside the door."

"Would she report us, I wonder?"

Paul only shrugged by way of reply.

THIRTEEN

The next day, Paul met Georg for lunch at an outdoor café in the Tiergarten, where the trees flung down their spangled impressions of sunlight and shade onto the tops of the tables. Georg was excited. His SS commission had come through, and he expected to be called up any day.

"Are you sure it's what you want?" Paul asked.

"Of course." Georg laughed. "The SS is at the forefront of German medicine. I used to have some reservations about National Socialism, but I've had a spiritual conversion. Why shouldn't man aspire to a vision of human perfection? Imagine a world in which disease and suffering no longer exist, and the process of natural selection can be engineered through bioeugenics so that all of humanity is uplifted. Can you think of a more powerful concept?"

"How does Leni feel about it?"

Georg smiled and replied, "She supports my decision—as any good German wife would do for her husband. But, of course, she's special. One of the Muses, I sometimes think, fallen to earth. She was meant to be worshiped—something I still find very easy to do."

"Then I'm happy for both of you," Paul said. The cynical ease of the lie surprised him. He was happy for neither of them, and least of all for himself.

"Of course, there was a bad period last winter," Georg went on, "after she lost the baby. She was in a deep depression for six months. Suicidal, at times."

Paul stopped eating and raised his head.

"I didn't know."

"A spontaneous abortion," Georg said, "at two months' gestation. The memory is still very painful for her. It might have been different if she'd gotten pregnant again straight off, but her illness made that impossible. In any case, she's come out of it now, thank God. She's her old self."

After they had finished their main course, Georg lit a cigarette. He looked trim and fit, having overcome by sheer will a tendency to take on weight, and though the fine blond hair was in early rout at his temples, the pink bloom of youth was still uncorrupted in his face.

"Tell me something," Paul said. "Have you ever heard of a medical project called T-4?"

Georg had been lifting the cigarette to his mouth, but now it stopped halfway in a sudden arrested motion. The sun flashed on his glasses as his head gave a slight jerk upward, and Paul could see the rounded surprise on the pupils.

"Where did you hear about the T-4 program?" he asked.

"I came across a file in my father's personal papers. A memorandum of understanding. It had von Stroelin's signature."

"What did it say?"

"It had to do with supplying large quantities of carbon monoxide gas to half a dozen state hospitals."

Georg shook his head and said, "You shouldn't have that paper. But since you do, you should know that the contents are officially secret and not to be repeated to anyone."

"Just tell me one thing. Does it have to do with killing mental defectives?"

"I really can't say anything about it," Georg insisted.

"We've been friends most of our lives. Doesn't that count for any trust at all?"

Georg was silent, like a judge taking an appeal under advisement. Finally he drew on his cigarette and blew a decisive stream of smoke.

"If I have your word," he replied, "that you won't repeat what I say to anyone."

"You have it."

"Then the answer to your question is yes."

"How did Krenek Chemicals get involved?"

"It was one of three firms considered as a potential supplier of the gas. Your father's bid was quite high. I don't think he wanted the contract. It was awarded to one of the others."

"Has the project started?"

"Reichsleiter Bouhler expects written confirmation from the chancellery within the week. The war makes it more imperative, of course. Hospital space may be needed for wounded coming back from the front."

"It takes a bit of getting used to—the idea of the state killing its own sick."

"There is no state decree," Georg said, "only executive permission. The decision to administer a mercy death to incurable patients is left to the medical community, where it properly belongs."

"Don't you have any misgivings?" Paul pressed him.

While the cigarette smoldered in a saucer, Georg unhooked his spectacles, leaving two butterfly wings pinkly indented at the bridge of his nose. He studied the lenses as he polished them with the napkin, as if the equation of terminating useless life could be reduced to an abstract principle, governed by laws of logic.

"The motivation is humane," he insisted. "As long as the project extends out of that principle, I don't see how it can be faulted. The men who conceived it were not murderers, but decent, caring physicians." He fitted his glasses back into place as if to reinforce his air of scholarly preciseness. "Some of our institutions have people in them who have to sleep on sawdust because of incontinence and sphincter dysfunction—people who eat their own feces and rub it in their hair. Think about them for a while and see if you change your mind."

But it was Liesl about whom Paul was thinking, not the others.

He smiled and replied, "Maybe I'm just having trouble getting used to carbon monoxide as a therapeutic agent."

"Oh, for God's sake, Paul, this isn't like you. And here we are, arguing like a pair of debaters at gymnasium. Come on. Let's take a walk and enjoy the day."

They left the café and stolled through the park. The air was still balmy, and there was no sign of the winds that carried the change of season in their brisk currents. Children sailed paper boats on a pond that in a few months would be frozen for skating. Paul could remember skating there with Leni on the icy crust in the lamplit darkness, the toy trees around the pond bent under the weight of snow in the branches so that it had the look of a Christmas scene come to life.

"What are you thinking about?" Georg said.

"Nothing," Paul murmured.

Georg glanced at his watch.

"Well, it's after three. Leni made me promise to bring you by for a glass of sherry."

Adultery, Paul thought, was a sin against God, but given a state of contrition in the adulterer, forgivable. Adultery between Aryan and Jew was a sacrilege against the state for which there would be no absolution.

"It's late," he said. "I should be getting on."

"Oh, nonsense," Georg protested. "Just one glass, and then you can be on your way. She'll say I'm to blame if I don't bring you. Come on. No more arguments."

The moment they set foot in the house, Paul knew something was wrong. As Georg closed the door, Leni called down from the top of the stairs.

"Georg! Paul! Is that you?"

Paul had a glimpse of her leaning over the balustrade, her long-sleeved blouse tucked into her skirt. He could make out some frightened tension in her, and then the rail was sliding under her hand.

"Where are the servants?" Georg frowned.

"I sent them home. Thank God you came by here first." She swept past them to the door and peered through the lace at the window. "You weren't followed, were you?"

"What is it?" Paul asked.

"Come into the sitting room."

After she had closed the sliding doors, Leni turned to Paul and Georg. She appeared to have been crying out of sheer vexation, her face pale with no trace of makeup, and Paul noticed the handkerchief nervously crumpled in one fist.

"Frau Kleist was here looking for you," she said to him. "Ernst was arrested a little while ago and taken away."

"Arrested?" Georg cried. "For what?"

"Two Gestapo men came for him," Leni said. "Frau Kleist was standing in the hall and heard them talking. Something to do with Ernst making statements against the Reich while he was in Florence. Someone reported him. The Gestapo have been watching him since he came back to Germany."

"Well," Georg said. "It's probably a mistake. They'll only question him about it and let him go."

"That's not all. They asked Frau Kleist about Paul." She gave Paul an anxious look. "Evidently they intend to pick you up, too."

"Did they search the house?" Paul said.

"I don't know. Frau Kleist didn't say."

Georg gazed at Paul.

"If they did," he said, "would they find anything improper?"

"Just a toy soldier," Paul said, "with one leg missing."

"Then why would they want to arrest you?" Georg said in a puzzled tone, as if he were asking himself the question.

"I once beat up a blackshirt. Maybe they got wind of it." Paul smiled wryly. "Naturally, that was before I knew you were going to be part of the SS Medical Service."

"Oh, don't make jokes about it," Leni cried.

"I wasn't."

Georg blew soundlessly through his pursed lips.

"There's always the chance you're right about that blackshirt, though I rather doubt it. In any case, you can't go back to your place until we find out what's going on. I'll give Fritz a call. He has contacts at the Wilhelmstrasse."

"No," Paul said.

"But why?" Leni protested.

"Because I don't want either of you involved."

"That's noble," Georg said, "but silly."

"Why risk your future? If we're accused of something political and you stick your neck out, it would be guilt by association. I'll find out what the trouble is. My own way."

"I think it's a mistake," Georg said.

"Probably. But that's the way I want it."

Georg sighed, turning his palms outward in a show of surrender.

"At least wait here until I go out and have a look round. We want to be sure the street's clear."

Georg was gone. The dilations of fear on Leni's pupils seemed to have widened even more.

Paul said, "It's possible they found out we're *Halbjuden*. I can't take a chance on turning myself in."

"Let Georg help," Leni pleaded. "We could hide you here."

"No." Paul shook his head. "Sooner or later you'd pay for it."

"Then where will you go?"

"If you don't know, it'll mean less trouble when they start asking you questions."

He saw the pain twist across her face, and tears forming, and put his hands on her shoulders.

"There are worse things in Germany to cry about."

Leni raised her head slowly, her cheeks wet, and suddenly her own arms were around his neck, and she pressed her mouth to his. One part of Paul resisted while the other remained passive, unable to break away, and even the wetness of her tears on his face seemed to be linked in their sadness to that day on the beach at Molos when their bodies had strained heatedly against each other. He reached up to pull her arms from his neck.

Leni sank into a chair beside the cold fireplace and buried her face in her hands.

"Why didn't you make me stay in Greece with you?" Her voice broke.

The sliding doors moved, and Georg stood in the opening. It was impossible to tell from his face if he had seen them, or heard any of the conversation.

"The street looks clear," he said. "But just to be safe you'd better leave out the back. The gate behind the garden isn't locked. You can slip through to the next block. Is there anything you need?"

Paul glanced once more at Leni, who sat with her hands folded on her knees, her legs slanting in a long diagonal from the hem of the dark skirt to the high heels that were dug close together in the Persian rug.

"No," he said.

FOURTEEN

Georg waited until Paul was out of sight, then shut the garden gate. Some jealous anger was heavy and hot in his chest, for he had seen the embrace between Paul and his wife, and it had only confirmed what he had always feared and refused to face. They had never stopped loving each other. Until now, he had accepted the idea that their estrangement had to do with Paul's insistence on living abroad in Greece. Clearly, that was a lie. But what was the truth? He knew he wouldn't get the answer from Leni.

That night he lay awake, brooding in the dark over what to do. Paul was as close as a brother. But he loved his wife more. Leni was an obsession. The possibility of losing her was unthinkable. All loyalties paled beside the prospect.

By afternoon of the next day, his conflict and sense of panic had resolved into a decision. He found Fritz on the range at Spandau. Von Stroelin was shooting against three Wehrmacht officers and an SS-Oberführer at targets set against an earthen berm fifty meters from the firing line. On the stand in front of him was a scope mounted on a tripod to check his hits, and several loaded magazines.

Georg stood well back and watched the shooters, but mostly his attention focused on von Stroelin. The bullish figure had an air of implacable calm and concentration, as if the power of his will and not the action of the pistol would carry each bullet to its mark, and his outstretched arm jumped only slightly under the recoil of each shot.

From the tower came the order to cease fire. The target detail went forward to score hits and put up fresh targets.

Soon the competitors were in their final phase of rapid fire. The shots crackled loudly across the open lanes between the baffles, and Georg covered his ears. Von Stroelin ejected a magazine, inserted a full one, and went on firing in a smooth, measured fashion. He was the first to finish the order, and he did not bother to peer through the scope. He knew the hits were grouped in the black.

He grounded his weapon, took off the yellow-tinted shooting glasses, and lifted the patch that had covered his left eye. Stepping off the line, he caught sight of Georg standing alone behind the tower.

"Fritz." Georg came up. "I need your help. It's about Paul."

"I suppose he's been arrested," von Stroelin said.

"No." Georg stared at the other man in surprise. "But the Gestapo are looking for him. How did you know?"

"I didn't. But it was predictable. He's too careless with his views."

"They took Ernst into custody, and Paul's on the run." Georg glanced at the other shooters, who were wandering downrange to check their targets. "Is there someplace we can talk in private?"

"There." Von Stroelin pointed. They stepped over to the shade of a tin roof and sat on a bench behind a long table with a sheet metal top for cleaning weapons. An odor of solvent and used oil patches rose from a waste barrel. "Now tell me what this is all about. When did you last see Paul?"

"I had lunch with him yesterday. We went back to the house for a drink. Frau Kleist had been there. She told Leni about the Gestapo, and Leni warned Paul."

"That was unwise of Leni." Von Stroelin shook his head. "It's dangerous to interfere in a Gestapo investigation. You should talk to her."

"I already have," Georg said. "But it would make things easier if we knew what it was all about. Leni begged me to see you. You have important connections—all the way up to Reichsführer Himmler himself. You could find out."

"I could," von Stroelin said. "But it wouldn't change anything. So what's the point of it?"

"The point is," Georg replied, "that I may be in a bit of trouble myself."

"You?" The other frowned. "What kind of trouble?"

"Two years ago, before Paul left for Greece, we had an evening out. Leni was there. In fact, it was the night we ran into you at the Pink Cat. Remember?"

"Vaguely," von Stroelin said, though Georg was sure he remembered it quite well, if only because of Leni's presence.

"After we left the cabaret, we stumbled into a roadblock. The Gestapo were raiding an apartment where some Communist Jews were hiding. One of them tried to make a break for it, and the SS sergeant at the roadblock stopped him. I still don't know what got into Paul. Maybe it was too much drink. Anyway, he knocked the sergeant down with his fists. The sergeant hit his head on the curb and got a nasty concussion. The Jew got away. Leni was hysterical. She kept begging us to get back into the car. I didn't want to see her involved, so we left the sergeant there and drove off."

"My God," von Stroelin murmured. "Do you realize what you've done? Keeping silent all this time?"

"I know," Georg said miserably. "I've been sick about it ever since. I was torn between friendship and duty. I made the wrong decision. Don't think it's been easy to live with, either."

"I always knew he was a Jew-lover," von Stroelin said.

"It may be that the Gestapo found out about it," Georg said, "and that's why they're trying to arrest him. In any case, I'd like to know. It could be nothing at all. Maybe they just wanted to question him about Ernst."

"I doubt it. They're both troublemakers. You should have broken off that friendship a long time ago."

"I've thought about going to the Gestapo with what I know," Georg said. "It would mean the end of my SS commission, but at least I'd have done my duty. Look, Fritz, I've always valued your opinion. You're the only one I know who can think clearly in a crisis. What would you advise?"

Georg could see the flattery make a direct hit. Already, he knew how von Stroelin would reply.

"What purpose would going to the Gestapo serve now? As a physician, you're more important to the SS than a sergeant who couldn't even defend himself in a street fight. It would be utterly stupid to put your commission in jeopardy."

"I suppose you're right," Georg said, and he knew that Paul's assault of the SS sergeant would be discreetly leaked to the authorities. He gazed at von Stroelin with abject gratitude. But behind the expression lay a smug triumph that he could manipulate someone of Fritz's stature. Fritz had other traits that Georg lacked and therefore admired—daring and fear-lessness and the ability to act coolly under pressure. Only his vanity could be made to serve another, and this Georg had discovered early on.

"Of course I'm right," von Stroelin said. "Don't forget, you have a wife to think about, as well."

"That's true."

"Now, think hard. Do you have any idea where the bastard might have gone? Did he say anything?"

"No. But he was shaken. I could tell that much. I wouldn't be surprised if he tries to slip across the frontier. He might even take Liesl with him. He couldn't very well leave her behind."

Two of the shooters, gripping their felt-lined pistol cases, were walking toward the cleaning pit. Von Stroelin stood up.

"I'll see what I can find out," he said. "In the meantime, you're to do nothing. Understand? Just keep your mouth shut. The Gestapo know what they're doing. They'll pick him up in twenty-four hours."

FIFTEEN

After his talk with Georg, Paul was more certain than ever that his father had been murdered to prevent his passing information about the T-4 program to the foreign press. But proving it would be impossible. His major concern, now, was to get Liesl out of Germany. He was sure the Gestapo would be watching his house. Probably they had been to the chemical works, too. The offices would not be safe. He decided to check into the Adlon, where he knew the night manager and could arrange for a room without signing his own name to the register.

"The lady is a married woman, Max," he said over the phone. "I don't want to be the grounds for a divorce."

"Of course," Max replied. "I understand perfectly. You are Paul Baum, a businessman from Bremen. The key will be at the desk."

"Thank you for your discretion."

"A pleasure, Herr Baum."

Later, Paul put through a call to his banker and arranged for a large sum of cash to be delivered in the morning by courier to the hotel.

"I'll be at a table in the courtyard restaurant at nine," he said.

The hesitation at the other end of the wire suggested a fine edge of suspicion on the other side of a courtly politeness.

"This is somewhat irregular, Herr Krenek."

"Secret government business," Paul said. "I expect your complete discretion, naturally."

"In that case, I will deliver it personally, of course."

Paul slept erratically, pulled by dark dreams into a landscape of struggle and flight, and he woke feeling tired. At nine o'clock he was at a table in the courtyard, driving the fatigue from his nerves with hot black coffee, when the banker arrived in homburg and pince-nez. The banker came through the crowd, sat down, and laid his hat on the table. He drew a brown envelope from the inside pocket of his coat.

"Do you wish to verify the cash amount?"

"Your assurance is quite enough," Paul said.

"Then I need only your signature on the receipt," the banker said, "to conclude our business."

It was late afternoon before Paul reached the convent. He waited in the reception room under a crucifix nailed high up in the gloom. From the chapel, a bell chimed vespers. Finally, Sister Clara appeared in the doorway.

"Herr Krenek." She gave him a look of surprise. "We weren't expecting a visit from you. Is anything wrong?"

Paul had already made up his mind to be truthful with the mother superior. He did not believe she would betray him to the authorities. Hurriedly, he related the situation.

"I've decided to take Liesl and get out of the country."

"Take Liesl?" She pressed her hands together as if in prayer, though it was a gesture of distress. "But is that necessary? Don't you think she would be better off here?"

Paul remembered his promise to Georg to say nothing of the T-4 program. But a promise was a worthless collateral these days in the inflated currency of lies.

"There's something I think you ought to know," he said.

The story itself had the sound of a monstrous fiction as he told it. Before he was finished, he saw the frown form below the stiff linen headband, and her compressed lips were white at the edges.

"A doctor from the Ministry of Interior has been here," she said. "He filled out a questionnaire on every child. I couldn't get any explanation from him about the purpose of the forms." She shook her head in disbelief. "But surely, even if what you say is true, it wouldn't apply to children."

"Liesl is a half-Jew," Paul said. "So am I. That may not be in any Gestapo file, but I can't take a chance. We've got to get out of Germany."

"But where will you go?"

"I have friends in Geneva."

"And what about a passport and visa?"

"I couldn't go back to the house for my passport. Not that it makes a difference. It's probably already on a list with the Customs police. We'll have to cross the frontier on our own."

"But Herr Krenek . . ." The nun hesitated, and Paul could see the conflict working its way into the creases of her face. Probably she was thinking about retaliation.

"You could say that I took her on another trip," Paul pressed her. "That
wouldn't be a lie."

Before Sister Clara could reply, one of the young novices interrupted
them.

"Reverend Mother," she said, "the police are here from Zossen."

The color went from Paul's face as his nerves absorbed the shock.

"On what business?" the mother superior inquired.

The novice glanced uneasily at Paul by way of reply.

"Ask them to wait," Sister Clara said.

"I'm sorry," Paul murmured. "I didn't mean to make trouble for you."

"I'll try to get rid of them." Sister Clara's manner was suddenly calm
and decisive. "You'll have to go out the side door. Hide in the woods
behind the playground. It's nearly dark. I'll bring Liesl out after they've
gone."

As he slipped down the hallway Paul heard the police talking to the
young novice in the front alcove. He had a glimpse, through the drapes,
of a uniformed figure, and a second man, in civilian dress, with a dead
white face like putty under the brim of a hat that he had not taken off.
Paul knew he must be Gestapo. It unnerved him to realize how they had
anticipated his movements. At the side door, Sister Clara pressed his arm.

"Be careful," she whispered.

Paul nodded, glancing left, then right. No sign of anyone. He ducked
low, sprinting across the yard, and was through the gate. Still crouched,
he worked his way along the stone wall until he was close to the woods.
He peered over the top of the wall at the main house. Nothing stirred in
the empty yard. Gathering himself, he bolted uphill into the trees, his
head low.

It seemed an interminable time before he heard voices drifting from a
distance. He parted the branches and gazed down at the police van on the
road. A nun came into view. He couldn't tell if it was Sister Clara. Only
her mantle and the starched band of her coif showed above the wall.
Behind her, the heads and shoulders of the police floated into sight.
Except for the man with the putty face, they were regular *Polizei*. They
said good-bye and climbed into the van. The driver turned down the road
to Zossen, the wheels lifting brown dust that hung in the air long after the
sound of the motor had died.

Another thirty minutes mounted their wait in Paul's nerves. The country lay with the color draining out of it in the dusk. At the windows of the

convent, the blackout drapes had been drawn. Paul heard the iron latch of a door opening, and a slice of light fell across the yard. Two figures hurried through the playground. At the edge of the wood they paused and Sister Clara called out in a soft voice, "Herr Krenek."

Paul stepped from behind a tree and said, "Over here."

Liesl let go of the mother superior's hand and ran to him. He knelt to hug her.

"Liesl, I thought we might go on a little adventure tonight. Just the two of us. Wouldn't it be great fun?"

Liesl nodded happily and squeezed Ilse in her arms. Sister Clara handed Paul a blanket tied in a roll.

"There are bread and cheese inside. A razor, too, and half a bar of soap. What about money?"

"I have plenty of Reichsmarks, and a Swiss account. I can always write a draft."

The nun thrust a paper into his hand.

"An address in Dresden," she said. "My brother is a priest. If you haven't any other place to go, he'll take you in." She hesitated, then added, "He's helped others get out of Germany. I'll telephone him."

Paul squeezed her hand.

"We're very grateful."

"You'd better not go into Zossen. The police have your description. You can walk into Luckenwalde and get a bus. It's only about fourteen kilometers."

"What did you tell them about Liesl?"

"That you took her away earlier today on a trip. An old woman's lie is always the best. It can even fool the Gestapo. Good luck, Herr Krenek." She stooped down and held out her arms to Liesl. "Come give me a kiss, Liesl."

A few moments later Paul watched the nun's figure melting among the shadows of the playground. At the door she glanced back toward the woods. Paul knew she couldn't see them but raised his hand anyway.

He set off with Liesl for Luckenwalde. Little traffic moved on the road. Once, they heard a car approaching and stepped into the trees, waiting for it to pass. It ground by slowly, headlights dark, and left a smell of dust in the leaves.

A few farms glimmered in clearings, and sometimes a dog barked. Nothing else stirred. The farmers would be to bed early and up before dawn to tend the stock. Clouds smothered the moon, leaving the road black, and the night wind smelled of rain.

Later, they rested on a log in a glade off the road. Below, in the trees, a brook ran past a stone farmhouse and they could hear the creak of a water wheel. A footbridge crossed the stream to a fenced pasture and barn. Overhead, a rumble of thunder sent the first drops of rain spattering into the forest. Paul glanced at the house to make sure no one was about.

"Liesl," he said, snatching her hand, "come along before we get soaked."

They hurried across the field to the barn, dark and high in the rain. The door squeaked on its hinges. A lantern hung from a peg on the wall, but Paul was afraid to light it. He waited while his pupils dilated to the dark. Objects took shape, a hay wagon, a tractor on blocks . . . Liesl still clutched his hand. They climbed the ladder to the loft.

Paul unbuttoned her damp coat and hung it over a beam. He opened the blanket roll and cut two slices of black bread and some cheese. Beyond the open shutter a ropy cataract of water streamed off the eaves. After they had eaten, they burrowed into the hay and listened to the rain on the roof close to their heads.

"Aren't you sleepy?" Paul asked.

The little girl nodded, her eyes wide. The rain drummed only a short time before it stopped. Finally Paul could hear Liesl's steady breathing and knew she was asleep. On the other side of his own tension, a deadly fatigue waited. He stretched his legs, burrowing deeper into the hay, and went to sleep.

Paul woke with a start. A cock was crowing. He touched Liesl, who stirred sleepily.

"Liesl, wake up. We have to go. I'll help you down the ladder."

They slipped out of the barn and circled through the woods to the road. Liesl said she was hungry, and Paul promised they would eat soon.

They tramped along the road in the dark. The first smudge of dawn showed in the east over Zossen. Igniting, it flared quickly across the sky. Birds woke as the country took shape in the first light. The grass alongside the road sweated with dew, and the hay stacked in the fields gleamed wetly at the first touch of morning rays. The scent of wet earth hung in the air, and smoke drifted from chimney vents.

Later, they found a spring near the road. The water welled up in a pool where the roots of a beech tree lay half exposed. They sat on the bank and finished the last of the bread and cheese. Paul rubbed a hand across his stubbled cheek. He badly needed a shave. Once they arrived in Luckenwalde, he did not want to look conspicuous.

He opened the straight razor Sister Clara had given him and made as thick a lather as he could from the soap. Shaving, he nicked himself in several places. He dipped his handkerchief in the spring water, wrung out the excess moisture, and used the wet linen to stop the bleeding. Bits of hay from the loft clung to their clothing, and these he brushed away before starting out.

At a junction, they met a farmer driving a vegetable cart into Luckenwalde.

"Car trouble," Paul said, glad that he had shaved and did not look too disreputable. "We're going into Luckenwalde to find a mechanic."

The farmer, who had several missing teeth and held the slack reins in his big gnarled hands, offered them a ride. Paul lifted Liesl onto the high seat and climbed up beside her. The farmer made a clucking sound to the horse. The ground gave a lurch, and then the country was gliding past. Behind the clop of hooves, they talked about the war in Poland and, once, the farmer let Liesl hold the reins. Around midmorning, the cart rolled into Luckenwalde.

At the station, Paul bought two tickets for Dresden. The bus would not leave until noon. He was afraid to wait in the station. The Zossen police might have alerted other units in the vicinity.

They walked up the street to a café and ate breakfast. It was still too early for the bus, and they crossed the square to a park and found a bench marked NUR FÜR ARIER—"Only for Aryans"—and sat in the shade. A few people passed the bench, but no one took notice of them.

SIXTEEN

In Dresden they went directly to the rectory. A housekeeper answered the bell, and Paul asked for Father Ludecke. She led them into a study crammed with books and papers where a window looked out into a garden. Two pendulum clocks filled the silence with their tick-tock beat, and the rosewood case of a third lay open, its serrated gears and pinions strewn around the base like harvested organs from a cadaver.

The pastor came in finally and shook hands. The cassock looked too small for his thickset, oversized figure, and the florid features in the broad, stolid face bore scant resemblance to those of Sister Clara. He gave an impression of general dullness, but Paul soon discovered this was only a pose that could serve as a defense with strangers or the authorities.

Paul pointed to the dismembered clock and said, "Is it broken?"

"Clocks are my hobby," Father Ludecke said. "Working on them is a fine exercise in patience."

Paul found it hard to imagine the powerful hands executing any task quite so intricate. After a few minutes, the priest handed Liesl a crayon and paper.

"Wouldn't you like to draw a picture?" he said. "Out in the garden, perhaps, where it's sunny?"

As soon as Liesl was outside, Father Ludecke said, "My sister telephoned from Zossen. She couldn't say much, of course. You never know who's picking up the conversation."

Paul went into detail about their situation while the priest listened, his heavy fingers laced across the front of his cassock. Afterward, both men were silent.

"I have to take care what I preach these days," Father Ludecke said, "if I want to keep my pulpit. So my sermons are dull and safe. I close my mouth, but not my eyes. We have hidden a Jewish family in this church, and one political prisoner who escaped from a camp."

Paul glanced through the lace curtain at Liesl in the garden. She had put down the crayon and was stooping beside the flower bed.

"Let's get down to practical matters," Father Ludecke said. "How do you propose to get across the frontier?"

"I thought we might slip across at night," Paul said, "around the Schaffhausen area."

"You'd have to swim the Rhine."

"Or steal a small boat."

The priest shook his head and said, "There are troops on both sides of the river. The place is swarming with patrols. Why don't you try to get through the ordinary way—a border checkpoint?"

"We have no papers or passport."

"I have a Jewish friend who was a mechanical engineer. The regime forced him into a different occupation. Now he is a first-rate forger of documents. They don't come cheaply, of course."

"I have money."

"You'll need a passport and visa," the priest said, "and ration cards. But, listen, Switzerland is full of refugees. If you're caught, the police will only deport you back here. There's another worry, too. The Gestapo has agents in the major cities."

"I have friends in Geneva," Paul said. "I'm not worried about deportation."

"I would avoid Schaffhausen. The Customs police there are very thorough. The best way to go would be by rail to Friedrichshafen and across Lake Constance by ferry. They say it's a quiet area, very little fuss."

"How long to get the papers?"

"Five days, perhaps six."

Paul agreed that the priest's way offered the best chance.

"In the meantime," Father Ludecke said, "you must try to alter your appearance. Let your beard grow. It will make you look older. A limp would help, too, and a cane."

"Wouldn't it draw attention?"

"No. People will look at you otherwise and resent that you are not in uniform. A limp dismisses the question altogether. Besides, you don't want to carry large sums of money through Customs. The cane will have a false bottom."

Outside, in the garden, Liesl had come back to the stone bench. She had the crayon, trying to draw a flower. On the paper, the petals were childishly misshapen, but Paul was sure the one she saw in her mind must be beautiful.

They spent nearly a week in the loft above the bell tower that looked out across the high slate roofs of the district to the Elbe, flashing in the sun. There were two straw mattresses, blankets, and a slop bucket for use during the day. At night, after the church was locked, they would descend the ladder into the vestibule and use the toilet and bathe at the sink.

Father Ludecke brought food and books and a change of clothing. Each night, Paul emptied the slop pail and made several trips up and down the ladder. A thermos of fresh water from the tap would last them through the next day.

To pass the time, Liesl drew pictures and played with Ilse, but she soon grew restless. Paul read to her from a book of fairy tales, and sometimes he talked about Switzerland.

"When we leave here to go to Switzerland we're going to play a game. Remember how we used to pretend things? One time you were a bird, and I was a cat, and when the cat crept close, the bird always flew away. That's like the game we're going to play on the train. This time we're both going to hide from the cat. We'll pretend to be other people so the cat won't be able to find us."

"Would the cat eat us?"

"Not if he doesn't know who we are. We'll have different names, and make up a story why we're going to Switzerland. We'll practice our story before we leave so we can fool the cat."

On the final evening, Father Ludecke climbed to the tower and called out softly. Paul lifted the trapdoor of the loft and saw the priest on the scaffolding next to the gleaming iron of the bell, his face upturned in the shadows.

"Herr Krenek, I have your papers. You and the child had better come down. We can talk in the vestry."

Paul descended with Liesl. In the windowless vestry behind the altar, two vigil candles flickered across the bare wall.

"I had your clothing cleaned and pressed. Everything is hanging in the armoire with the holy vestments. You can change before we go."

"What time do we leave?"

The pastor had shed his cassock and wore dark trousers and a collarless white shirt. He drew a fob watch from his pocket and opened the faceplate.

"In six more hours," he replied. "Six hours, precisely. It's the night train from Berlin."

"And our papers?"

"A first-class job. Your name is Schmidt. Apart from passport and visa, you have a book of ration tickets and a Party card to identify you. Your story is this. You are on your way to a clinic in Zurich where your daughter will undergo certain neurological tests. You'll carry a letter on the clinic's stationery, signed by the neurologist, to support those facts. It will underline the urgency of the tests. Should you be questioned, the authorities will more than likely attribute nerves or faltering speech to the anxiety of a father for his daughter."

Paul nodded. He had nothing but admiration for the man who liked to tinker with clocks.

"I have packed some things into a suitcase for you. It wouldn't do to go through Customs without luggage. By the way, you'll find a scissors on the shelf with the altar linens—to trim your beard. You'd better sleep here in the vestry tonight. That way we can get off more quickly."

SEVENTEEN

Paul and Liesl boarded the train in the dark. A brakeman swung a lantern with a red filter over the glass, and the passengers crowding the platform jostled each other amid the scraping of feet, hissing of steam, and measured clank of a boiler valve.

It was another twenty minutes before the train rolled out of the station. One other passenger occupied the compartment. He dozed in the seat, hands folded across his belly. Paul pressed the clips together on the window shade and started to raise it.

"*Nein, nein,*" the other man snapped, not asleep after all. "Have you forgotten blackout regulations?"

"Sorry," Paul murmured.

He settled back on the high seat and put an arm around Liesl. The whistle gave another shrill blast as the train picked up speed on the outskirts of Dresden. Liesl fell asleep with her head on his lap. The aisle lamps had been dimmed. In the compartment's gloom, Paul couldn't distinguish the features of the other passenger, only the white hands folded below the belt of the trenchcoat.

Later, they waited forty-five minutes on a siding for a troop train to pass. While they were sidetracked, the first daylight started to seep around the borders of the shade. This time no one protested when Paul raised it. The country stretched away, black beneath the swirl of dawn streaking the glass.

Now Paul had his first clear glimpse of the other man. He looked thirtyish with a few thinning locks of sandy hair stranded across his high forehead. An inflamed patch on one cheek smelled faintly of eczema cream, and around the nostrils of his thin nose were tiny burst veins like pinworms under the skin. He turned out to be a lawyer from Berlin on his way to Ulm.

"Traveling far?" he asked.

"Zurich," Paul said.

"For business or pleasure?"

"My daughter is visiting a specialist at a clinic."

"Do you live in Dresden?"

The questions had the clipped rhythm of a cross-examination. Paul thought it best to be truthful since the lawyer might know Dresden.

"Just visiting a relative in the Altstadt," he replied. "We're from Berlin."

He hoped that would arrest the dialogue, but it was not to be. The lawyer glanced at the cane hooked over the armrest and said, "I noticed you limping when you came into the compartment. Were you wounded at the front?"

"Nothing so noble, I'm afraid. A motorcar accident."

"Bad luck," the lawyer said. "What work do you do?"

"I teach philosophy at the university."

"I have a friend who teaches law there. His name is Rausch. Perhaps you know him?"

"I'm afraid not."

"That's odd. He's been there for several years."

"The faculty is quite large. Actually, I haven't started yet full-time."

The lawyer continued to stare, his mouth drawn into a tight smile that reinforced the impression of a prosecutor scoffing at a lie from an accused. The arrogance behind his scrutiny made Paul worry, but he couldn't let it show.

The other man drummed his fingers against the briefcase on the seat beside him. He asked if Paul thought the war would spread, and Paul said he didn't know.

"The British are at fault," the lawyer said. "They can't curb Chamberlain."

Paul would have smiled at the joke, only it was not intended as humor. The lawyer was mouthing Dr. Goebbels's moral outrage at British aggression.

Paul decided to follow the Party line and replied, "Chamberlain had his chance to listen to reason."

The ticket inspector tapped on the glass and came in. Grateful for the interruption, Paul inquired about the dining car. The inspector told him it was open for the breakfast service.

As Paul stood up to leave the compartment, the lawyer said, "Wait!"

Paul turned his head sharply. The lawyer leaned across and unhooked the cane from the armrest.

"You've forgotten this," he said. Above the lipless smile, his stare challenged Paul with its bright curiosity.

"So I have," Paul said, and for the first time wondered if the other man might be Gestapo.

In the dining car, a waiter seated them. Beyond the window, morning light streaked the country. A village streamed by, high-roofed houses and fenced fields, and a hill of dogwood. But Paul couldn't get his mind off the lawyer. He knew the Gestapo sometimes put agents aboard trains. Or the lawyer might be one of those zealous citizens of the Reich constantly vigilant for deserters, or Jews on the run, or defeatist talk.

On the menu, half the items had been crossed out, and there was no fresh fruit.

"It's the war," the waiter apologized. "All this rationing. They haven't got it straight yet."

"We all have to make sacrifices," Paul said, "like good Germans."

The waiter had white hair and dentures that slipped. The linen of his jacket had lost its starch, turning yellow at the lapels next to his bow tie. He wrote down their order on his slate, then gestured toward Liesl's doll.

"And something for this *Fräulein?*"

Liesl stared at the waiter who kept a serious face. Suddenly she burst into giggles, shaking her head and clutching Ilse.

On their way back to the compartment, Paul said, "Don't forget our game. We have to be careful."

"So the cat won't get us?" She gazed up at him.

"He can't get us as long as we keep pretending."

They found the lawyer getting up to go to the dining coach.

"How is the service?" he asked.

"Not much of a menu, I'm afraid," Paul said. "It's the war."

"We all have to make sacrifices," the lawyer gave the standard response, "like good Germans."

Going out, he swung his briefcase hard into Paul's knee.

"How clumsy of me! I haven't aggravated your injury, I hope?"

"No," Paul said.

Did he only imagine the suspicion on the other side of the bright stare? Paul knew he had to bring his nerves under control. Already, his anxiety had made him careless.

At Ulm, the lawyer left the train. Paul watched him cross the platform in the sun, walking briskly, the trenchcoat folded over one arm, the briefcase dangling from the other. He paused outside the main concourse, glancing back at the coach as if he had forgotten something, or perhaps remembered something. Paul could see him frowning before he turned once more and disappeared in the crowd.

The train did not move for another fifteen minutes, but at last Paul felt the lurch of steel as the couplings tightened, and the station rolled off the window.

An older man stepped into the compartment. His face was lead heavy and had deep ridges scored into it, and his eyebrows and mustache were silver-gray. He looked vigorous, despite his years, and big blue veins wormed across the backs of his heavy hands.

The newcomer smiled at Liesl, and the creases took on a benign arrangement. Whatever worries lingered in Paul's mind were quickly dispersed by the blue twinkle under the thatch of brows. The man turned out to be a manufacturer of Swiss chocolate from Geneva.

"But I know Zurich well, too," he said. "Do you have a hotel?"

"No," Paul said.

"Let me give you the name of one." He took out a card that identified him as Otto Schutz and wrote down the hotel on the back. "Just give this to the desk. They know me well there. You'll get a good room."

Paul looked at the card and thanked him.

"There are more refugees every day," Herr Schutz said. "Jews, mostly. The government won't be able to handle the problem for long, I'm afraid."

"Will Switzerland stay neutral?" Paul asked.

"It is our policy, of course, but there is worry in Bern about all the German divisions along the Rhine. The newspapers talk about an invasion. I hope it doesn't happen. It would be a disaster for business."

"Do you export much chocolate to Germany?"

"Our best market! Hitler himself has a sweet tooth, you know."

They talked of the war, but the older man seemed bent on avoiding controversy. Soon, he turned his attention to Liesl. First, he made a grandfatherly fuss over her doll. Then, for a while, he played a game, hiding a pfennig in his hand and extending both fists for Liesl to guess which one contained the coin. Finally, he spoke of a dog named Hugo.

"Where has Hugo gone? He was here a while ago."

Herr Schutz flexed his knobby hand, extending a misshapen forefinger straight out. This became Hugo's head and neck. The thumb and remaining three fingers served as legs. He walked Hugo across the seat and onto the point of his knee.

"Isn't Hugo a friendly dog? Wouldn't you like to pet Hugo?" Herr Schutz coaxed Liesl, using his own free hand to stroke the extended forefinger.

The little girl patted the forefinger with care. Suddenly the dog flew at her ribs. The playful dig was accompanied by a deep snort from Herr Schutz.

Liesl shrieked, bursting into laughter. They repeated the game, and again the child giggled. At last Herr Schutz opened his briefcase and held up a piece of candy.

"Is she allowed sweets?"

"Yes, certainly. Thank you."

"It is very delicious chocolate." The older man winked at Liesl. "Little girls always like it."

The afternoon was sinking across the landscape when the train coasted down through the rolling country above Lake Constance to Friedrichshafen, the terminus of the rail line and the checkpoint for Customs. From the compartment they had their first glimpse of the lake, blue and shining, with clouds above it. On the Swiss side the foothills vaulted back from the shore into the hazy distances where the Alps soared, the snow-chinked crags toppling among the sky reflections on the water. A thrill shot through Paul. Their first view of Switzerland! The lofty nearness of it teased them, as if the promise of their future waited beyond the sparkle of the lake.

"Pretty, eh?" Herr Schutz remarked, all the while staring at Paul.

"Yes." Paul couldn't take his gaze from it, any more than he could restrain the joy stretching the smile into his face. How improbable it seemed. Across the lake—no blackouts, rationing, or war, only sanity and safety.

Later, the train rolled into the harbor station near the ferry slip. The ferry was tied up at the pier and waiting to board passengers. It would put across the lake to Romanshorn on the Swiss side, where connections could be made for Saint Gall and Zurich.

Paul claimed their suitcase in the Customs shed. He looked in the crowd for Herr Schutz but saw no sign of him. Two Customs inspectors worked the counters. On the other side of the barrier slouched a round-shouldered figure who had the look of a Gestapo man. His expression conveyed a smug, all-powerful air. Paul took pains not to stare, but remained achingly aware of the other man's presence.

The queue moved forward, and Paul handed over passport and visa. The Customs inspector carried a roll of beefy fat under his shirt, and his neck swelled over his collar.

"Destination?" he asked, leaning close enough for Paul to smell the mixture of beer and *Sauerbraten* on his breath.

"Zurich," Paul said. "We're taking the electric train from Romanshorn."

"Your business in Zurich?"

"My daughter is seeing a neurologist for some tests." Paul reached into his coat. "I have a letter here from the clinic that will verify—"

"Open your luggage, please." The inspector did not seem interested in explanations.

Paul unsnapped the suitcase. There were clothes, toilet articles, and a copy of *Mein Kampf.*

"Have you read it?" The Customs officer glanced at him. Was it wry amusement on the other side of his smile, or simply patriotic zeal?

"Of course I've read it." Paul tried to give his tone a fervent ring, but not a disrespectful one. "Every page. It's brilliant."

"Everyone seems to carry a copy through Customs these days," the inspector replied. "Close your bag, please."

He chalked the suitcase and waved them through.

"What about our passport and visa?" Paul said.

"They have to be stamped. You'll get them back at Swiss Customs across the lake."

"Thank you," Paul said, and thought to add, "Heil Hitler."

"Heil Hitler." The inspector did not even look up.

Outside, on the tree-lined esplanade, a porter spotted Paul's cane and trotted over. Paul gave him the suitcase to carry to the boat. Gripping Liesl's hand, he limped out from under the copper burnish of the September leaves toward the ferry slip. The porter waited below the gangplank, and Paul tipped him. A purser checked their tickets and motioned them aboard. A breeze blew off the lake. On the open deck, Paul drew a deep breath into his lungs and could almost smell the intoxicant of freedom mingled with the cool touch of the distant snow fields.

"Remember our last boat trip?" he asked.

The little girl nodded, holding Ilse at the railing as if the doll were another passenger.

"Will there be stars that fall down and turn into flowers?"

"We'll keep a sharp watch out for them."

More passengers boarded the ferry. Paul drew the pocket watch from his vest. The boat would be late leaving Friedrichshafen. He glanced back and caught sight of the Gestapo man who had been in the Customs area and the inspector who had chalked his luggage striding together across the esplanade. He felt suddenly cold, as if a cloud had passed over the sun. Wind-driven swells beat against the boat's hull with a sloshing sound like warning whispers, but he could only wait.

"Liesl," he murmured. "Don't forget our game."

The two officials climbed the gangplank, mounting the companionway steps to the upper deck.

"Herr Schmidt," the Gestapo man called out, "and Fräulein Schmidt."

The Customs inspector pointed them out even as Paul lifted a hand.

"Yes? I am Schmidt."

"Come off the boat, please. Your daughter, too."

"But why? Our papers were checked."

"Quickly, please."

"Shall I leave our luggage aboard?" Paul said.

"No, bring it."

Paul's hope vanished in one sickening inner wrench of feeling. Already, his pulse hammered wildly in response.

"Come, Liesl," he said, and picked up the suitcase. The Gestapo man watched critically. The sneer on his mouth seemed proof enough he did not believe Paul's limp to be genuine. The Customs inspector stepped forward and took the bag.

"Thank you." Paul nodded gratefully.

He gripped Liesl's hand, his mind trapped in the blind corners of its own racing as they crossed the esplanade back to the terminal. This time they went to an unmarked office on the gallery above the main floor. The windowless room was rank with cigarette smoke that hung in layers across the sallow light. At a desk sat Herr Schutz, the chocolate manufacturer. Paul's nerves could scarcely absorb the shock. In the cigarette's wreathing, the older man's face looked altogether different. Gone were the kindly smiles and benign manner. The lines had hardened into a merciless vigor.

Behind him, leaning against the wall, an SS captain in black blouse and flared breeches fingered a swagger stick. Herr Schutz had Paul's passport open on the desk, studying the markings through a magnifying glass. He did not bother to glance up.

"It's a good job," he murmured. "Where did you get it?"

"At the passport office, of course."

"They don't do forgeries at the passport office."

"I tell you it's genuine. I'm taking my daughter to a clinic in Zurich. Here," he insisted, reaching inside his coat, "I have a letter to prove it."

Herr Schutz took the letter from him and dropped it on the desk. He did not open it, but gave Paul a contemptuous smile as if he were tired of the performance. In the corner, the round-shouldered Gestapo man murmured something to the SS officer. Paul was dimly aware of the officer's visor gleaming and the watery shine of his boots.

Herr Schutz reached for a clipboard and thumbed through a sheaf of dispatches. He studied one for several moments, then lowered the board and smiled at Liesl. The face became once more that of the chocolate manufacturer, lacerated with kindness.

"Liesl," he said, "don't you miss your little friends at the convent? Sister Clara says they are crying because they are so sad since you left. Poor Sister Clara. Don't you miss her, too?"

The little girl nodded gravely. Suddenly, confusion mounted on her face. She glanced at Paul, not sure what to say.

"Will the cat get us now?" she whispered.

"No." Paul shook his head. "We're not playing the game anymore."

The smile had dropped from Herr Schutz's mouth, drawing the stern lines together again. He put a rubber band around the passport and papers Paul had surrendered. Then he turned to the SS officer and nodded. More panic poured into Paul's nerves, leaving his throat dry.

The SS officer pushed away from the wall with his shoulder. His manner had the bemused indolence of absolute power. Paul saw that he wore the rank of Hauptsturmführer—a captain.

"There is a sedan outside," Herr Schutz said to Paul. "You're to go with Hauptsturmführer Hoess."

"Am I arrested?" Paul asked.

Herr Schutz did not reply. At the desk, his head was bent into the pluming of the cigarette. He was already absorbed in another matter, as if Paul did not exist.

As Paul started to follow Liesl and the Gestapo man out into the hall, the SS captain held his swagger stick across the doorway and said, "Before we go down, I have something for you."

Paul gazed at him, half anticipating what was to come even before the leather quirt slashed at his cheek, cutting into the flesh. The blood ran under his hand, pressed to the burning welt.

The SS officer smiled, speaking with no more emotion than if he had swatted a fly.

"That is for daring to strike an SS lance corporal with your fists in the street two years ago. I only wanted to be the first to remind you."

While Paul groped for a handkerchief to stem the flow of blood, the other man motioned with the quirt for him to proceed into the hall. Only Leni and Georg knew about the assault on the blackshirt. Going out, Paul wondered which of them had betrayed him, though something in him rejected the idea that either one could have been responsible.

Downstairs, two cars were parked at the curb under the trees. The SS officer motioned Paul to the first one.

"What about the child?" Paul asked.

"She won't be going with us."

Liesl was standing a short distance away with the round-shouldered Gestapo man. She had her doll clutched under one arm, and the breeze from the lake lifted a few strands of hair like spun gold across her chubby face.

"Herr Hauptsturmführer," Paul said, "may I speak to her?"

"No time for that."

"I don't want her to be alarmed," Paul pleaded. "It won't do you any good if she's terrified, will it? Let me have a moment, that's all. It'll mean less bother for you in the long run."

"Well," the captain said. "Make it quick, then."

Paul went back to Liesl. He knelt, smiling, on the shade-drenched pavement and held her shoulders, but it was hard to control the shaking in his fingers.

"You have a hurt." She pointed to the gash in his cheek.

"Just a scratch," he said.

"From the cat?"

"No, I chased the cat away. Listen to me, Liesl. Some urgent business has come up. I have to go along with the other man. It'll only be for a little while."

"Can't we go on the boat?"

"Of course we can. As soon as this other business is taken care of. I'll come for you."

Her lip trembled and she lowered her head. A tear spilled down her cheek, then another. Paul quickly took out his handkerchief.

"What's this? Real tears? But listen, it's only temporary. We'll still have our boat ride. In the meantime, you'll be looked after." He folded the linen so that the blood smears did not show and dabbed her cheeks. "Think of Ilse. You've got to be strong and brave for her. She depends on you."

The little girl stared at him through the film of tears.

"There's something else," Paul said, wiping her nose with the handkerchief. "I want you to remember to smile always, and don't make a fuss. That's very important. Will you promise to do that for me?"

Liesl nodded unhappily.

"Wonderful!" Paul smiled. "Now give your brother a big hug. Until we see each other again, eh?"

He felt the squeeze of her arms about his neck, and then he stood up. Liesl climbed into the sedan with the Gestapo man. Paul could only see her face and shoulders and the glint of her hair. He waved as the car pulled away, and Liesl waved too. In a few moments the road was empty except for the windblown shade of the trees lining the esplanade.

"We're wasting time," the captain called.

Paul climbed into the back seat. The captain ducked in beside him and nodded to the driver. A dozen possibilities tumbled through Paul's mind. He might wait for a chance to bolt, or try to overpower the SS officer and take his weapon, or twist the steering wheel and cause a wreck. One by one, his better senses canceled each option. The captain seemed to have a telepathic understanding. He opened the flap of his holster, and his hand rested on the pistol grip. As they swung away from the station, Paul had a final glimpse of Switzerland across the lake and the tiny cluster of houses on the hilly shore that was Romanshorn.

"Where are we going?" he asked.

"Don't worry." The captain smiled as if their destination were a splendid joke. "A place you're sure to like. Plenty of fresh air and exercise."

PART THREE

BELSEN

ONE

On a clear summer night in 1943, Sturmbannführer Georg Viertel, newly promoted to SS major, crept home along the blacked-out streets of Berlin in his prewar Mercedes 540 coupe. Only two blocks from his house, he had to swing wide around a crater ringed by barricades where a British bomb had fallen. It unnerved him to know that death could have come that close to Leni on the whim of a gloved thumb in the blue light of a bombardier's Plexiglas bubble. But death was capricious in its choices, and in the game of war it had switched allegiance after Stalingrad.

Georg left the car in the dark behind the house and picked his way on foot under the trees to the front, letting himself in with his key.

A dim light fell across the upstairs landing as Leni came out of the bedroom tying the cord of her silk dressing gown at the waist. Georg paused at the foot of the stairs, absorbed in the sheer pleasure that the first sight of his wife always gave him after they had been apart. The light shining through the gown gave an ascendant glow to her form so that he could perceive the long solid shape of her legs, and her breasts, loose in the silk. He called out to her as his head and shoulders came up out of the shadows.

"You look lovely at midnight," he said, and kissed her cheek.

"And you look tired at midnight." Leni smiled.

"It's been a day," Georg said. "Hamburg is in flames. The worst bombing yet. The decision has already been made to evacuate Berlin, except for essential workers."

"There hasn't been any word over the radio," Leni said.

"It'll come soon enough."

In the bedroom, Leni sat at the dressing table, her back to the mirror. Her hair, which she no longer cut short, spilled into a soft knot at the nape of her neck and shone in the oval of glass. Georg took off his tunic, sat on the side of the bed, and began to pull off his boots.

"I've found you a small villa outside Potsdam," he said. "It's only a matter now of getting packed and moved."

"But I don't want to leave the city," Leni protested.

"It's not a question any longer of your wanting to stay," Georg said. "Orders must be obeyed. You'll be safe from enemy bombers, and I can stop worrying about you."

"It's silly to worry. If it's your time to die, there's nothing you can do about it." One corner of her mouth twisted down in a wry embittered smile. "And if it's not your time, you can stand under ten falling bombs."

"You sound as if you want to be where the bombs fall. I couldn't bear it if anything happened to you."

"Anything is bearable." Leni shook her head. "If you give it enough time."

Georg stood up, gripping his boots, and said, "Well, I have an unbearable craving for a hot bath—and my wife."

Leni glanced down, brushing the fingertips of one hand across the painted nails of the other, which rested on her crossed legs.

"I'm in my cycle," she murmured. "A very heavy flow."

Pausing beside her, he touched the side of her neck with his curled fingers. The grazing caress was his way of saying he still wanted her.

The bathroom door closed. Leni heard the water running into the tub as he drew his bath. She could imagine him on the other side of the door, putting his boots down with the heels flush to the wall, taking off his glasses and folding the blades before resting them on the ledge above the sink, then undressing and draping his uniform neatly over the back of a chair. In a chaotic universe, Georg's life was a center of order, precisely arranged.

Leni stood up and went slowly to the bed. Her fingers seemed inexorably heavy as they unfastened the cord of the dressing gown. The silk garment slipped from her shoulders to the floor, and for several moments she stood, feeling cold, like a statue undraped. The sanitary belt demarked a line over the curve of her hips, and the pad crossed a field of crinkled gold like a chastity lock soon to come off. Still wearing it, she slipped under the sheet and lay on her side, her shoulders exposed above the linen cuff.

In the bathroom, Georg finished toweling dry and straightened before the mirror. His grub-white, hairless body sported a pink flush from the hot bath. Four years had put thirty pounds on him, and the disbursement of weight to the hips now gave them a pear shape. Beneath a slight roll of belly fat, his male part hung against an imperfect scrotum where only one testicle had dropped. Even the crop of brown pubic hair around the boyishly penile shape looked as if it had thrived with some difficulty in poor reproductive terrain.

He slipped hurriedly into fresh pajamas. At the sink he hooked on his glasses and brushed his teeth, rinsing his mouth, then examining a speck of black rot that had eaten through the enamel at the gum line of his left incisor. He splashed cologne into his palm and rubbed it over his face, his eyes watering from the astringent fumes, and finally he took a tiny amount of the fluid into his mouth and swished it about his teeth to conceal the odor of decay.

Coming out, he had a glimpse of Leni's bare shoulders and her arm outside the sheet, and the shine of her hair in its soft convoluted bun against the pillow. He switched off the light and crept into bed beside her. A shiver went through her as he brushed her shoulder with a kiss. He could only hope that it was a tremor of pleasure, for she kept her sexual emotions encrypted in silence. His hand stole along her flank to the sanitary belt, and she made no effort to stop him as he drew it down. In his gentleness, he might have been removing a gauze pack from a tender wound, still unhealed. At last her legs stirred and she turned to him, the female scent strong—stronger even than the cologne in which he had drenched himself—and he found himself partially erected in its sexual ether. For once there was no difficulty in penetration, no inhibitions of dry resistance, for the sluice of the menses was its own lubricant.

Intercourse with his wife was always too swift. She made no sound at all, and it was like an expedition into arctic terrain where one became icebound after a short distance. Always, his emission came too soon, before he could make repairs. It made him wonder how far the frozen landscape in her extended, and if it were possible to get beyond it to the fault line of some true sexual upheaval that would crack the crusts of ice.

For all of her unresponsiveness, he found the beauty of her naked body erotically thrilling. Nude before him, she remained somehow clothed in a cold serenity, like a chaste denial. She was submissive rather than cooperative. The protocols of marriage did not extend beyond a physical collaboration, and so the sexual treason of psychological resistance could not be held a crime. Now, once more, he felt himself ejaculating prematurely, alone in that sexual wilderness of wasted sperm, snow-blinded by his own seed that was already freezing into ice blocks in some trackless region of his brain.

Leni was gone from the bed into the bathroom. Georg could see her shadow moving across the crack of light under the door. He was perspiring in his scalp behind his ears, as if his frustration had condensed into these few oily droplets exuded from the pores. He heard water running from the tap. Leni would be washing the pink blood from her inner thighs, and the sleety thaw of his own seminal debris that her uterus rejected and expelled. He felt oddly resentful, as if he had been cheated. Since he was not sure where the anger should be directed, he pushed it deeper inside himself.

Sleep would not come. He could only wait on the impotence of his own wakefulness while his nerves carried the chemistry of failure to his brain. Sexual inadequacy worked on him like a stimulant. The effects would take time to wear off and be absorbed into the psyche of disappointment. Leni was fast asleep, her breath warm and sweet, like an intoxicant. Sometimes he would inhale it, as if he were stealing a bit of her life to possess without her knowledge.

On the pillow, her head stirred, and a small sound came from her throat. She was caught in a dream—one of those odd transactions of the night, conducted in secret, like espionage. But tonight her lips would leave behind a clue, carelessly dropped from the dream, which could be seized as evidence—Paul's name—twice repeated in a whimpering tone. Then she was quiet. Jealous fury gripped him, as if he had stumbled upon an act of infidelity. It was stupid to feel that way, for surely she could not control her dreams. Still, he brooded about it in the dark, the need for sleep blocked up behind the outrage of his suspicion. Even after he had brought it under control, the thought crawled around like a worm in his head.

At dawn, shaved and dressed, he sat in the kitchen, his legs crossed in the flared trousers above the black gleam of his boots, and watched Leni brew ersatz coffee.

"Did you sleep well?" he asked.

"Quite well."

Her head was bent over the steeping pot, her hair trailing half down her back in a loose, unknotted sheaf.

"No dreams?" Georg said casually.

It seemed to him that her hands stopped moving for a brief moment before they continued pouring the coffee. He wished he could see her face. Her eyes could not hold a lie steady on the pupils.

"None," she said.

When she turned with the coffee, her eyes were empty, the evidence destroyed.

"I thought I heard you talking in your sleep," he said. "It must have been my imagination."

"Where are you off to today?" Leni asked.

"The KZ at Bergen-Belsen. I'll be there overnight."

Her cheeks suddenly had a touch of color.

"Will you see Ernst?" she asked.

Georg's gaze was locked on her face like radar waiting to pick up a sortie—the blips of untruth on the oscillating screen of his own doubt.

"That's not likely," he answered. "Ernst was sent east more than a month ago—to Auschwitz."

Leni's head came up sharply.

"You never mentioned it."

"I didn't want to upset you with the news."

"Why did they ship him to the east?" She frowned.

"All Jewish prisoners in Germany were transported to camps in the east last year."

Her eyes skated away from his, then came back.

"But what does that have to do with Ernst?"

"Ernst was a half-Jew," Georg said. "On his mother's side."

"That's ridiculous," Leni scoffed.

"I thought so, too, when I heard it. But it's true."

"How did the SS find out?"

"From a fellow prisoner. They inform on each other more than you'd think. It's a way to curry favor."

"It could have been a lie."

"He had a book of Jewish prayers in his possession."

Leni glanced toward the window where the first gray light of morning pressed against the panes.

"At least Paul got out," she murmured finally.

Georg stared at his wife, his face blankly composed over some raw, savage feeling of betrayal. For the first time ever, he wanted to hurt her—not in any physical way, but to inflict psychological pain—and his reaction horrified him. On a cerebral level he struggled against it, but the compulsion was too strong, as if it were the only way he could break out of his own pain.

"I'm afraid he didn't," Georg said. The ease of the lie surprised him, but the suppressed shame discharged itself in a small thrill of satisfaction as he saw some cold hysteria come into her face.

"Do you realize what you're saying?" she asked.

"Paul was killed four years ago. The border police shot him trying to get across the frontier."

The emotions on her face were no longer identifiable, lost in the devastation of the news. She dropped her head slowly onto her forearm, which rested on the table.

Georg came around behind her and put his hands on her shoulders. A single anguished sob wrenched through her body the moment he touched her—one more bit of perjured testimony. His fingers caressed her shoulders in a comforting way.

"I tried to tell you then, but I couldn't. After all, you were in love with him, once."

"You should have told me." Her voice was little more than a choked whisper. "You had no right not to tell me."

"I did what I thought was best for you."

When she raised her head, he was surprised to see that her cheeks were dry. The grief twisted into her face was beyond tears.

"And Liesl? Did they shoot her too?"

"She was taken to a children's home in Bavaria. I can't say if she's still there or not."

"Paul was your best friend," Leni said miserably. "Can't you at least find out something about his little sister?"

"I'll put through a call when I get back if it will make you feel better." He paused, and added. "I suppose he never told you about his Jewishness?"

This time he saw the lie harden on her stare and not go to pieces, like the others.

"No," she said.

"It could have made a lot of trouble for us, harboring a Jew. I suppose that's why he refused to let us help him."

"And died instead," Leni said.

"At least it was a quick death," Georg said. "That's one thing to be grateful for, isn't it?"

"Since when does death deserve our gratitude?" Leni asked.

Georg shrugged and replied, "No one ever knows when he may have to choose it for a friend."

TWO

The ride to Bergen-Belsen in a motorcycle sidecar was hot and dusty, but the roar of the machine at open throttle along the road at least spared Georg from a dialogue with the driver. The wind cut his face around the goggles, and he sat low in the pod and watched the country racing across the windscreen. Time was racing too, for Georg as much as for Germany, and the destination was disaster. But only a few bright minds could conceive defeat, even after Stalingrad. Since February, in league with a handful of senior SS officers, he had been working out a plan of escape to South America in the event the war should be lost. Now, the operation had taken on a new irony, for if it were to succeed at all it would do so partially through the efforts of a Jew—Ernst Krenek.

On a raw winter day, five months earlier, Georg had visited Ernst outside the concentration camp. The meeting had taken place in an empty railroad coach on a siding in the rail yards where Ernst had been on a work detail unloading coal from gondola cars into trucks. From the frosted compartment window, Georg had watched the guard bringing him across the switchyard over ground covered in crusts of frozen slush. Ernst looked rail thin against the pane and moved with his head bent into the chill wind, arms folded across his chest, and hands clamped into his armpits. Then the pane was empty, a snowscape of tracks and standing boxcars under the lead-heavy sky, and the guard's fist rapped once on the door.

"The prisoner, Herr Hauptsturmführer," he announced.

"Leave him," Georg said. "Come back in thirty minutes."

"Yes, Herr Hauptsturmführer."

The sight of Ernst up close gave Georg a mild shock. Loss of weight had left sunken hollows below the high cheekbones in the gaunt face, and the pale eyes, rimmed with coal dust, had a guarded look. A filthy sweater, worn under his striped prison garb, gave only a little warmth from the numbing cold, and the fingers were rotted off the woolen mittens. His nose was running, and he rubbed the back of a mitten across the mucus of clear fluid.

"For God's sake, sit down," Georg said.

"Thank you," Ernst murmured. His tone had a low decibel of distrust, and he added, "Herr Hauptsturmführer."

"Don't be a fool, Ernst." Georg smiled. "We're alone. I'm your friend."

The coal had left a grimy shine on Ernst's face, and his clothing had a rank smell.

"I've been advised in rather strong terms," he replied, "that friendship is a form of contraband."

"No one can search you for it," Georg said.

"It wouldn't matter. I'm not concealing any."

"You look half starved."

"The camp has a limited menu. Soup and bread. No dessert."

"And what about Paul?"

"A bit worse off than me. He talked back to a guard. They beat him up and put him on half rations. He'll do it again, of course. The next time it happens, they'll shoot him."

"I'll have a word with the chief physician. We'll make him fit again. How are your hands?"

"My hands?" Ernst gave him a puzzled look. "So cold, the fingernails ache."

"Let me see them."

Georg tested the articulation of the fingers. The left thumb had been smashed, leaving the dead nail misshapen and purple, but the injury did not look to be disabling. Ernst's hands were supple and sinewy in Georg's own, which were smooth and white as a woman's.

"How long since they've held a paintbrush?" Georg asked.

"That was another life." Ernst shook his head. "Didn't you know? Artists are cast into hell when they die. That's where I am now. In a state of damnation, surrounded by an electric fence, and the SS are the black angels."

"Maybe it's time to think about your resurrection." Georg let go of his hands.

"The dead here don't rise," Ernst said, "except through a chimney."

"I have a special job," Georg said, "that requires a live artist, not a dead one. You'll be out of the camp every day, and get special treatment. Soap. Decent food. Cigarettes. No other work details."

A flicker of hope, almost like a twinge of pain, passed across Ernst's stare.

"And Paul?" he murmured.

"He'll be taken care of," Georg said. "The first swine of a guard who lays a hand on him will dearly regret it, I promise you. Of course, Paul will have to keep his mouth shut and not antagonize people. I'll leave it to you to persuade him."

Ernst gazed at the insignia of rank on Georg's greatcoat and asked, "How does a captain have that kind of authority?"

"Don't worry about my authority. It comes from higher up. Now tell me, as an artist, could you reproduce masterworks from the nineteenth and early twentieth centuries that might fool, say, an art expert?"

"It's always possible," Ernst said. "But very difficult. Especially the earlier century."

"Describe the difficulties to me."

"They would depend on the medium."

"Oil on canvas, for instance?"

"You'd have to find another canvas of similar size that was painted in the same decade and still mounted on the original stretcher. It's possible, after soaking the canvas in an alkaline solution, to remove the original paint with a palette knife, but it is a very slow process. One slip, and it's ruined."

"At that point," Georg said, "you could copy the original?"

"If I had the original to work from. A print is too deceptive. It doesn't show the thickness and texture of the paint. But that's only the beginning. The oil can take years to dry after the painting has been hung. In the process, the colors blend to their own chemistry. In five to ten years they may have aged in a way that's inconsistent with the other works of the original artist. An expert could spot the difference."

"Suppose we were dealing not just with oils, but pastels, and pen-and-ink drawings?"

"Vintage paper is the main problem. The watermark would give it away. Picasso and Dufy were fond of *papier d'arche*. Quite a lot of their early work was done on it."

"Where could vintage paper be found?"

"Paris, most likely. If you poked about some of the art supply shops on the Left Bank, you'd probably find a few pads gathering dust on a shelf. Most of the major artists, from the impressionists on, worked in Paris. It's where they bought their art supplies."

"Assuming we could provide you with everything you need for the job, and a place to work, would you be willing to do what you've just described?"

"What's behind it?" Ernst frowned.

"That's not for you to be concerned about," Georg replied.

"You're asking me to participate in something that may or may not be morally acceptable, and in the same breath telling me not to be concerned."

"I'm asking you to participate in something that can make your life easier. Yours, Paul's, and Liesl's. It's a chance to do important work, the kind you were born to do, not piling lumps of coal into a truck. I'm in a position to help you survive, but only if you let me. If you have any sense, you'll seize the opportunity—if not for your own sake, then for the others."

"How many paintings?"

Georg gazed at him and said, "Dozens."

"Where would I work? It couldn't be done in the KZ."

"There's an old estate on the river this side of Celle, the property of an SS colonel on duty in the east. His wife and a maid occupy the manor house. The servant quarters are empty. They'll make an ideal studio. You'll be driven to and from the place every day. It's not far."

"What will the other prisoners think?"

"Only what you tell them. As far as anyone else is concerned, you're on a special work detail—restoring old works of art brought into the Reich from captured countries. It's the truth, after a fashion."

"And Paul?"

"He's to know nothing more than the others. It's for his own good. If the information were to leak out, the project would be as good as finished."

Ernst gazed across the switchyard to the skeletal figures passing chunks of coal by hand out of the gondola into the truck. Their breath froze into white puffs that the gusting wind tore away as if it would not permit them even to keep that.

"I'll need paints and supplies," he murmured.

"Give me a list of all your requirements."

"First, I'll have to know the artists and paintings."

"You'll have those details today, before I leave."

Ernst's mouth twisted down in a reflective smile.

"I've always thought that copying another artist's work was a bit like stealing from the dead. Now I seem to be engaged in the practice."

"I'll only require one other thing from you," Georg said. "Your word of honor that you accept the conditions as I've described them, and promise to keep silent."

"Honor is the first thing that goes in the KZ. You turn it in with your other valuables, and they don't issue you a receipt for it."

"No one can confiscate a friendship," Georg said. "I'll take your word based on *that,* not our present circumstances."

It seemed a long time before Ernst made up his mind, as if he were borrowing against his integrity in the full foreknowledge that the loan would default. But in the end it could only be another debit in the ledger of survival, and at last he nodded his head in agreement.

"Good," Georg said. He drew his own black, fur-lined gloves from the pocket of his greatcoat and tossed them onto the seat beside Ernst. "Wear these when you go out. Your fingers won't be any good with frostbite."

"They'll say I stole them," Ernst said.

"Nobody will bother you from now on," Georg said. "I promise you."

Now, the memory of the rail yards smothered in old snow under the gray gantries and cast-iron sky faded off the dirty windscreen of the motorcycle sidecar and left only the racing fields and forests on the Plexiglas. The white hands in Georg's lap were tightly clenched on impatient fury. Five months of work were suddenly at risk of being lost, the project terminated, all because of a stupid Jew prayer book found among Ernst's things in the prisoner barracks. Worse still, he had admitted being half-Jew, almost as though he were proud of it. Only a damned Jew could be capable of such a cheap deception! But if they were to salvage the project from disaster, Georg knew he would have to put his bitterness against Ernst aside and work out a solution to satisfy all interests. Even as the gleam of the summer day went to pieces on the windscreen, his mind stayed busy with the problem.

THREE

The estate lay behind a stone wall on a wooded bluff above a bend of the Aller. It was a beech wood, and the grounds had a copper gleam from the wet compost of dead leaves under the trees that were still twisted and bare in the cold of March when Ernst began painting in the servant quarters. Working, he had a view of the river streaming off the casement panes, and higher up, beyond the talon grip of bare branches, the manor house squatted low against the sky.

The SS sergeant who escorted him to and from the estate each day was named Otto Holst, and among the guards at Belsen he was less despised than most because he was corrupt. Favors could be bought from him at the fair market value of special treatment.

Holst had come out of the coalfields in the Ruhr, and in the cavernous sockets beneath the low slope of his forehead his eyes were bright and black like those of some burrowing animal, and the crooked nose owed its shape to a blow from a pick handle during a fight in a mine shaft. The sergeant saw at once that Ernst was involved in a project that ascended to some higher corridor of power, and his attitude changed from one of overbearing dominance to sly respect. He knew nothing about art, and so the aesthetic mystery of it impressed him unconditionally. On the trips to and from the camp, he seemed more a benign protector than a guard, and sometimes addressed Ernst as Herr Krenek and joked with him in a bluff, coarse way.

Each morning when Ernst arrived at the stone cottage he found a thermos of hot coffee beside a covered dish of sweet pastry. Wrapped in newspaper for the noon meal were black bread, cheese or a piece of salted fish, and sometimes dried fruit. The hearth had been swept clean, and logs piled over kindling on the iron grate so that he had only to open the damper and strike a match to start a fire. He had been told to write down his needs on a pad by the easel. This he did, and the items always appeared in a day or two, though he had no idea who procured them.

By mid-May the manor house had gone into hiding in the beech leaves, and the river ran sparkling in spring sunlight below the bluff that sloped down through grass and wildflowers to the moving sheen of water.

One afternoon he caught sight of a woman walking a pair of Dobermans in the wood. Her bright red hair was drawn back severely into a banded sheaf, and she wore riding breeches and boots and an English tweed coat, and gripped a switch. At that distance her mouth was only a spot of red paint in a blank of flesh like an unfinished portrait. The dogs, sleek and high strung, bounded ahead of her. Then she passed out of view into the shady dappling of leaves, the gleam of red hair going out like an ember on Ernst's stare.

Later, the canvas on which he was painting suddenly brightened under an intrusion of warm sunlight that streamed across his shoulder from behind. He turned to find the woman standing in the open doorway, the dogs on either side of her so that their blackness seemed to flow from the riding boots below the flared trousers. The fangs of the Dobermans flashed, and their low snarling had scarcely erupted when the woman said icily, "Be still!"

The animals shied back, perhaps out of respect for the switch, cut from a green birch, dangling in front of them like a fencer's foil.

"I am Frau Hesse," she said. "This is my husband's estate."

"I'm afraid you startled me, Frau Hesse. I wasn't expecting a visitor. My name is Krenek."

"You are the prisoner Krenek," she corrected him, "from Belsen."

He saw now that she was older than he had thought, probably in her forties, though her body had remained deceptively youthful in its angular thinness. The red hair came from a commercial rinse, and the invasive lines beneath her eyes were like the tiny cracks that form in old alabaster. More deep lines curved down from the corners of her mouth, as if the severity there had been forced to extend itself. The effect was one of flawed beauty that time was just now taking beyond the repair of creams and lotions and the ordeals of exercise.

"You're right," Ernst replied. "I'm one of the *politicals* from the KZ. A dangerous influence, according to all reports."

"My husband is an SS Standartenführer," she said, "serving in the east."

"Doing his duty for our sacred Fatherland," Ernst said, careful to keep the derision out of his tone.

Frau Hesse spoke softly to the dogs, then walked slowly up to Ernst. Her eyes were quite large, which made the coldness in them all the more startling, though her mouth had a trace of contemptuous humor.

"If I thought you meant that cynically," she said, "I'd have you shot."

"You might be doing me a favor," Ernst replied.

The switch rested across her shoulder, and he half expected it to slash across his face. But she only touched the tip of it to his cheek like a threat of punishment.

"If you really thought that, you wouldn't be here painting."

"Better than a labor gang at Belsen," he said.

"Only if you remember your place."

"I won't forget, Frau Hesse," he said, not daring to flinch away from the tensile strength of the birch against his face. "Memory is the one thing they don't confiscate from you in the camps."

The switch fell away, like a reprieve, and the woman turned to examine the half-finished canvas on the easel.

"Where did you study?" she asked.

"The Academia di Belle Arti in Florence."

Among the tubes of paint strewn over the worktable lay his sketch pad. Frau Hesse leafed through several sheets, pausing over one.

"Braque," she said. "But I don't recognize the drawing."

"I do some work in the style of the artist before I try to copy him. It gives me a better feel for the line." He hesitated, adding, "I see you know about art, Frau Hesse."

"I studied two years at the academy in Antwerp." She thumbed through more of his sketches.

"Why did you give it up?" he asked.

"It was a wasted effort. Why indulge failure?" She raised her head, and he saw the combustible heat of some unpredictable emotion on her stare. "You have the quality that I lacked. It shows in your work. Now you have an opportunity to do something with it."

"For what?" he asked. "The glory of the Reich?"

The antagonistic smile had come back into her mouth. The domineering air was inborn, he thought, not acquired—a legacy of too much privilege that included a codicil of superficial elegance.

"You have an insolent manner," she said in a half-amused way. "Be grateful that I have enough respect for your ability to tolerate it—for now."

"Only the paintings deserve respect," he said.

"Is that what you think?" she asked. "We'll see."

From the window Ernst watched her moving with the dogs away from the cottage into the beech wood. An odd sort of tension had gripped his nerves, and he tried to exorcise it with a cigarette. Clearly, the woman enjoyed the arrogance of power, and whatever neurotic conflicts lay at the core of her personality, he was now hostage to them. She might as well have been appointed the curator of his freedom. She would be the sole critic of his work, like one of the experts *auprès du tribunal,* and her certification would apply to his survival as well as his canvases. Even as he dragged the cigarette from his mouth, he had a premonition the whole affair would turn out badly.

On the drive back to the KZ, Sergeant Holst glanced at him and said, "What's the matter? Didn't it go well today?"

"Fine," Ernst lied.

"What are you painting?"

"I'm restoring old canvases."

The sergeant's blunt hands gave an impression of clumsy power on the steering wheel, and in the fading light his nose had the look of clown's putty where it swelled at the base.

"But you have fresh paint on your hands and clothing," he said. Behind the observation lay a sharp curiosity.

"That's true," Ernst said. "Sometimes I have a bit of spare time, waiting for a chemical to dry, and I can paint. I was painting today, as a matter of fact."

"Did you sell many pictures before the war?"

"A few dozen, I suppose."

"Did they fetch a good price?"

"Sometimes."

"How much would one of them be worth?"

"It's hard to say. Pictures increase in value if the artist is any good."

"Like old brandy, eh?"

"Yes," Ernst said. "Tell me something. What do you know about Frau Hesse? I met her today."

"I've never seen her," Holst said. "They say she was something to look at, once. Her husband is a colonel doctor at Auschwitz. There's a joke that he volunteered to go east because she wouldn't let him keep his pants on."

"Auschwitz?" Ernst frowned.

"Where most of the Jews were transported," Holst said. He winked at Ernst. "They send them up the chimney to make room for more."

Ernst did not reply, and the vehicle ground along the road lined with trees where the last light of the day was going to pieces in the leaves.

Holst said, "Too bad you can't still paint the pictures and sell them."

"What's the point of stewing over it?" Ernst could sense the proposition coming. "There's nothing I can do about it."

The windows were down, making a pleasant breeze after the hot day, and the side mirror reflected a plume of dust lifting behind them into the trees.

"If you could paint them," Holst said, "I might be able to sell them for you. On the sly, of course. We could split the profit."

"What good are Reichsmarks in a KZ?"

"But, Herr Krenek, you won't always be in a KZ. One day you'll walk out. I could put away your share. You can trust old Otto."

"What if you were caught? I couldn't let you take a risk like that." Ernst shook his head. "But, look. You've been decent to my brother and me, and I want to do something for you. If you like, when I get a chance, I'll paint a first-rate canvas for you. One that could be worth something in a few years, if you hang on to it."

"Of course I'd hang on to it." Holst nodded vigorously. "I'm no fool. I know about the value of great art."

The road veered to the west, and the barracks of Belsen, low in the distance, streamed across the windshield.

"Then it's settled," Ernst said.

Before the week was out Frau Hesse came again to the cottage while Ernst was at work. The window was open, and this time he heard the dogs and saw her coming downhill through the trees in the embers of wind-blown light on the ground in the late afternoon. Under one arm she carried a portfolio, as well as the switch.

Ernst stood up and snubbed out his cigarette as she came through the door.

"I've brought some new work for you," she said.

"I'm still working on the Braque," he said. "I'm not satisfied with it."

"I am." She gave him a long, cool glance. "You only have to satisfy me—not yourself."

"Whatever you say, Frau Hesse."

She cleared a place on the table, opened the portfolio, and arranged the pictures. There were two pencil-and-crayon drawings, a third in ink, and a gouache.

"Modigliani," Ernst said.

"I've brought you a number of good prints, as well. I want you to try some original work in his style."

"I agreed to do copies," Ernst said, "not forgeries."

"Why should it matter? In the end, it's all the same."

"A copy isn't a forgery until someone misrepresents it as an original. That's your affair, not mine. But a new work in the style of the artist doesn't leave any doubt, does it?"

"What a pity," she said with a derisive smile, "that your poor suffering conscience has to undergo such an ordeal."

"Suppose they don't turn out to your satisfaction?"

"It's your job to see that they do."

"Modigliani was a Jew. His work could never be exhibited in the Reich."

"Where it might be exhibited is not your concern. The fact is, none of the early work from his days on the Rue Caulaincourt was cataloged, and he destroyed a great deal of it himself. He was fond of sketching prostitutes and patrons in cheap cafés on the Left Bank. It shouldn't be hard to duplicate. Once you've mastered his line, we'll try something more ambitious. Perhaps an oil . . ."

"There are artists from that period whose styles would be easier to do. Why pick Modigliani?"

"Because he's a great painter. The value of his art will soar in a few years. Besides, he usually drew directly on the canvas and thinned his paints with terps before he applied them. That means drying won't be a problem."

"I'll have to think about it," Ernst said.

No sooner were the words out of his mouth than his hand was clamped over the searing pain of a raw welt high on his cheek, and he could feel blood on his fingers. He hadn't even seen her pick up the switch.

"That's for the impertinence of imagining that you have any part at all in any decision made here. I'll choose and assign your projects. You have no rights. You only have a talent. At the moment, your talent belongs to me. Consider yourself an article of personal property. Your only function, apart from painting, is obedience."

"Is that all, Frau Hesse?"

A smile dragged the corner of her mouth into a line of scornful amusement, but the heat on the fixed stare went to some deeper pleasure that had to do with inflicting physical pain and humiliation.

"You have blood on your face and neck," she said. "Go in to the other room and rinse at the sink before you make a mess. I'll be back tomorrow to see what you've done."

* * *

But she did not appear the next day, as if her absence were an assertion of authority, a subtle exercise in dominance. The morning after, he found a note beside the thermos of coffee. Unsigned, it told him to come to the house at nine o'clock.

An hour later, he tramped uphill beside the low stone wall, warm in the sun, where the bluff slumped down to the river. Wildflowers swam on the water in flecks of reflected color. The scene was deceptively tranquil, as if nothing could be wrong in the world, least of all his own situation, but that was the cheapest forgery of all.

The first impact of the brass knocker drew barking from the dogs inside. Almost at once it became a snarling rage on the other side of the door. Abruptly, the sound went dead, and a latch slid out of its iron cuff. He had expected to confront a maid, but instead it was Frau Hesse. She saw his surprise and said, "The maid is in Celle. She won't be back until noon. There is something I want you to see."

Thick drapes, drawn at the windows, gave the house a false sense of night. Frau Hesse wore a wraparound garment that had the look of an artist's smock, tied at the waist with a cloth cord, and a pair of flat, open sandals. The dogs had been banished to the wide stone hearth. Ernst followed her through the deep gloom, aware of a musky, perfumed scent and the glitter of earrings where the red hair was drawn back and clamped behind her head and the whiteness of her legs, which were still elegantly curved, though flawed above the swell of the calves by red rivulets of collapsed veins.

Narrow stone steps descended to a vaultlike door rising out of the shadows. At the touch of her hand, it swung back soundlessly on its bearings, but all Ernst could see was a cavernous dark.

It was a gallery, and it came up slowly in soft light controlled by a rheostat, as if the glimmer itself would intrude respectfully on the vivid colors of the canvases that covered the walls. Ingres, Cézanne, Renoir, Monet . . . the collection was dazzling in the sheer array of genius, hidden away like refugees from the Führer's pedestrian vision of art.

"I wanted you to see it," Frau Hesse said. "Not one at a time, but like this, all of it together."

"Incredible," Ernst whispered. A thick Persian rug sank underfoot as he stepped to the room's center and turned slowly, the excitement hammering at a vein in his throat. He could not tear his gaze from the spellbinding beauty.

After a few moments, the lights dimmed to a low glimmer, as if the paintings were being taken away from him, and he turned to see Frau Hesse still standing beside the rheostat. She had stepped out of the sandals, and now she unfastened the cord at her waist until the loose smock fell open, and he saw that she wore nothing underneath.

"How long has it been since you've had a woman?" she asked.

On his way back to the cottage, Ernst stopped at the low stone wall in the noon shade. The river streamed into the sunny distance where the tiny parcel of brilliance burned on his stare like an enticement to freedom. But escape was out of the question. Paul's life, and possibly Liesl's, were the escrow that would be forfeited, apart from his own word to Georg. And now the contract had been altered to include a nymphomaniac. Already the memory was buried in his stare—her wiry, naked body writhing with a hard, vicious force in the motions of copulation and the dry upheavals of evasive pleasure, streaking close but never quite caught in the wet salt wave that broke too soon on the false tremors that formed it. Still, she had seemed not wholly dissatisfied when it was done, a gleam of promiscuous triumph in her gaze as she sat up, the tips of her small breasts hard as unopened buds that swelled only a little in their sexual antagonisms.

In the cottage, he could not focus on his work. Thoughts of Frau Hesse spoiled his concentration. Finally he put down the palette, took up his sketch pad, and penciled the first lines of the picture he meant to paint for Otto Holst. The project had suddenly acquired a creative urgency. It would be his posthumous apology to the artists whose work he had been forced to copy, and with a bit of luck, Holst would deliver it. Already the lines on the paper were fusing together in his vision of them—a dead landscape of surreal terror, not unlike his own existence.

He worked for a full hour on the concept before it occurred to him that he should have a place to conceal what he was doing. It would not do to have Frau Hesse find the drawing and question him.

He settled on the attic-like space between the ceiling and the slate roof. The only access to it was a ceiling trap in the hall outside the lavatory. He found that he could easily reach it from a chair, unseating the trap, then heaving himself up through the gap into the crawl space among the support timbers. The air was stale, and just inside the gutter of the first joist he caught sight of a dusty black book. He lifted it from the snare of cobwebs, blew the dust from the cover, and saw that it was a Jewish prayer book. On the first blank page was a name—Herschel Marx—and scrawled beneath it a line from a psalm:

> Light will shine on the righteous
> And joy upon the upright of heart

But the light had gone out, Ernst thought, and it would shine nowhere, least of all on the righteous. He left the prayer book, rolled in his preliminary sketch, between the cross timbers, dropped down from the crawl space, and fitted the trap into place above his head.

The next afternoon, Frau Hesse came alone to the cottage, and Ernst asked, "Have you come to see the sketches?"

"No," she said.

The heat went into his face, but she only smiled contemptuously, locking her fingers in his hair, and then she put her mouth against his and entered it with her tongue. It seemed to Ernst hardly more than a minute before they were naked on a tick mattress on the stone floor of the next room where the sun streamed through the window above their heads onto the bare wall. There was no tenderness in her, only appetite, and some harsh sexual anger meted out in the explicit aggression of her fingers forcing his maleness into her and the impatient straining of her body. Afterward, he did not withdraw from her, knowing from the pressure of her hand lingering on the back of his neck that he was not yet dismissed. The flicker of pleasure on her stare had less to do with carnal satisfaction than some joy of ownership, the interest in a new possession, and he winced as she ran the fingers of her other hand across the unhealed welt in his cheek. The antagonisms, spent in sex, were only a little inflamed on her smile as she said, "It's a work of art. Perhaps I'll give you one on the other cheek to match it."

Through the early weeks of summer, an afternoon hardly passed that she did not turn up at the servant quarters. The direction of her desire was often unpredictable, subject to quirks of deviant curiosity, and, always, the dry contractions were blocked up behind a prurient anger so that the sexual disbursements were paid out in devalued currencies of pleasure.

Sometimes he was able to bring her to climax, usually at the expenditure of his own shame, but since he no longer placed any value on his pride, it did not matter. On these occasions he could feel the anger break inside her, and, once, in the aftermath of that sexual release, he took advantage of her mood to ask about the man whose name was in the prayer book. She was lying on her back, her forearm across her closed eyes, the shine of semen still wet on her thighs. Ernst sat upright, his curled back to her, and lit a cigarette. Her free hand rested on his spine, not so much in a caress as in a claim of ownership, and he asked, "Did you ever know a man named Herschel Marx?"

The hand that had been moving slowly over the small of his back stopped altogether, and he could sense instant curiosity in the arrested motion.

"Where did you hear the name?" she asked.

"From another prisoner," he lied. "In the camp."

"What prisoner?"

"I never knew his name. He was sent east."

"What did he tell you?"

"Nothing, actually. It was something I overheard him say to another inmate while we were on a work detail. Just that this person—Marx—had some connection to the Hesse estate."

Once more, the hand on his back began to move, the painted nail of one finger tracing an aimless pattern.

"Marx was a gamekeeper here. It was about eight years ago that he came looking for work. He had letters of endorsement under a different name. He was here for two years before the police arrested him. It turned out that he was a Jew trying to hide his identity."

. "Really?" Ernst asked. "What happened to him?"

"What do you suppose happened to him?" Her tone had a scornful edge, as if the question were unnecessary. "He was taken off to a camp, of course."

"Where?"

For a moment she was silent while the fingernail traced a large letter A across the column of his spine.

"Where he won't have another chance to lie about his Jewishness."

Ernst remained motionless, his arms encircling his upraised knees, the cigarette dangling from his long mouth as he stared vacantly into its plume. Her fingernail constructed another A across his lower back, and he could feel the letter burn like a brand of shame through the skin all the way into his loins, where the dissipations of pride could be comfortably ejaculated. Afterward, he was sure that was the moment when he formed the intent to smuggle the prayer book back into the camp with him. It was almost as if a part of him wanted to be caught.

FOUR

After his talk with the commandant at Belsen, Georg went directly to the servant quarters on the Hesse estate and waited for Ernst. He heard the car on the road and stepped into the open doorway. Sergeant Holst was driving, and Ernst sat beside him on the front seat. The leaves hurled their speckled reflection onto the windshield, and in the gloom behind the glass Ernst's face was only half formed, like an image on a film negative.

A deep sadness overtook Georg—a sense that he had been somehow betrayed. Both Ernst and Paul had played an important part in his life, but now the relationship was closing on itself like a circle, and he viewed its passing with an ambience of regret.

The car rolled to a stop in the shade, and as Ernst and Holst got out, Georg motioned to the SS sergeant to stay with the vehicle. He said nothing to Ernst until they were inside, the door shut. Then he demanded softly, "Why?"

Ernst replied with a fatalistic smile, "You live in fear of something for a long time. One day it happens, and then you're not afraid anymore."

"You're a fool," Georg said.

"There are worse things to be, these days."

"It was stupid to take a book of Jew prayers into the camp. But the stupidest of all was to admit being *Halbjude*."

"They already knew it when they questioned me."

"That was a bluff. An interrogator's trick. You could have denied everything. You could have said someone planted the book in your things. I would have defended you."

"I'm sick of living a lie. The price is too stiff."

"Dying isn't exactly a bargain."

"Neither is living."

Georg threw up his hands, turning half away in exasperation.

"I can't help you if you're going to take that attitude."

"I'm not asking for your help," Ernst said.

"Let's talk about the project," Georg said. "How much longer to finish it?"

"What difference does it make? I won't be involved in it."

"For God's sake, Ernst," Georg snapped, "just give me a simple answer, will you?"

"The time frame would have depended on the working conditions. You run into delays waiting for certain paints and supplies that may be required—and other interruptions."

"How long?" Georg pressed him.

"Under ideal conditions, perhaps four months. Realistically, six."

Georg sighed and moved slowly to the window. For a long time, the river on the glass took his stare into the bright distances of the day. At last he turned and said decisively, "There's only one way it can be managed. Too many people at the camp know the truth about you—prisoners and guards, both. Paul will have to be sent off to a different KZ. Mauthausen, perhaps. The chief doctor there is a personal friend. I can arrange the transfer. None of the guards or inmates at Mauthausen will have to know about this *Halbjude* business as long as Paul keeps his mouth shut. In the meantime, here at Belsen, we'll put out the story that he was transported to Auschwitz with the rest of the Jews."

"And me?"

"You'll stay here at the cottage, full-time, until the project is finished. There isn't any other way. As far as anyone at the camp will know, you were sent to Auschwitz, too, with Paul. I'll talk to Frau Hesse myself."

"And tell her I'm a half-Jew?" Ernst smiled.

"My God, no! It would ruin everything. Do you imagine for one minute that she'd let a Jew stay here? It's going to be hard enough as it is to persuade her."

"I'm sure," Ernst said with bitter amusement. "And when the project is over, what then?"

"You'll be sent to another camp."

"Where?"

Briefly, Georg's stare slid away, then came back.

"I don't know."

"Wouldn't it be easier for you just to find another artist?"

"I *can't* find another artist," Georg said quietly.

* * *

The words fastened themselves into Ernst's nerves like a terminal pronouncement. For the first time, he realized they meant to kill him, or let
him be killed. His Jewishness would provide the grounds. But the heart of
his crime was that he knew too much and would have to be silenced.
Probably he had been working under a sentence of death all along. The
odd part was, he didn't care.

Still, his hands shook a bit as he took a cigarette from the pack on the
table.

"Suppose I had to refuse?"

Georg snapped a cigarette lighter and held out the flame.

"Then it's over for you. I won't be able to help you. Or Paul, either." He
added in a tone of regret, "Or Liesl."

Ernst took a deep inspiration of smoke and exhaled it slowly.

"Can you guarantee our lives?"

"Paul was my best friend," Georg said. "If it were only up to me, neither
of you would be in a camp. Do you think it matters to me that you're
Halbjude? Didn't we grow up together?" He shook his head. "But it's not
that simple. It's a collective decision, and I only possess one vote. If you
go on with the project, Paul and Liesl can be protected. I'm in a position
to give my word on that. As for you, I can only promise that I'll do my
best to keep you from harm."

Ernst sat on the edge of the plank table and smoked in silence. Finally
he said, "I want to see Paul."

"That wouldn't be wise."

"It's my condition for saying yes. I want him brought here."

"You can't tell him anything about your work."

"I only want to see my brother before he's sent away," Ernst said. "All
Paul knows is that I'm cleaning and restoring old canvases."

"I'll have to be here when you talk to him."

"I gave you my word once before," Ernst said. "I didn't break it then."

"But things are different now," Georg insisted. "I'll have to be here.
There's no other way. It's for Paul's protection. Don't you see? I can guarantee his safety only as long as I can guarantee his ignorance."

Ernst blew another reflective stream of smoke.

"All right." He crushed out the cigarette, but he was thinking that only
death could put a warranty on silence, and only the dead kept their
promises.

FIVE

The soft shades of the dying day were stretched across the estate by the time Sergeant Holst returned from camp with Paul in the car. Ernst was smoking another cigarette on the plank bench near the easel, and Georg was sitting on the wide stone sill of the casement windows, his gray SS tunic framed in the light of the panes. Coming in, Paul caught sight of both men at the same time and stopped in his tracks.

Georg slipped off the sill to his feet and said, "Hello, Paul."

Ernst watched his brother carefully. The cold resistance in Paul's stare had a familiar antagonistic glint. Finally his mouth dragged down in a half smile, full of contempt.

He said to Georg, "What are we waiting for—one of your mobile gas vans?"

"Hardly," Georg replied.

"You never had much use for Jews," Paul said.

"You're misdirecting your anger," Georg said coolly.

"I thought it was high praise," Paul said.

"Stop it, Paul," Ernst said. "Georg is a friend, no matter what you think."

"The Sturmbannführer, you mean?" Paul asked.

"Do you realize," Georg said, "if anyone at the Reich Central Security Office knew why I was here that I would probably be taken out and shot?"

"It's true." Ernst nodded. "Georg ran a risk coming here. The least you can do is listen to him. Sit down, and don't be so hardheaded."

The infiltrations of shadow lengthened across the stone floor of the cottage while Georg spoke of the arrangements he proposed to make.

"The people at Belsen who know you're a half-Jew will have to suppose you're being sent off to Auschwitz. That way, no one will think any more about it, and there's less danger of someone informing. I can arrange to divert you to another camp in Germany while you're in transit. Probably Mauthausen. You'll be just another political prisoner."

"And Ernst?" Paul asked

"I'll be staying here for a while," Ernst said, "until I've finished the work I'm doing."

"Restoring old canvases?" Paul said with a cynical amusement directed not so much at Ernst as at the project itself.

"It's the only thing that's keeping us alive," Ernst wanted to say, but did not. Instead, he left his cigarette in the crimped tin that served as an ash-tray and went to the easel, lifting away a half-finished canvas to reveal another—this one his own. Drawing attention to it with Georg looking on posed a risk, but one that had to be taken. Openness would have to serve as its own camouflage. Unless Paul took away a visual impression of the canvas, the stratagem Ernst had conceived would have no chance of suc-cess. It was why, under the pretext of saying good-bye, he had insisted Paul be brought to the cottage.

"This is an oil by Chirico," Ernst said, "painted in Paris before the First War. It's called *The Court of Blue Shadows*. The canvas had some damage in the upper right corner, but I was able to repair the flaw. After that, it only needed a proper cleaning to restore the original colors. It looks as if it were painted yesterday, don't you agree?"

The dead landscape of crumbling arches and topless pillars, strewn with broken busts and classical statuary, could pass nicely as a Chirico, Ernst thought. It had the same static mystery of the artist's work—the sense of an ominous but unseen presence.

It was Georg, not Paul, who stepped to the easel for a look. The knot of nerves in Ernst's belly tightened.

"One of the surrealists, I suppose," Georg said.

"Actually," Ernst replied, "his work anticipated theirs. He was a Greek who studied in Munich. Don't you remember, Paul? The summer we visit-ed Munich, I took you to an exhibition of his work at the Pinakothek Museum. You were impressed enough, at the time."

Paul gazed at Ernst, then moved closer for a look at the painting.

"It was a long time ago," he replied, frowning at the canvas. "It's all pretty vague, now. But I think I remember."

"Memories are all we have these days." Ernst smiled sadly. "You shouldn't be careless with them."

Later, on the drive back to the camp, Paul stared reflectively at the red strokes of twilight on the horizon, trying to interpret the signal Ernst had sent. The text was undecipherable, but one thing was clear—the two of them had never been together in Munich.

PART FOUR

THE COURT OF BLUE SHADOWS

ONE

The painting in the window of the consignment shop streamed across his own face on the glass, and the two images merged like a double exposure. The pain swelled in his head to an unbearable pressure, and burst, and whole pieces of memory floated up out of some interior recess. From somewhere across the desolate reaches of the painting, it came to him: Your name is Krenek. . . .

The man who called himself Josef Neumann was suddenly gone—stepping into a shadow of the mind—unable to confront Paul Krenek, who stood alone now before the shop window. The two had met only for an instant among the toppling columns and maimed marble figures in the blue surreal distances of the canvas.

After the sunlit street, the shop was dark. The cluttered shelves settled slowly out of the gloom onto his pupils. Some dizzy aftershock of self-discovery hit him, and he gripped a shelf with both hands. An older woman in dark clothing stepped through the beaded curtains into the aisle.

"Are you ill, *mein Herr?*"

"Just give me a minute." Paul shook his head.

"You look pale. You'd better sit down. There's a couch in the back of the shop."

Her hands were on his arm, guiding him through the dry rattle of the beaded curtains into a dim back room.

"Sit here and I'll get you a glass of water."

Stuffing poked from the sofa in hernias of soiled cotton where the fabric had split. Paul heard water running from a tap. He leaned his head back against the wall and shut his eyes.

In his mind he saw clearly the railway siding outside Dachau as the sliding door of the boxcar rolled open, and he could hear the shouts—"*Out!*

Out!"—along the ramp where guards with attack dogs stood in the gray mist of the morning.

Prisoners spilled from the string of freight cars onto the platform. An old man lay dead on the floor of the car that Paul was in. He had no teeth, and his mouth made a sunken hole in his face where the eyes were rolled up under half-closed lids. His sphincter had expelled the black watery waste of his bowel, and people stepped around the corpse as if it were a stench pile of rags and flesh.

A week earlier, the prisoners had left Mauthausen in a group of five hundred on a forced march to Dachau. Starved and sick, fewer than half had reached Munich. There, the survivors had been packed into boxcars and left overnight before starting the final leg of the journey.

Now, on the platform, Paul blinked in the mist of cold sunlight. The black stubble had gone to seed on his face, and his scalp and groin itched where lice were feeding. There was pain, too, in his forearm where the tattooed number had been cut from the flesh, four nights earlier, in a temporary camp on the outskirts of Passau. It had been performed by a prisoner doctor who apologized because he had no procaine to deaden the site, and two prisoners had held Paul's arm immobilized while the scalpel did its work, and then the doctor had sewn the wound to close it. No one could tell Paul why it had been done, and even the doctor could give no explanation other than, "Orders." The few grains of sulfa sprinkled over the sutures had not prevented infection, and soft abscesses of pus were forming around the catgut under the dirty gauze.

All along the ramp the prisoners stood like skeletons clutching blankets and staring vacantly ahead. An SS captain raised a loud-hailer.

"As your name is called, respond with your serial number and form a rank to my left."

Halfway down the list, Paul's name was called, and he fell in with the new group and stood, unmoving, the buttonless jacket hanging open on his lanky frame, which had dropped fifty pounds in these last months of the war.

"What's it about?" the man beside him whispered. The sallow skin was stretched tightly over his skull, his cropped hair riddled with bald patches from ringworm of the scalp.

"Who knows?" Paul asked.

The officer finished calling out names. Orders were barked at those who had been left standing in front of the boxcars, and the first ranks tramped off toward the machine gun towers of the camp. The captain spoke again to Paul's group.

"The American Seventh Army is advancing from the west. The KZ here is filled beyond its capacity to feed and care for its prisoners. Also, there is an outbreak of typhus. You have been selected to move on to a camp farther south in Bavaria where conditions are much better."

They set out across an empty field away from the rail siding and struck a dirt road. The cold air burned into Paul's lungs like acid, and he could hear the faint boom of artillery from the west. The mist was starting to lift off the flat country, and there were scattered woods along low rises of land and patches of marsh and a few farmhouses, their roofs sinking on the distance. Flanking the column on either side were the attack dogs on their leather work leashes. There were no power lines along the road, which was rutted and looked to be abandoned.

"Do you believe it?" the man with the scalp infection softly asked Paul. "About the camp to the south?"

The sergeant who had charge of the column called out like a drillmaster, "No talking in ranks!"

Ahead, where the land swelled into a knoll, a khaki sedan was parked in some trees. The SS captain from the rail siding stood outside the vehicle. He was leaning on the open door and talking to someone in the back seat.

"There's your answer," Paul said.

The sergeant halted the formation and stepped forward, a short whip in his grasp. Three times the lash sang down across Paul's neck and shoulders.

"I said no talking! Don't you know how to follow orders?"

The welts burned like a jellyfish sting. Paul saw the captain striding downhill from the sedan.

"What's the trouble, Sergeant?" the officer called out. "Why have you stopped?"

"A prisoner ignored an order to be silent, Herr Hauptsturmführer."

Paul gazed at the captain and said, "What difference does it make? You bastards are going to shoot us anyway."

The officer's mouth fell open. The other prisoners stared at the ground, trying to distance themselves from Paul. The sergeant drew back his whip, but the captain lifted a hand to stop the blow. He replied in a surprisingly calm voice, "I give you a choice. Either march and be silent, or I'll turn the dogs loose on you. They'll rip your throat out, and your balls, too. Before it's over, you'll beg for a bullet."

On the knoll, two more SS officers had climbed out of the sedan, and Paul frowned. One of them was surely Georg. The features below the visor of the peaked cap had the same even cut, though the sun was behind both figures, obscuring them in the cold rays of light that pierced the haze and hung in the tall branches of the trees like sun-javelins.

"Carry on with the march, Sergeant," the captain said.

As they tramped off, the man next to Paul whispered, "You fool. You'll get us all killed."

Paul did not reply. They were already condemned, but the others could not accept it. They would hold on to their denial until the end, and believe whatever they were told.

A shallow culvert looped around the base of the knoll, the banks rising gradually above their heads. The sergeant halted the column and went forward. The first four prisoners were detached at once and marched out of sight around a blind curve. A guard and his dog went behind them.

In the west, the batteries had stopped firing. Despite the April chill, the man with the ringworm patches had a sheen of sweat on his gaunt face.

Suddenly, rifle shots rang out. The dogs strained forward on their short leashes, hackles bristling, and Paul could hear their low, whining excitement.

The handler who had escorted the four prisoners came back into view with his Alsatian. The sergeant ordered the next four to move out. The man next to Paul began to cry.

At regular intervals the crack of carbines shattered the stillness. Finally, it was Paul's turn to go. The skeletal man stumbling along beside him was sobbing loudly now.

As they rounded a second bend, Paul saw the SS captain and four riflemen standing behind an open trench. The top of the knoll where the sedan was parked had drifted back into view. The two officers had come around to the other side of the car, but now they were too far off to distinguish their features. Even as Paul stared at the man he thought was Georg, he began to have doubts. Perhaps it was only someone who looked like Georg from a distance.

"You are too slow," the captain called out. "We haven't all day. Make a single line along the edge of the pit, and don't look around."

Paul stepped to the rim. Below, bodies were sprawled over each other, limp and obscene in their postures, mouths slack. A skull had been blown apart, and a few bloody gouts of brain matter shone among the tangle of arms and legs.

The man who was sniveling dropped to his knees, a slime of mucus hanging from his nose. He had lost control of his bladder, the wet stain spreading down one leg of his striped pajamas.

Paul stared straight ahead into the sun that had the look of a sore on the cold mist. The captain barked a command, and the snap of rifle bolts sliding into battery drew another loud sob from the man on his knees. Paul heard the scrape of boots coming close, and the soft click of a pistol hammer being cocked behind his head.

"You deserve special treatment," the captain murmured, "you Jew scum."

"Go fuck yourself," Paul said.

Then the sun exploded in a white solar flash on his eyes, and he could feel himself dropping away from a great roar behind his ears.

In the dim room behind the shop the woman's face hovered in front of him. He could smell oil of camphor from a cold sore on her lip. He asked, "What place is this?"

"Don't you know?" she replied. "It's Celle."

"Celle? Near the camp?"

"Camp?" She gave him a puzzled look. "What camp are you talking about?"

"The KZ at Belsen."

A new wariness came into her expression.

"Well, of course, it was emptied after the war."

"The war." Paul frowned. "That's right. It's over, isn't it?"

"It ended more than a year ago. The country is under military occupation. We're in the British zone."

"I know."

After a pause, the woman said, "I think perhaps you need a doctor. You've had some sort of attack that's left you confused. Do you know who you are?"

"Yes." Paul ran his fingers gingerly over the scar behind his ear. "It's as if I just woke up from a long dream."

"Do you have a family?"

The question seemed to jerk him back into the moment.

"That painting in the window of your shop. Is it yours?"

"No, it's here on consignment. The owner is a gentleman named Holst."

"Otto Holst?" Paul said, and even in the gloom he could see the startled reaction in her.

"You know Herr Holst?"

"What price does he want?"

She hesitated, pressing her hands together under her chin as if in prayer.

"Herr Holst is asking three hundred marks, plus the consignment fee of ten percent." She evidently took Paul's silence to mean a loss of interest. "Of course, it might be possible to obtain it for less."

"Where can I get in touch with him?"

"I'm afraid that isn't permitted. Perhaps I could contact him in your behalf and make an offer."

He could see the gleam of serous fluid on the erupting sore as she pursed her lips.

"You'll get your fee," he said. "Tell me where to find him."

TWO

The address turned out to be a dingy frame shack with a tiny garden plot next to the switching yards. Paul knocked three times before a blowsy woman came to the door. In the dusk her face made a pale oval on the other side of the screen, and he asked for Otto.

"He isn't home yet." A missing front tooth put a wet slur into her speech. "He works over there in the yards. Sometimes he's late. You could ask the superintendent where to find him."

Paul crossed the switchyard toward the lights of the signal house. Boxcars and gondolas stood along the tracks, and the gantries were dark against the sky. A locomotive and tender chugged by, blowing white steam onto the blue darkness, the *tramp-tramp-tramp* shaking the ground. After it had gone by he stepped across the rails and all at once caught sight of Holst and two others on a spur track below the water tower. They were working on the cinder embankment in the glimmer of acetylene flares. Two were swinging picks while the ex-sergeant leaned on the handle of his shovel. There was no mistaking the stocky figure in the one-piece overalls. The misshapen nose, swollen at the base like a clown's, was as unique as a fingerprint.

Holst was joking and talking with the others and did not see Paul until he had come to the edge of the moving half-lit shadows. No more than twenty meters separated them when the ex-sergeant raised his head, and Paul saw the shock register on the other man's face in the bright glint of the flare. Holst threw away his shovel and bolted down the far side of the track bed into the dark.

Paul scrambled over the embankment of loose ballast and could not see him. A string of freight cars stood along the track, leaving the ditch beside it awash in shadow. Then he spotted the running figure, ahead, where the track curved.

"Hey!" one of the workmen shouted. "Who the hell are you? What do you think you're doing?"

But Paul was already racing down the ditch. He saw Holst clamber up the bank and duck beneath a gondola. Paul went under it too, low enough to smell the creosote on the ties next to the carriage wheels, and then he was out the other side into the dry weeds beside the track. Holst was in the open, crossing the lines, and the signal lights threw his moving shadow across the rails. Paul sprinted after him, gaining all the time as the stocky figure ran out of wind. Near the gantry, Holst stumbled and went down. Paul overtook him while he was still on the ground, his shoulders heaving. There was no flight left in the other man, only harsh sobs of breath. It was several moments before the ex-sergeant managed to push up on his hands, turning his head slowly to gaze at Paul.

"What's the matter, Otto? Aren't you glad to see old friends?"

Sweat ran down into the coal dust on Holst's face, and the cowering expression was no different from the cringing fear Paul could remember on the faces of camp inmates who had once been under the other man's thumb.

"Why are you chasing me?" he gasped.

"Why are you running?" Paul replied.

A look of confusion mounted on the features, smothering some of the fear.

"I don't know," Holst stammered. "You gave me a start, that's all. I thought you were dead. I have enemies. . . . I have to be careful. . . ."

He got to his feet, his chest still rising and falling.

"What made you think I was dead?" Paul asked.

Holst's hands shook as he untied his bandanna, leaving a white circle at his throat. He used the cloth to wipe the sooty grime from his face and the back of his neck.

"You were sent to Auschwitz," he replied. "For most Jews it was a one-way trip."

"And my brother?"

"I thought he went there, too."

"How do you know? Who told you?"

"It was the officer at the estate—that last day when I took you to your brother in the servant quarters. Don't you remember? The Sturmbannführer from Berlin . . ."

"Sturmbannführer Viertel?"

"That's him!" Holst proclaimed as if he were identifying a criminal in the dock.

"You must have seen my brother again," Paul said. "Otherwise, how did you get hold of his painting?"

"It was a gift," Holst said. "He painted it for me because I'd done favors for him. You remember, don't you? I looked out for both of you."

His tone had the hopeful urgency of a murderer trying to establish an alibi.

"When did he give it to you?"

"It was the next day. I was told to collect his personal effects and take them out to the estate. They said he wouldn't be coming back to the barracks."

"Was the Sturmbannführer still on the estate when you got there?"

"No. Only Herr Krenek." Holst frowned. "I thought it was strange. Business as usual, you know. He told me to take the painting and said he wouldn't be seeing me anymore. He was right. It was the last time I laid eyes on him."

"Then you can't say for sure that he was sent east?"

"I only know that *you* were. I saw the order."

Another switch engine chugged around a distant bend, the headlamp sweeping them briefly out of the darkness. At least there was a chance, Paul thought, that Ernst and Liesl were alive. Hope would always survive on possibilities, even if they were in short ration.

"I want the painting," he said.

"But it's mine," Holst protested. "Herr Krenek gave it to me. He said it might be worth something one day."

"You'll get your three hundred marks later."

The ex-sergeant had lost his fear. Some of his old bravado came back. Beneath the sloping forehead, the bloodshot eyes in the cavernous sockets had a wily glimmer.

"What proof do I have that you'll pay?"

"None," Paul said.

"Then why should I trust you?"

"The Allied War Crimes Commission is looking for SS who worked in the camps. I could give them your name and some facts."

"I didn't say you couldn't take the painting," Holst replied quickly. "It's just that these are hard times. A man has to be careful."

"I know," Paul said. "That's what they used to say in the camp."

THREE

The British captain had a wart the size of a pencil eraser on the cheek of his broad face under overgrown brows.

"And you were carrying this letter of identification from the American CIC in Munich?" He held up an envelope.

"Major Ward." Paul nodded.

"But he only knew you as Josef Neumann?"

"That's right," Paul said. He had claimed the painting that morning from the shop in Celle and come back to the headquarters of the British Military Authority in Bergen-Belsen.

"Extraordinary business." The captain gave him a look that did not seem altogether convinced.

"Josef Neumann was carrying this, too." Paul held out the business card from the Levin Gallery.

"Alina Levin," the captain said, reading the name on the back. "Do you know her?"

"She's a Jewish doctor in Munich. She can verify what I've said about myself."

"About Josef Neumann, you mean."

"Right now I'm only concerned about my sister and brother, not Josef Neumann."

"There are survivor lists from the camps. Refugee centers maintain a register. Beyond that, missing persons aren't easy to trace."

In the yard, three British troops were scrimmaging with a soccer ball. The bantering exchange on the other side of the glass had no connection at all to a world of death camps and missing persons.

"The last time I saw my brother was in 'forty-three. He was assigned to a special work detail on the Hesse estate."

"The Hesse estate is a military billet. The SS colonel who owned it is on a list of war criminals still at large. His wife went into hiding, as well."

The Third Reich, Paul thought, was like some vast crime scene with the fingerprints wiped clean. He said, "If my brother survived, he would have gone back to Berlin. Everything we had was there."

"If you want to go on to Berlin, I'll see you get a border-crossing permit. But first I'd like a chat with your Major Ward. . . ."

A few days later Paul stood in the street in front of the pile of stony rubble that had been his home. The houses along the block were mostly gutted shells, the mortar blackened and glass gone from the windows.

He climbed over the ruins that scavengers had long since picked clean. Here and there a piece of iron poked from the debris—the twisted frame of a bed, a singed clump of piano wires.

Toward the back he found the summerhouse half intact. Chalky dust sifted down as he ducked under the sagging roof. He used his shoe to probe the litter behind the smashed bench and saw the shine of oilcloth. The rotting material flaked away as he unwrapped it, and two pfennigs dropped out, leaving the maimed lead figure in his hand. It seemed to him a final irony of the war that a toy soldier would survive when so many real ones had been lost.

In the Soviet zone, a truck crammed with refugees dropped him off at Zossen. He found Sister Clara still at the convent school, empty now except for a handful of nuns.

"Herr Krenek." She stared hard at him. "It *is* you, isn't it?"

"I would have called, but there's no telephone."

"And Liesl?" she asked.

Instantly, his hopes fell. The disappointment had a cutting edge, like anger. Anger at whom? God? Sister Clara? Or his own expectation that Liesl would be here?

"We were caught before we could get across the frontier," he replied. "They sent me off to a KZ. I was hoping Liesl might have been brought back here."

"No, Herr Krenek." The nun shook her head sadly. "She never came back."

He started to speak, but broke off. What was the point in going on?

"Sit down, please," Sister Clara said. "I'd offer you tea, but these days we haven't any. The new government has only one god—in the Kremlin—and he doesn't tolerate rivals. So we go without."

They sat on high-backed chairs in the dim room, and Paul noticed a bare, faded spot on the wall where the crucifix had once hung.

"Russian soldiers were here," she said. "They took everything of value when they left."

"What happened to the children?"

She did not answer at first. The years had given her a distracted, troubled air that he did not remember.

"They are gone to Our Lord in heaven," she replied.

"Dead?" Paul could not believe it.

"The authorities came one day with an order from the Ministry of Interior. They took all the children away in a bus. I remember their little faces at the windows. They were excited and smiling because someone told them they were going on a picnic in the woods. We never saw any of them again."

The furrowed ridges in her face did not change shape, as if they were beyond sadness.

Already, Paul was anxious to be on his way. The talk, like the surroundings, could only inflict more pain, and Sister Clara could be of no further help. He waited for a chance, and made an excuse to leave. On the way out he asked about her brother, and she told him that he had survived.

"Perhaps God will work a miracle in your life, too. You mustn't give up hope about Liesl."

But a God of divine justice, Paul thought, would waste no miracles or mercy on Germany, and hope was only a temporary reprieve from the truth.

The Krenek Chemical Works had been leveled in the last days of the war. All that was left of it now was a field of weeds in the Russian sector. Paul found Frau Kleist nearby in the working district of Prenzlauer Berg. Dusk was settling, and the electricity was off in the shabby apartment building when he knocked at the door. He hardly recognized the gaunt, gray face that appeared in the opening, and her first words were the same as Sister Clara's: "Herr Krenek. It *is* you, isn't it?"

The flat smelled of boiled cabbage, and after Frau Kleist had lit a candle in a saucer, she faced him and said, "The electricity is only turned on for an hour in the evening. You must excuse me if I lie down while we talk. They say I have a tumor. It hurts to sit up."

Paul helped her to the bed, then drew up a chair. The medication she was taking for pain made her responses somewhat slow. He asked if the Gestapo had come back to the house after he had fled Berlin.

She nodded. "They went through everything. I stayed on for a month, Herr Krenek, hoping you would come home. Then a Gestapo man showed up again and said you were both in a concentration camp. He told me I was dismissed and not to come back."

"Did the Gestapo ever say anything about Liesl?"

"They wouldn't answer my questions."

Paul gazed around the flat in the wavering glow of the candle. There was only an electric ring for cooking, and no hot water. A covered chamber pot in the corner served as a toilet.

"I thought you must all be dead," she went on. "That's why it was such a shock to find you at the door."

"What about Frau Viertel?"

"Then you haven't heard?" The old woman clucked her tongue sadly. "Poor Frau Viertal. So young and beautiful, too. She was in their house the night the bombers came. It was in mid-April when the battle for the city began. The whole block was leveled. Wave after wave of enemy planes. The people caught in it had no chance. . . ."

The news stunned Paul, shutting down the circuits of feeling so that no emotions could be processed. His body was full of dead connections, his mind dark. The burned-out wiring would not carry the overload of pain.

After a long silence, he murmured, "Are you sure?"

"Ja, Herr Krenek. It was her husband who identified the remains. He buried her the next day. The poor man was completely broken by it. That very night at her grave he took out his pistol and shot himself."

Paul frowned. The thirty-nine prisoners outside Dachau had been executed, as far as he could fix the time, on the twenty-seventh or twenty-eighth. If Georg had killed himself in mid-April, who was the SS officer on the knoll?

"Everything is gone, Herr Krenek." A tear rolled from the corner of her eye onto the white braid on the soiled pillow. "Old friends dead. Nothing is the same. Hitler was a curse from God." She lifted a hand weakly and crossed herself. "He must be burning in hell for all the suffering he's caused."

The curator at the cemetery was a bent-shouldered old man, deaf in one hairy ear.

"Yes, I remember quite well. The Sturmbannführer shot himself at the grave of his wife. He was buried beside her."

"Was a date recorded?"

The old man ran a crooked finger down his ledger.

"He was interred on the twentieth of April, 1945."

"Did you see the body yourself after he shot himself?"

"I saw them take it away on a litter."

"I'd like to see the graves."

The curator gave him directions.

"They are easy to find. The marker for the Sturmbannführer is in the rune shape for the SS. It's the only one in that section of the cemetery."

At the site, Paul stood gazing down at the markers engraved only with the names and dates and a common epitaph. "Beloved wife of . . ." "Beloved husband of . . ." Other stones encroached on their privacy. All the deaths had occurred in the last two weeks of April. In the final days of the war the district had filled up quickly, leaving no vacancies.

FOUR

The first week he was back in Munich Paul went twice to see Major Ward, who pressed him for details of his experience in the camps. The talks led each time to a trench outside Dachau, like a blind ending in a maze. The missing parts of his memory had been recovered and put together, but there were no clues left behind in it that might be used to mount a search for Ernst and Liesl.

Alina Levin had given him the sitting room where Josef Neumann had spent the night, but that event seemed as if it had occurred years ago, rather than weeks. Several times they had tea in the walled garden where the white birch took the glint of the morning sun on its leaves. It was not that she was aloof, but rather that she had a way of deflecting questions about herself. Above the prominent cheekbones, the gray eyes had only an empty sheen of dead sadness. Even the cold intelligence was worn like a protective mask. She struck Paul as less herself than a perfect duplicate of the person she had once been, but missing some life force within, like one of Gogol's dead souls.

More than once they talked about the painting Paul had brought back.

"It looks like something Chirico might have done," Alina said. "Only it's not. There's no *Court of Blue Shadows* in any catalog. Besides, if it were a copy, why would your brother sign his own name on the back? No . . . it's an original. Probably he said it was a Chirico to throw your SS friend off the scent."

They were in the sitting room, where the twilight on the windowpanes threw a soft glow across the canvas.

Alina asked, "What sort of project was Ernst working on?"

"Something to do with the restoration of art damaged in the war."

"That sounds a bit vague, doesn't it?"

"Everything was vague at the time. Including survival." Paul had been staring at the canvas. Now he looked directly at Alina. "This surgery that Ernst underwent—how would it have changed him?"

"Severing the fibers of the prefrontal lobes was an experimental procedure. Before the war, it was tried on a small number of patients subject to violent episodes that couldn't be controlled by other means. The early research produced some destructive side effects. Loss of motivation. Apathy. A depressed range of emotions. . . ."

"A total change of personality, you mean." The anger knotted itself into Paul's jaw.

"There's always a possibility the surgery was never carried out."

"Suppose it wasn't. Could he have survived?"

"You're asking me to speculate. I could answer that anything is possible. There was a mass escape from Auschwitz in the summer of 'forty-four. About six hundred prisoners got through the wire. All but a few were hunted down and killed. Yes, it's possible your brother made it out of the camp, but even if he did, the odds that he survived are very slight."

"It only takes a bit of luck to beat the odds." He might have been a gambler placing his last chip on a number.

"If you believe in luck," Alina said.

"What else is there to believe in?" Paul asked.

One evening they went out for a walk in the warm dusk. The block of houses had not been badly damaged except for one, at the far end, where a stray bomb had lit. The devastation seemed out of place, like another contradiction of odds. They climbed out over the rubble chinked with dirt and dry weeds and sat down on a broken block of concrete. The sky was spread above them in a strata of pure blue, as if the sediment had settled out of it, and a few stars burned.

"I wonder if Liesl can see them," Paul said.

"Perhaps."

"Major Ward sent a message to the refugee centers. They'll post inquiries on their bulletin boards. Maybe someone knows. . . ."

Alina gazed at him and replied, "The camps are full of messages pinned to boards. It's a form of despair, not hope. Don't expect anything, and you won't be disappointed."

"You think she's dead," he said flatly.

"I didn't say that. But I think you have to face the fact that she was either sent to a camp or to a state hospital. The chances that she could have survived either situation are slim."

"She would have grown tall by now. Her features must be different. Sometimes I try to imagine what she looks like, and I can't get a picture."

"Have you thought about contacting the War Crimes Tribunal in Nuremberg? They've collected evidence against SS doctors. A number of them are going to be put on trial. I know one of the American prosecutors. I gave him a deposition on what I saw at Auschwitz. It may be that Liesl's case is somewhere in the records. I could speak to him, if you like."

Paul gazed at her in the dusk and said, "You've already done more than I can repay you for."

"It's not you I'm doing it for," she replied sadly. "It's myself."

Paul could not sleep, and around midnight he lit the lamp on the table where *The Court of Blue Shadows* rested in its heavy frame and picked up a magnifying glass. The sterile terrain of the painting swam through the lens, and the faces of the marble busts jumped out at him. The silent rage in the blind sockets and on the screaming mouths cried out for attention. The magnifying glass passed across a pedestal, and came back to it, hovering for a long time while Paul's frown deepened. Another pedestal swelled into the lens, and another.

A soft knock at the sliding doors unlocked his mind from the painting.

"I saw your light." Alina stood in a long robe and slippers in the opening. "Are you all right?"

"Have you a sharp tool?" he asked.

Her shadow withdrew. He heard a drawer open and close. In a moment she was back, holding out a screwdriver.

He took it from her and said, "I've found something in the painting that I never saw before. You need the glass to pick it up. Inscriptions at the base of each pedestal."

Alina bent over the canvas. Her hair, spilling forward, had a platinum gleam in the lamp.

"They're written in Greek," she said.

"The word on the pedestal in the foreground is *frame*." Paul used the tip of the screwdriver as a pointer. "Over here, on this one, is the Greek word for *list*. The third one has a number—*seventy-four*."

Alina raised her head and murmured, "List of seventy-four *what?*"

Paul turned the painting facedown on the table and used the screwdriver to take out the staples that secured the canvas in the back. He held the empty frame to the light and ran his fingers along the beveled groove but could find no flaw in the wood.

"Try opening the corners," Alina said.

Paul forced the flat head of the screwdriver into the hairline crack where the diagonal faces of the wood were cemented. He rocked the blade gently back and forth until the adhesive split. Soon, all four arms of the frame lay side by side. One surface was less even than the others, and he scraped the residue of dried adhesive from the diagonal joint and found the plug of soft putty. It flaked out in pieces, leaving a hollow slot that went deep into the frame. A scroll of thin paper had been stuffed into the bore, and Paul had trouble working it loose.

"Careful," Alina said, her face close to his.

Even after it had been freed, the paper seemed to resist scrutiny, the edges curling closed until he weighted them down. Scrawled in India ink, cursive and neat in Ernst's familiar hand, were titles and names.

"What do you make of it?" Paul murmured.

"Most are works of modern art," Alina replied, "and the names of the artists who painted them."

Paul had been leaning on the edge of the table with both hands and staring at the paper. Now he pushed away and said bitterly, "It doesn't tell us anything about Ernst."

"I'm not sure what it tells us," Alina said through a puzzled frown. "But I think Major Ward might have an interest in it."

FIVE

"Most of the works on your list," Major Ward said, "match the inventory of stolen art found near Merkers. They were two thousand feet down in a salt mine. Your list is only a portion of the total recovered, but the paintings on it are the most valuable of the lot. It's as if somebody went through and picked out only the best."

"But you couldn't trace all of them?" Paul asked.

"Twelve are still a puzzle. The titles don't match any catalog of known works."

Alina said, "That wouldn't necessarily rule out their authenticity."

"The trouble is," Major Ward said, "none of the artists are alive to confirm or deny it."

The three were sipping coffee in the drab office of the War Crimes Commission on the Ludwigstrasse. On the wall behind the desk was a photograph of President Truman. It did not altogether cover a faded spot where in the past another picture must have hung, probably the Führer's. But history, Paul thought, evicted politicians like bad tenants. He said, "What happens now?"

"Most of the art recovered from the mine shaft has gone back to museums and private collections. All we can do is track down the paintings on your brother's list and have them examined by an expert." The American took a swallow of coffee and said, "I understand you're off to Nuremberg. . . ."

"Tomorrow," Paul said.

"I hope you turn up something. Maybe I'll have some news about the paintings when you get back."

The hostel in Nuremberg was old and dim and had survived the bombing with only a little damage, and they were each given a room off the hall at the top of the stairs. There was a working telephone at the desk, and after

153

they had unpacked, Alina put through a call to the headquarters of the U.S. prosecutor and spoke with the officer who had taken her deposition some weeks earlier.

"He'll see us in the morning," she told Paul. "There's nothing we can do until then."

They went for a walk along the river past the ruins of the red-roofed houses that had belonged to wealthy burghers, then wandered back along the cottage lanes, bathed in shade, and stopped to rest on a stone bench in a patch of sun at the top of the street. The Germans who were out looked shabby and unkempt beside the Americans and the foreign press that had invaded the town nine months earlier at the start of the war crimes trials. The twenty-one men in the dock who had led the Reich were there, now, to ratify the defeat.

"This place stinks too much of Hitler," Paul said. "You can feel his soul rotting in the rubble."

"We're all rotting a little on the inside, aren't we?" Alina remarked sadly. "Cheap compromises were the price of survival."

"Not if you refused to pay."

"Everyone paid. Even your brother when he agreed to do what they asked."

"I don't know what Ernst did," Paul said, "or why."

A breath of air came off the dying day, stirring the hair against her motionless face.

"Collaboration is just a word," she murmured. "An abstraction. As a behavior, it can't be applied to a situation that exists without a moral center."

"Like Auschwitz?"

"Auschwitz was a system that you either fitted into as a victim or as part of the working apparatus. Suppose you were a doctor, and the chief SS physician ordered you to choose fifty prisoners from the sick block for the gas chamber. How should you respond? You could refuse, in which case you would become one of the fifty, and the selections would then be made at random. Or you could carry out the order and at least separate those who were going to die anyway from those who had a chance at survival. In that context, you could look at your own involvement as a means of saving lives."

"Or complicity in murder," Paul said.

"The point is, you could never really distinguish right from wrong, because you couldn't measure your decisions against conventional moral values. They were always cleverly removed from the situation so that your actions were purely utilitarian." She had been gazing toward the river beyond the rooftops of the district. Now she turned to stare at him and said gravely, "What would you have done?"

"Seen them in hell," Paul said.

"Yes," she murmured. "But you're different."

The young JAG captain—one of several assistants to the American prosecutor for the War Crimes Tribunal—doodled on a scratch pad as he listened to Paul's story. Twice, he glanced at the sleek line of Alina's crossed legs below the hem of her dress, and it was clear that his interest went beyond the deposition he had taken from her at their first meeting. That was enough, when matched with Paul's CIC credentials, to relax the rules of access to the evidentiary files.

"I'll call the office of the chief investigator," he said, "and tell them to expect you."

For two days, in a windowless basement lit by bare ceiling bulbs, they sifted through documents crammed into cardboard boxes and cabinet drawers. But they could find nothing related to Paul's arrest at Friedrichshafen, or where Liesl might have been taken.

The second afternoon, they left the building and found an open-air café near the Schöner Brunnen and had a sausage and a *helles Bier* at a table under a ragged umbrella that looked across the fountain square to the cathedral. Paul stared reflectively at his saucer, and finally Alina asked, "What are you thinking?"

"I was just remembering a cruise Liesl and I took along the Rhine. In one town where we tied up there was a hill covered with wildflowers behind the church. She wanted to pick some, so I took her up there." He raised his head slowly, his gaze lost on the blue gleam of the day. "I think it was a special time for her."

"And for you," she said. "It's one memory you kept."

He shrugged and said, "I suppose what makes it special is the impossibility of ever going back to it."

They fell silent. Only one other table was occupied, by a patron reading a newspaper and smoking. From the side, he reminded Paul of someone, *but who?* Then it came to him—Herr Schutz, the Gestapo agent on the train to Friedrichshafen.

Alina saw his frown.

"Is something wrong?"

"When the Gestapo arrested us at the frontier, we were carrying papers that identified us as Paul and Liesl Schmidt. Do you think she could have been sent somewhere under that name?"

Alina thought about it for a full moment and replied, "It wouldn't do any harm to go back for a second look."

It was well into the evening when Paul suddenly found himself staring at a document—a list of twenty children assigned to the Special Department of the Kinderhaus at Eglfing-Haar outside Munich. Over a two-day period in the summer of 1943 they had been killed by lethal injection of iodine. Among the victims was "Schmidt, Liesl," age eleven.

The name jumped out clearly from the rest of the print, which was only a blur. Paul stared at it for a long time in the dim light before running his finger down the paper to check the source. "Deposition by ERNA HOFF—given this 21st day of April, 1946, at Freising . . ."

"What is it?" Alina gazed at him across the table.

Without a word, Paul handed her the document and left the room.

Outside, she caught up with him in the street.

"Wait, Paul."

He halted abruptly in the dark beneath a stone arch, leaning against it with one arm, his head bent. His shoulders did not move under the touch of her hand, the muscles flexed and rigid.

"They killed her."

"Yes," Alina said tonelessly. "I know."

From a tower, a clock struck the hour. After the last chime had faded into the night, Paul turned. The shadows touched out Alina's face, but her hair picked up the reflected shine of the moonlight from the cobbled street behind her. In the dark, her fingers closed gently on his arm.

"Come back to the hotel," she said.

"I'd prefer to be alone for a bit."

"No," she insisted softly. "This is no time to be alone."

He gave in to the pressure of her fingers on his arm. They walked back along the narrow street past the darkened shops and crossed the square, empty now under a cold blaze of stars.

In Paul's room, Alina opened the window under the attic gable that looked down over the slate roof to the street below. There she remained, staring out at the night. Paul sat on the side of the bed in the dark, his head in his hands.

Finally, Alina turned away from the window and came over to him. She knelt down, and he felt the cool touch of her fingers at the side of his face.

"Shall I stay with you tonight?" she murmured.

Paul shook his head slowly and replied, "I wouldn't be of any use to a woman."

"That doesn't matter."

* * *

For several hours they lay side by side and spoke in whispers, and sometime after midnight they slipped into an intimacy that was spontaneous and wholly unexpected, though it seemed to follow naturally a moment when Paul suddenly broke off talking, as if the words could not get past the ache in his throat, and Alina leaned forward and grazed his mouth with her own parted lips in a kiss that was impossibly tender in its simple charity and reassurance. It was as if their souls had drifted together like the shadows of two windblown clouds comingling on the ground, and she whispered, "Come into me now."

SIX

Once during the night Paul woke with Alina curled against him. Her arm was across his chest, the fingers relaxed beside his neck, and he could feel the warm swell of her breast against him.

From the very start, even as her fingers had guided his maleness between her legs, her body had seemed to resist pleasure, as if the flesh were bound by some monastic vow of purity and cold denial. Yet there had been a practical knowledge of sex in the straining of her hips, the frank and explicit movement of her hands that almost too swiftly brought the flow of seed from him. But he could sense no climax in her, only the gift of unpurchased compassion that her body had tendered in the motions of love and false sexual heat. When it was over, he lay in the warm clasp of her arms, alone in the wet mystery of that flooded salt pool of himself where his pain had been released into her, and he could remember the soothing whisper close to his ear, "Be still—don't move— stay in me for a while."

Now, in her sleep, she stirred against him, but did not wake, and he was aware of the clean scent of her hair on the pillow. He breathed it in like a warm sweet intoxicant, and before long he, too, drifted back to sleep.

When he woke again, she was gone, and dawn had broken into the room in streaks of light. Nothing remained of the night except his sharp memory of it, though his nerves were still warmly steeped in the erotic tenderness of her naked body, which had acted on his pain like a narcotic producing a state of tranquilized release.

He had a wash at the tin basin and gave the black stubble on his face to a razor. Rinsing, he dried at the window, where the roofs and rubble of the town were bathed in the pink glow of morning, slipped into his clothes, and stepped across the hall. No one answered his knock.

Downstairs, he caught sight of Alina in the walled garden on the other side of the French doors. She sat by herself at one of the iron tables, her back to him, a cup of black coffee in front of her. Paul went out through the glass doors and quietly spoke her name. Some air of troubled reflection did not wholly vanish from her upturned face even as her mouth formed the smile to disperse it. The gray stare gave up only a trace of some new emotion, like encrypted material not meant to be deciphered. Whatever it was, she seemed deliberately to be pushing away from it, holding it at a distance from both of them.

"Last night . . ." Paul began.

"Was last night," Alina said before he could go on. She added gently, "This is today."

Paul drew a chair and sat down.

"All right," he said.

She started to speak, but the reply aborted itself on some interior conflict. Instead, she shook her head and asked, "Now that you know about Liesl, what do you intend to do?"

"Go to Freising."

"Why?"

"To find the woman who gave the deposition."

"But you've got what you came here for. Isn't that enough?"

"No," Paul replied coldly.

The sun coming over the stone wall warmed the garden and left a gleam on the table where they sat.

Finally, Alina said, "If you've made up your mind, then I suppose the best route to Freising is by way of Regensburg. I know an artist there, a friend of my father. If I can get a call through, I'm sure he'll put us up for the night."

The old man who greeted them was tall and unbent with hawkish features under thick, silver hair, and Alina introduced him as Herr Kruger. His sight was going, and he told them that now a woman came in every day to cook and clean for him.

"She's left a covered pot on the stove for us," he said. "I hope you're hungry."

They dined at a bare table lit by a candle, and Paul asked Herr Kruger if he still painted.

"These days I can only see shadows. It's like looking at the world through a cloudy glass." He paused. "But, of course, the world isn't the same place, is it? I think I prefer to remember it as it was."

Alina asked, "Like Paris?"

"Paris." The old man smiled. "When I first saw it, there were only horse-carriages, and the streets were lit by gaslight. What times we had! I used to drink absinthe with Modigliani at a café in the Rue Caulaincourt. We once fought over a girl. I wanted to paint her. He wanted to sleep with her. He ended up doing both."

Later, clutching a branched candlestick, the old man led them back through a court to his studio above the garage. Beneath a heavy skylight, canvases covered the walls. He set the candle holder down on a table strewn with half-squeezed tubes of paint, old brushes, and a bust of Ingres. A sofa, draped in velvet, floated out of the half-lit shadows, and the light struck a gleam from the brass rail of a bed.

Herr Kruger said to Alina, "Your father was here, once. He took away a drawing. It was a pencil sketch of the girl I told you about, the one who went off with Modigliani. I drew it from memory. I suppose I was in love with her myself." He gave them a look that seemed to say people in love should not be apart. "If I could go back, I would do things differently."

After the old man was gone, Alina and Paul looked at each other in the glimmer of the candles. Color came into her cheeks, and her gaze fell away. Paul's mouth shaped a wry smile.

"Don't worry," he said, "I can sleep on the sofa."

"That isn't necessary," she replied.

"I thought you didn't want to sleep together."

She shook her head and murmured, "It has nothing to do with what I want." Her downcast stare lifted slowly to his and held fast. "Would you mind if we just held each other for a while?"

Paul was silent, aware of the pain in her eyes. He stepped to the table and blew out the candles. A few stars pressed against the skylight, and the moon bathed one side of the studio in its pale radiance. In the shadows by the bed Alina was already taking off her clothes, her back chastely turned to him. Paul looked away and started to undress, too.

Under the thin quilt, she clung to him silently, her body tense. He could almost feel the barrier of some frozen hysteria in her nakedness. She said, "I have to tell you something that happened to me in the camp."

A warm tear fell into the hollow of Paul's shoulder, and another.

"You don't have to tell me anything unless you want to."

She went on in a low, flat monotone that did not change at all. "There were always pregnant women in the camp. If they were Jewish and the SS found them, they were sent off to the gas chamber. It was the same if they delivered, only, then, the infant would be killed, too. So we brought these women to the infirmary, usually in the middle of the night, and aborted them. I remember a girl of fifteen who was close to term and had managed to conceal it. Labor had to be induced. The baby came. A boy. He had blue eyes. I covered his mouth and pinched his nostrils shut. That's how it was done."

Paul started to speak, but her arms only tightened about his neck to keep him silent.

"One of my duties as a doctor was to select female subjects for gynecological experiments. First, the ovaries were radiated, then surgically removed so the effects of deep X-rays on the reproductive system could be studied. Conditions in the operating room were crude and septic. The subjects who developed infections from unsterilized instruments were taken later to another block and injected with a lethal product. I was made to go along to keep them calm. They had no reason not to trust a Jewish doctor. They were told to sit with an arm raised across their eyes. I assured them that the syringe was only medicine to cure their infections. It's what I was ordered to say, but I would have said it anyway. Wasn't it more humane to give them the comfort of a lie instead of the truth? An SS medical orderly injected them with phenol. It was introduced through the fifth rib space directly into the heart ventricle to produce death in seconds. . . ." Her voice trailed off to a whisper, but the grip of her arms remained strong, her body rigid. "Sometimes I dream about the victims. The corpses are heaped together in that room, and I can't get past them. I see the little boy, too, with the blue eyes—staring at me—asking why."

A convulsive shudder passed through her body as something broke in her, and she wept bitterly while Paul held her. It seemed an interminable time before the flood of tears slowed and the sobs no longer wrenched her shoulders.

"You did what you had to do." Paul stroked her hair. "It was the best anyone could have done under the circumstances. Try to let go of it."

"I can't," Alina said. "I feel dead inside—like the victims who developed complications after surgery. Only mine is a psychological infection, and untreatable. The other night, I found that I couldn't respond sexually. Maybe that's my punishment. Probably it is." She raised her head to gaze at him. "Because I want to love you that way, too."

Paul brushed the tears from her cheeks with the backs of his fingers and kissed her softly on the mouth. They might have been entering into a compact, one that obligated them to each other with the understanding that the sexual clauses would be written in later.

SEVEN

The next day, they reached Freising as the sun was going down. Paul had Erna Hoff's address, and they found the flat, but the concierge told them she was out.

"Fräulein Hoff is a Catholic. She goes to the cathedral every Saturday evening. It's just up in the next street."

Dusk was settling over the town as they went up the wide steps beneath the soaring spires of the church. The altar was dark beyond the communion rail, but here and there in gothic alcoves the blaze of candles gave up a gleam of marble sculpture. From the photo Paul had seen in the deposition, it was not hard to pick out Erna Hoff's robust, big-boned figure in the line of penitents outside the confessional. Beneath the blond, braided loops of hair, the round face had a clean, scrubbed look, like a forty-year-old schoolgirl.

They slipped into a back pew where the shadows were darkest. No one took notice of them, not even the saints staring down from their marble perches in disinterested silence. Finally Erna Hoff left the confessional and went down the aisle to kneel before a statue of the Virgin in the crimson flicker of vigil candles. She prayed for a long time, her chin on her folded hands. What penance would the priest impose for killing children? Practiced on a mass scale, most evil would dilute itself to venial proportions. At last, she crossed herself and pushed up from the kneeler.

"Stay here," Paul whispered to Alina. "I'll talk to her."

He waited for Erna Hoff to go past the pew, rose, and followed her outside into the cool night.

"Fräulein Hoff," he called out.

She turned, frowning into the shadows above the steps where he stood. "Who is it?"

Paul came down to her and replied, "You were a nurse in the Kinderhaus at Eglfing-Haar. I have some questions."

"I've already told the investigators everything I know. You should talk to them if you need information. Besides, who are *you* to be asking me questions?"

Paul decided to use his CIC credentials as a bluff.

"I work for American Counterintelligence. If you prefer, I can have the military police take you in, and then we'll talk. It's up to you."

Some of the arrogance went out of the blond Teutonic features. She was the type who would always be obedient to authority.

"We can't talk here," she said, as if a dialogue about murdered children would defile holy ground. "There's a park up the street."

The bench under the shade tree had a faded spot in the backrest where the Only for Aryans sign had been bolted into it, and the wind blew leaf shadows across the wood.

"You had a child named Liesl Schmidt in your care."

Erna Hoff nodded slowly, and Paul saw the puritan force in the white face give way to some small apprehension.

"Tell me about her," he said.

"What can I tell you? She was a placid child. Not so retarded as the others."

"Then why was she killed?"

"Her case came up for review, like all the rest. The doctor recommended that she be kept on for further observation, but . . ."

"Which doctor?"

"Dr. Wesser. He was in charge of the department. Each case required the opinion of three outside experts, and I remember that Dr. Wesser was surprised when the file came back overruling his recommendation. He even called Berlin because he thought it was a mistake. I was there when he spoke to the physician who was responsible for the order. That was the first indication we had that the child was a *Mischling*, because, of course, she looked quite Aryan, not at all like a Jew half-breed."

"Who was the physician in Berlin?"

"Von Stroelin was his name. He was very high in the Ministry of Health, and so there was no doubt that the information was accurate."

The anger that had accumulated in Paul since the day at Friedrichshafen when the SS had taken Liesl should have exploded and come out. But it remained locked up in him, still under pressure.

"What did Dr. Wesser do about it?"

"What *could* he do? The order had to be carried out. I told Liesl the doctor had to give her some medicine and took her down to the treatment room myself so that she wouldn't be frightened. But as soon as she saw the syringe, she began to fuss and cry and wouldn't hold still. The more I tried to calm her, the more hysterical she got. The doctor was very clever with children. There was a red geranium in a pot on the window ledge, and finally he pointed it out to her and asked if she'd ever seen such a pretty flower." Erna Hoff paused, frowning in a puzzled way. "The child was sobbing, but she looked at the flower and blurted out something that made no sense—something about the flower being a star. Anyway, it was enough to distract her, and he got the needle in."

For a full moment Paul stared at the calm, guiltless face in the wind-blown shadows. He wondered if Liesl had ever found comfort in the mountainous breasts behind the clean crackling of starch in the chalk-white nurse's uniform. The park was empty. He was thinking how easy it would be to choke off a scream and leave her dead on a bench that had once been marked NUR FÜR ARIER.

"Was she cremated?"

"Normally she would have been, but she was one of four children on whom a new euthanizing agent had been used. Those bodies were kept in the morgue. An SS doctor did some postmortem tests to determine the effects of the iodine concentrate on the organs and tissues. By the time he'd finished, the crematory wasn't operating. The hospital was always concerned about pestilence, so one of the groundsmen was brought in to bury the remains."

"Who?"

"His name was—let me think—oh, yes—Graeber. Max Graeber. I believe he's still at the institution."

"Yes, I'm Herr Graeber. What can I do for you?"

The old man was bent and wiry in a peasant's collarless shirt with billowing sleeves, and he walked with a limp. Now he took off his cap out of respect to Alina, who stood beside Paul. The three were alone in the storage annex on the hospital grounds. A parcel of sunlight, slanting through a transom, fell across medical equipment and spare bed frames stacked against the walls.

Paul gave their names and the reason for their visit. The old man was suddenly fearful.

"But I was only carrying out an order when I buried them. I told the investigators about it. The crematory wasn't operating."

Suddenly Paul's gaze went past the other man to a wire bin piled high with debris. Wedged among the artificial limbs and braces was a rag doll, the cotton stuffing soiled and popping from the seams, but with a familiar smile stitched into the round face. He walked slowly to the bin and pulled the doll from the tangle.

"Show us where you buried the children," he said.

They drove out in a dray, sitting on the high seat. Herr Graeber had no need to coax the horse, which seemed to know the route. The site lay only a short distance outside the walls. They stopped in the trees off the road, and the old man pointed downhill to a sunny glade.

"See that pile of stones? That's where I marked the grave. It was a terrible business, those children. Whoever did the autopsy didn't bother to sew them up. I tried to give them a decent burial. There was a cross, from sticks tied together, but it's gone now."

Paul helped Alina down from the dray and told the old man they could find their own way back. The cart rattled off, its wheels creaking. As soon as it was out of sight, Paul said, "Wait, will you?"

He tramped downhill into the glade where a breeze stirred the locks of yellow grass. The sunny sparkle made him think of Liesl's hair flying behind her the day he had pushed her on the swing in the yard of the convent school. He stood for a long time, lost in thought, beside the pile of stones. Finally, he dropped to one knee.

"Liesl," he whispered. "I've brought you Ilse."

From the trees, Alina watched the figure climbing toward her. The moment she saw the look in the upturned face she knew it was not the same person who had left her a short while before. The flat hatred in the pale eyes gave no ground, as if no other emotion could ever again coexist there, and some dangerous force had come alive in him. She caught her breath, not quite sure why she was suddenly afraid.

EIGHT

"The canvas," Major Ward said, "is a Monet. One of his water lilies series, painted at the turn of the century. It was among the stolen art recovered at Merkers and given back to the French government. Your brother had it on his list."

The afternoon was clear, scoured by breezes, and Paul and Alina were once more alone with the American in his office above the Ludwigstrasse.

"Two weeks ago," the officer went on, "the painting was sold at private auction in Rio de Janeiro. It seems the one we gave back to the French was a copy."

Alina asked, "Have you examined the others on the list?"

"Seven, so far. All fakes."

"How could they have gone undetected all this time?" Paul asked.

"For the simplest reason of all. No one thought to examine them before now."

"You think Ernst painted them," Paul said.

"Most likely." Major Ward dragged on his cigarette, and a wet cough broke from his lungs, expelling the smoke in gouts.

The sound of a jackhammer drifted up from the street, and a wrecking ball on a crane slammed into a wall. The remains of the Third Reich, Paul thought, were being knocked down and carted off a little bit each day. Still, pieces of it survived, as far away as a Rio art gallery.

"But he was able to tell us about it," the American went on. "That's all that matters. We know what paintings were taken. The people who have them don't know that we know. They may even assume that the sale of the Monet went unnoticed."

Paul asked, "Do you think Ernst was sent off to Auschwitz because he knew too much?"

Major Ward frowned through the plume of his cigarette. Some private conflict worked across the tough features where even the freckles looked as if they had been rammed into the uneven planes. He pushed up out of his chair and stepped to the window, his back to them.

"I think maybe it's time you had a look at something," he said.

They drove south out of Munich into the lake country and rolling hills, Major Ward at the wheel of the jeep, Alina beside him in the bucket seat, and Paul in the back.

"You know," the officer said, "I organized my first counterintelligence operation at a parochial grade school on the Chicago South Side. The janitor caught me smoking in the lavatory. It was a third offense, and they were going to expel me. I had to sign a pledge before God and Sister Agnes to give up cigarettes. The nuns couldn't set foot in the latrine, so they used the janitor as a spy. The first thing I had to do was set up a surveillance apparatus. When the janitor showed up in the halls, a signal came in, and we flushed the evidence. It didn't take him long to figure out what was going on, but he was an amateur. Instead of developing informants, he talked Sister Agnes into assigning student monitors to the lavatory. Most of them you could bribe or intimidate to keep silent, but a few were incorruptible. It's always the pure of heart who pose a menace, isn't it? Then, one morning, we found the janitor dead drunk in his trailer. That was the key to the whole thing. It was simply a matter of turning a spy into a double agent through blackmail and forcing him to work for you."

"You're trying to make a point," Paul said.

"Only that counterintelligence is a dirty business. We deal in a commerce of deceit. But I never lied to you. I just didn't tell you everything."

Paul asked with a wry smile, "What did you leave out?"

"It began with that scar on your forearm. Why would they go to the trouble to remove a serial number? There had to be a reason."

Alina said, "It was done on a forced march. They weren't stopping to bury corpses. Someone didn't want him identified in case he died along the way."

"We didn't know that at the time. Josef Neumann had no past to tell us about. It was almost too convenient. We thought for a while he might be faking."

"Why would you imagine that?"

"Because skepticism is a prudent measure in my business," the American replied, shifting his gaze briefly to Paul's reflection on the rearview mirror. "Actually, we never lost track of you after you left the DP camp. It was pretty obvious, as long as you stayed working on a farm, that your condition hadn't changed. Then Dr. Levin showed up with the photograph from Auschwitz. That was our first break. It sent you running off to Belsen, and your memory came back. Once we knew who you were, the pieces started falling together."

The jeep had topped a rise, and Major Ward pulled off the road into a shady wood that dropped down past a sunny patch of meadow. Below, there was a fine view of Starnberg on the near shore of the lake that stretched off, blue and still, with high mountains beyond it.

"What pieces?" Paul was faintly amused.

The American lit another cigarette and hesitated, as if he could not decide where to begin.

"A month before the fall of Berlin, a U-boat put in to the coast of Brazil near Belém at the mouth of the Amazon. The vessel was carrying large quantities of medicine, gold, and stolen art. Three passengers were aboard her. Two males. One female. Passengers and cargo were transferred to a riverboat, and the sub set a course for Kiel. She was sunk by a British destroyer off the west coast of Africa near Dakar. Three of the crew were picked up. That's how we learned about the voyage."

"What does it have to do with Paul?" Alina asked.

"Once his memory came back and we got his name, it wasn't hard to trace Paul Krenek who had a record at Mauthausen. Would you like to know what became of him after he was shot behind the head? In May of 'forty-five, while Josef Neumann was recovering in a DP camp near Dachau, Paul Krenek was released from another camp near Linz. The tattooed number on his arm matched the serial number from Mauthausen, and he was given identity papers—which meant he could travel without fear of being interned."

"Who was he?" Paul frowned.

"Someone who obviously knew quite a bit about you. For instance, he knew you had no living relatives who might come forward to contradict his identity. If for any reason he found himself detained for questioning, he knew enough about your background to give the right answers. He was a man on the run—probably SS." He pulled on his cigarette as if it were part of his thought process. "You had a close friend in the SS who was attached to the Ministry of Health and directed medical experiments on prisoners."

Paul shook his head and replied, "I saw his grave in Berlin, next to his wife's."

"Both were exhumed ten days ago. One coffin contained the remains of a blond female killed in the bombing raids. The other one had rocks in it."

A familiar image worked across Paul's stare—an SS officer in the misty sunlight on a hill near Dachau.

"If he's not in his grave, where is he?"

"I'd guess Brazil," Major Ward said.

"Carrying a passport with my name on it?"

"Probably," the officer said. "By the way, have either of you ever heard of ODESSA?"

"The port on the Black Sea?" Alina asked.

"The ODESSA I'm talking about is an acronym for an escape apparatus set up by former SS. The U-boat that put people and supplies into Brazil near the end of the war may have been part of it. One of the crew the destroyer picked up was able to identify a passenger aboard the sub. It seems he was a former medalist in international small arms competition. Von Stroelin is his name."

Paul said, "He signed the order that killed my sister."

"The best guess is that he was sent into Brazil to set up a dispensary and safe haven at some remote site. He was a qualified plastic surgeon. Wouldn't it be useful if some of the SS elite on the run from war crimes could have their features altered?"

"Who were the two with him?"

"Until you came forward with that list, we had no idea. Now one of the paintings on it turns up in Brazil. It may well be that all seventy-four were aboard the U-boat. If that's true, then quite possibly the other male and female were SS Colonel Stefan Hesse and his wife. Greta Hesse was something of an art expert, and your brother worked on the Hesse estate. The SS would have needed someone like her to dispose of the paintings." Major Ward drew on his cigarette and glanced at Alina. "I take it you knew Hesse at Auschwitz?"

Her face had paled in the sunny dappling of leaves, and she stared down at her hands in her lap.

"Only by sight," she murmured.

"You never worked with him, then?"

"No." She shook her head, still not looking up. "He was assigned to a different block." Her gaze skated briefly across Paul's before coming back to Major Ward. "He was a neurologist."

"I know," the American said. "We're going out to have a look at one of his patients."

The sanitarium had once been a private villa. The road, passing through the gates, skirted a small, marshy lake and climbed through a birch wood to the house of whitewashed stone and heavy timbers where flower boxes left their colors on the windowpanes. Major Ward killed the motor and swung out of the jeep.

"Aren't you coming in?" he asked Alina, who had stayed in her seat.

"I prefer to wait," she replied tonelessly.

In a small office-library, the chief nurse glanced up from her station.

"We're here to look in on Herr Adler," Major Ward said.

"He's resting in his room. He had another seizure this morning. You should keep the visit as brief as possible."

As they mounted the stairs, the American said, "Most of the patients here are exhibits for the prosecution in Nuremberg. They survived the camps, but they'll require custodial care for life. The one thing they have in common is that they were subjects of medical experiments."

Upstairs, an orderly carrying a bedpan passed them in the hall outside a room. The door was open, and Paul had a glimpse of a larval figure under a sheet, his head turned toward the window.

"Good day, Herr Adler," the American said in passable German. "How do you feel? Do you remember me?"

The head on the pillow swiveled toward them. A shattered cheekbone had left a concave depression on one side of his face, and a surgical scar ran across his forehead near the scalp line of steel-gray hair.

"The usual lobotomy," Major Ward said in a low voice, "involves the insertion of a long, thin instrument through the eye sockets to cut the fibers of the prefrontal lobes. At Auschwitz, Stefan Hesse preferred to go in through the skull. Probably he was doing other things, besides, but no medical records were left behind."

Paul gazed at the scar. It had been clumsily sewn and beneath the trilobite shape of infertile tissue, Herr Adler's stare had a dull vacancy. No recognition broke from it, only placid disinterest. After a moment, his head shifted back to the window.

"Before Jews were purged from teaching posts," Major Ward went on, "he was a university don and the author of a book on quantum physics. Today he can't concentrate long enough even to carry out a simple task. Stefan Hesse had a special interest in Jews who possessed superior creative intelligence. But he got a bit careless with this one, and the operation left destructive lesions in the anterior of the brain that cause petit mal seizures. When the Russians overran the camp, Herr Adler was the only lobotomy patient still alive. We know there were other subjects, but, as I say, the records were gone."

"And Ernst was one of them?" Paul stared at the listless figure under the sheet.

"In all likelihood."

* * *

Outside, they stood in the gravel drive in the sun next to the jeep. Alina had gone downhill to the lake where the spears of marsh grass in the shallows along the bank flung their yellow glint on the water.

"Why did you bring me here?" Paul asked.

"To help you make up your mind."

"About what?"

"Going after the people who were responsible."

"Von Stroelin? Georg?"

"And Hesse," Major Ward added. "The man who probably killed your brother."

"I've never laid eyes on him."

"Dr. Levin has."

Paul gazed at the officer.

"You mean you've already talked to her about this?"

"No."

"Then what makes you think she'd want any part of it?"

"I know she would—if *you* were to ask her." His head was bent toward a match in his blunt, cupped hands, and another wet cough rattled up from his tar-filled lungs at the first intake of smoke. "Sister Agnes was right. I should have honored the pledge."

"Why didn't you?"

"Because it was more fun to outwit her. She was all-powerful, like the SS."

Both men were staring downhill at Alina, who was idling along the lake, her head bent.

"She knows the art world," Major Ward went on. "It was her father's profession. What better cover could we ask for? Right now, the whole business hinges on that Monet that was sold through a gallery in Rio. If we can identify the seller, there's a good chance we can pick up the trail of ODESSA."

"And if we can't?"

"We'd be no more in the dark than we are now."

Below, Alina had turned, standing motionless against the sunny glimmer where the reed grass impaled the water. She gazed uphill at them, shielding her eyes.

Some embittered humor in Paul twisted into another wry smile.

"You needn't have brought me here," he said. "I would have gone after them anyway—on my own."

"I know." Major Ward nodded. "But you'll find it's easier if you have an organization behind you. There's only one constraint. We're looking to cripple ODESSA in Brazil. From a counterintelligence view, that's our primary objective. Settling any personal score along the way is secondary. That may be hard for you to understand, because you have a lot of rage in you, but it's a condition you have to accept."

Paul glanced over his shoulder at the sanitarium rising above the white birches.

"I understand," he said. "Now maybe you should explain it to Herr Adler."

PART FIVE

ODESSA

ONE

The aerial tram lifted away from the station and climbed on its cables toward the granite dome of Sugar Loaf. The bay slid into view, and Paul could see scraps of sail tacking to the wind and the congested sprawl of Rio de Janeiro out to the mountains that lunged steeply into clouds.

Only five other passengers sat on the two long benches that ran the length of the car. Their cameras and smiles gave them away as tourists. At the lower station, Paul had taken care to see who boarded the coach before getting on himself.

As the car swung higher into the sky, the boats on the bay melted to toy size, and the glint of sun on the water sent flashing rays across the city to the horizon that swayed gently on the axis of light.

Paul turned to gaze at the solid dome of Sugar Loaf on the sky above the car, the web strands of cable stretching up to it. On the summit, the station swelled slowly to size, the granite face of the monolith spreading across the front windows of the coach until it filled the glass.

As soon as they docked, Paul stepped out onto the terrace. He caught sight of Alina standing by herself at an observation point and drifted over to her. They might have been two strangers, intent on the same view.

"How did it go at the gallery?" he asked. "Did you meet the director?"

"His name is Hoffmann. I bought a small Corot from him. It was over-priced. I let him think he was taking advantage of me."

"Then he believed your story?"

"I told him I was an agent for the Grüenig Hall of Modern Art in Zurich and we were interested in a South American exhibit for our new wing. He'll have some paintings for me to look at tomorrow morning. I left a business card. He may decide to call Zurich, but I doubt it."

The sun was warm on Paul's face, and the wind blew from the sea. It was now five days since their ship had docked in Rio. Both carried Swiss

passports issued from the German-speaking canton of Zurich. Paul's identified him as Josef Neumann, and Alina's bore the name of Vicki Linz
Neumann.

"It doesn't matter if he calls Zurich," Paul said. "That's been covered.
What was your impression of him?"

"He's a rather aseptic little man, and his hands sweat when he talks
about money. Evidently he emigrated here from Germany before Hitler
came to power, but I could tell from his attitude that he was pro-fascist."

"They wouldn't deal with anyone who wasn't," Paul said, and he gazed
across the bay at the dark mountains jackknifing down into massive pits of
shadow. The city spilled away from them to the far-off gleam of beaches in
the south and silent scrolls of surf. "What time do you see him tomorrow?"

"Nine o'clock."

"Buy two of the Brazilian paintings. You can bargain a little, but pay
him more than they're worth. Then inquire about the Modiglianis. See
what his reaction is."

They fell silent as a family of American tourists passed behind them on
the way to another observation point.

"Oh, look, Henry," the wife cried. "There's Copacabana!"

"That's Ipanema," the man said.

"No, silly!"

The breeze snatched away the arguing voices. Below, the blue plane of
the bay had the look of a solid on which the boats seemed barely to crawl.

Alina smiled and said, "I wonder what American Counterintelligence
will do with a Corot and two Brazilian oils."

"Sell them, probably, to get their money back."

"Not all of it, I'm afraid."

Paul shrugged. "They'll settle for a piece of ODESSA."

The gallery lay in one of the narrow shady streets off the Avenida Rio
Branco, and at nine o'clock the next morning Alina knocked at the glass
door, which was still locked. A shadow drew up on the curtain, the latch
rattled, and Herr Hoffmann opened the door.

"Ah, Frau Neumann, you are so prompt. I was just coming to unlock."

"You have the paintings?" Alina stepped inside.

The director slipped the locking bolt back into its cradle and said,
"This way, please."

The locked door sent a momentary anxiety into her nerves until she
realized it was still half an hour to opening. She followed him past walls
draped with paintings and felt the stale wash of a fan off the high ceiling.

The shop was very old, but impeccably tidy, like Herr Hoffmann himself. The lapel of his white linen suit sported a fresh carnation, and a few thin strands of brown hair were pasted straight across the top of his head. Even the mustache, worn to conceal a harelip, seemed part of some orderly arrangement.

Except for two stuffed chairs, a wall mirror, and brass urns containing flowers, the room was bare—like a chapel in a funeral parlor where the dead were put on view. On display instead were a dozen oil paintings.

"The three artists represented here have a national reputation," Herr Hoffmann said. "Two have had exhibits in New York and Lisbon."

Alina moved slowly from panel to panel, studying each group. All the paintings were listed in the range of fifteen thousand cruzeiros, or about three thousand U.S. dollars. They were technically well executed, she thought, but worth about a third of the price.

"This one is rather nice." She touched a picture—a slash of white water amid tropical leaves.

"It's called *Bridal Veil*," Herr Hoffmann said. "One of the lovely spots of Rio. A place where lovers used to meet."

"And that one." She pointed to a canvas of bursting red and yellow forms. "It has a certain energy."

"*Carnival* is the title. A steal, Frau Neumann, at sixteen thousand cruzeiros. I can assure you that all of these paintings will appreciate handsomely in value. A wise investment. Better than diamonds."

She stepped back from the folding screen and gazed at the display once more.

"I should like to take back those two. Unfortunately the Grüenig Society has limited the amount to be spent. I'm afraid we can't meet the price."

Herr Hoffmann pressed his hands together, touching the fingers to his spoiled lip.

"Perhaps Frau Neumann could make an offer . . ."

"I was thinking in terms of twenty thousand cruzeiros for the two," Alina said, and she could almost feel the slick of moisture coming out on the director's palms.

"Oh, but I am afraid that is much too low. I would say it is only a matter of time before these artists are known internationally. Then watch the price of their art soar."

"The society might agree to twenty-five thousand cruzeiros, but no more."

"Twenty-five thousand. . . ." The director's stare took on a hard glitter.

"To have a painting on display in Zurich would be the best possible advertisement for an artist trying to build a reputation in Europe," Alina said.

Herr Hoffmann stroked his chin above the bow tie. At last he sighed.

"Very well. Twenty-five thousand. But only because I know the paintings will be in good hands."

"You can be sure of it," Alina said, thinking they would end up, with the Corot, in a CIC vault—not so different from a salt mine at Merkers.

She sat in one of the stuffed chairs, her legs crossed, and wrote out a check on the armrest.

"I must tell you," Herr Hoffmann said, "that until your arrival, I had never heard of the Grüenig Hall of Modern Art in Zurich."

"The society was formed after the war by a group of wealthy patrons. One of them is even an expatriate Jewess." The faint smile she gave the director had a conspiratorial air of derision. "Of course, married to a Swiss financier, one can conceal that sort of background quite well."

"A Jew," Herr Hoffmann said. "Interesting."

"This one is obscenely rich and has a passion for Modigliani. She already owns several of his paintings and a sculpture." The fountain pen hovered over the check as Alina glanced up. "In fact, she asked me privately to be on the lookout for any work by him. I can tell you she'd pay dearly for one. But I imagine sales of his art in South America are rare."

"My dear Frau Neumann, you are quite mistaken. Rio is a cosmopolitan city. This very summer the gallery disposed of a Monet for one hundred seventy thousand cruzeiros at a private sale. Would it surprise you to know I have a patron who is in possession of not one, but several, Modiglianis? She might be induced to let one go for the right price."

"Really?" Alina watched his palms draw together once more as if beseeching a deity. "What a pity I didn't know before today. I have a plane to catch this evening for Buenos Aires."

"Perhaps, if Frau Neumann would wait, I could place a call to the owner. It's possible a viewing might still be arranged on short notice."

Herr Hoffman was out of the room. She could hear him speaking faintly—in German, not Portuguese—on a telephone down the hall. She stood before a mirror and adjusted an earring. The borders of cloudy glass were cemented to the wall, and she wondered if someone was staring through her reflection at her from the other side. An odor of rotting vegetation rose from the brass urn of fresh lilies. The stems of older flowers had decomposed in the water, which had not been changed. Herr Hoffmann appeared in the glass, as if his figure had materialized on the mild essence of decay.

"The owner could have one of the Modiglianis here at two o'clock this afternoon," he said. "Would that fit into your travel plans?"

Alina turned from the mirror and said, "Yes, but no later than two. If you would be kind enough to give me a receipt for the paintings I've just bought, I'll pick them up when I come back this afternoon."

TWO

From his table on the gallery above the main floor, Paul saw Alina come into the coffee shop. After a moment, she caught sight of him and climbed the stairs along the plush runner and sat down.

"I have another appointment with Herr Hoffmann this afternoon to look at a Modigliani. He made a telephone call, and the owner agreed to bring it by at two o'clock."

A waiter came up, the white of his starched jacket gleaming in the panel of dark, polished wood, and Alina ordered coffee and a pastry.

"Did you hear the conversation?" Paul asked.

"He was too far down the hall. But he talked to me about the sale of the Monet. I got the impression that the person who has the Modiglianis probably had the Monet, too. In any case, it's a woman, and he spoke to her in German."

"Greta Hesse?" Paul asked.

"We'll know soon enough."

On the main floor, below the gallery, the tables were filled. The swell of voices rose into the cut glass of a chandelier hanging like a huge paste jewel beyond the railing where Paul and Alina sat.

"When I was leaving," she went on, "I inquired about the title of the painting. All he would say was that it was an early work done when the artist was living on the Rue Caulaincourt."

"Or the Hesse estate," Paul said.

"What about funds? After the check I wrote this morning, there's not much of a balance left."

"Once you've seen the painting, just say you have to get in touch with your Jewish client in Zurich so she can cable funds into the account. Tell them you'll be in touch with them when you get back from Buenos Aires.

You can always say later that the arrangements broke down. The important thing now is to keep the contact open."

The waiter served Alina's roll and poured coffee from a silver service. Below, the mirrored walls on the main floor gave a false sense of space and distance, like another forgery. It was hard to tell which were real, the figures at the tables or the multiple reflections of themselves in the glass.

As soon as the waiter was gone, Alina said, "Suppose it *is* Greta Hesse this afternoon . . . and suppose her husband comes with her? He's bound to recognize me."

"Don't worry. He won't come out of his hole, wherever it is. He's the one wanted for war crimes, not his wife. The game's different now." On the white tablecloth, Paul's brown hand tightened into a fist. "It's us they're afraid of, not the other way around."

The Avenida Rio Branco was very wide, and shade trees lined the broad sidewalks as well as the islands that ran down the center of the boulevard. A little after one o'clock Paul took a table under an awning at a sidewalk café and ordered tea. From the table he had a view, across the boulevard, of the art gallery steeped in shade near the mouth of the narrow side street. A breeze stirred the striped canvas overhead, and Paul took a newspaper from his coat pocket and unfolded it to read while he sipped his tea.

At ten minutes to two Alina passed by the tables without looking at him. He watched her cross the boulevard in the traffic, one gloved hand steadying her hat as the breeze caught the wide, furled brim. She went into the side street, her figure melting into the shade that gave back only a gleam of her light, two-piece suit before the stone portico of the gallery took her from sight.

At precisely two o'clock, a black Lincoln-Zephyr sedan pulled to the curb on the far side of the avenue, and the driver got out. The coat looked too small for his brawny frame, the fabric tight across the shoulders, and his thick neck bulged over his shirt collar. He circled to the far side of the sedan and opened the rear door. A woman stepped out, and Paul saw a flash of red hair as she straightened, and an overpainted mouth glistening below dark glasses. The driver handed her a large portfolio, and she moved briskly off past the shops into the side street. Before turning into the gallery, she glanced back, and Paul could see the black shine of the dark glasses in the dense shade that gave her face the look of some preying insect.

A shiver of anticipation went through him. He was sure the woman must be Greta Hesse. All his nerves were iced down in some homicidal desire that stretched back in an instant of time across three summers to the Hesse estate and his last meeting with his brother.

The burly driver stood on the pavement beside the sedan. He was looking both ways on the boulevard, and his gaze swept past the sidewalk café but did not pick up Paul in the crowd at the tables. He climbed back into the car and sat at the wheel, the heavy bulk of his arm resting on the frame where the window had been rolled down.

Paul left money on the saucer to cover the bill, folded the newspaper under his arm, and walked up the boulevard away from the tables. At the end of the block, he crossed to the island strip of the avenue where taxis were parked under the sunlit leaves. There were no German-speaking drivers, but he found one who could communicate in English and said, "I want a car followed. I don't want the other driver to know. Can you manage it?"

"What you ask is very difficult, senhor."

Paul held out a large cruzeiro note.

"Would this make it easier?"

The driver stuffed the bill into his shirt pocket.

"I am your man."

For another twenty minutes, they waited in the leafy shade. Alina was the first to appear on the boulevard. She had the paintings, wrapped in brown paper, that she had purchased that morning, and she flagged a taxi from the curb.

It was not long before Greta Hesse came into view in the moving crowd. The beefy driver sprang from behind the wheel to open the door for her. Paul saw the glint of dark glasses as she bent into the back seat. He touched the taxi driver on the shoulder.

"I see them," the driver murmured.

They cruised down the boulevard in the traffic behind the Lincoln-Zephyr. In a short while it turned off toward the heights of Santa Tereza, and Paul could see the red-tiled roofs of the villas amid the green splash of tropical foliage on the hillsides.

The street climbed into the old Bohemian quarter and swung past an ancient aqueduct, its massive stone arches eroded and darkly leeched with mold. The structure had been converted to a viaduct for electric trams that ground along the tracks at the top, and vendors had set up stalls in the shade under the lower tier of arches.

The road lifted past the whitewashed stucco of a church into the residential area, where the balconies of colonial mansions were steeped in the shady dappling of trees and lush vegetation. Ahead, the Lincoln-Zephyr turned off the road into the drive of a private villa. As the taxi passed,

Paul had a glimpse of the burly driver unlocking a pair of iron gates in a high stone wall.

"You wish me now to stop somewhere?" the taxi driver asked.

"No," Paul said. "Keep going."

THREE

From a patch of woods near the top of the hill there was a clear view of the district spilling down toward the little church, white in the sun, that squatted like a boundary marker above Lapa. Paul lifted a pair of field glasses and adjusted the focus until a tram, climbing along the viaduct toward Santa Tereza, jumped into the eyepieces. The *bonde* ground silently along the narrow-gauge track in a bright, bending distortion of thermal waves. He shifted the glasses away from it, past the church and houses half hidden in the streaming greenery, to the Hesse villa. The red tiles of the roof came up sharply on the lenses, and he could see the graveled drive looping up through the trees from the gates, and the garden, drenched in leafy shade and hidden from the street by the high wall that had shards of glass cemented into the top. A pair of big Alsatians drowsed in the sun beside a reflecting pond.

Paul lowered the binoculars to glance at his watch. Two minutes to ten. He had come every day for two weeks to the hillside park and watched from the shade of the stone bench where he now sat, and he could predict the routine. He waited for the second hand to pass twice around the dial, and lifted the glasses again.

In the garden, the dogs were on their feet, ears thrust forward. All at once they bounded out of sight under the thatched roof of the patio.

After a moment, two figures came out from beneath the overhang into the sun. One was the thickset bodyguard who had driven Frau Hesse to the gallery. He was pushing a robed, pudgy invalid in a wheelchair. As they turned toward the pond, Paul was able to pick up Stefan Hesse, the spectacles perched crookedly on his nose as if they had been placed there by someone else. But that was only an aftereffect of the stroke that had left the muscles paralyzed and slack on one side of the round, chinless face. The mustache seemed hardly more than a pencil scribble above the drooping, moist mouth with its excess of vermilion pigment.

Paul noted down the time, though there was hardly a need to keep a log any longer. The pattern of activity varied scarcely at all. At ten each morning the two men would appear on the garden path beside the floating pads of water lilies. For half an hour Stefan Hesse would be left alone among the gleam of tropical flowers in the shade of a lattice arbor, the guard dogs resting on the ground next to the wheelchair, and then he would be taken back into the house.

Monday through Friday a male therapist came to give an hour of massage and exercise. At five minutes to four, the bodyguard would stride down to unlock the gates and wait for the panel truck that bore the marking FROMM CLINIC. The therapist wore a white uniform and carried a medical bag into the villa. The bodyguard went inside with him while the dogs stayed in the yard.

Two afternoons a week, while the therapist was working with her husband, Greta Hesse left the villa on foot with her prayer book and rosary. Several flights of stone steps along flowered terraces took her down to the church. Her visits were more corporeal than spiritual, for the appointments were not with God but with a lover waiting in a gray coupe. Once, Paul followed in a taxi. They drove to an apartment above a nightclub off the Avenida Mem de Sá in the quarter. The man was younger than Greta Hesse and wore a flowered shirt open on his tan chest, tight dungarees, and flat beach sandals.

Now, on the stone bench, Paul closed the notebook and stared down over the tops of the trees at the figure in the wheelchair. Only the legs and hands of the crippled man were visible in the shade under the lattice arch. Paul waited through the half hour before lifting the field glasses again and at once picked up the bodyguard striding out from beneath the roof of the patio. His stocky legs were slightly bowed under the thick brawn of his torso, and his arms were short and thick, too, and swung out to the sides when he walked. Paul smiled. The villa, he thought, operated with the same German efficiency and passion for order that had sent six million Jews to the ovens.

Alina asked, "Are you sure there isn't anyone else in the house? No cook or housekeeper?"

"A mulatto girl does the cooking and cleaning," Paul said. "She doesn't live in, and she's off on Mondays."

It was now evening, and they had come out into the cool darkness on the covered porch of the bungalow they had rented at Leblon Beach.

"How will you get past the dogs?"

"The dogs are left outside while the therapist is there. If I could take his place in the panel truck . . ."

"What about Frau Hesse and the bodyguard?"

"Frau Hesse has a lover. She's gone two afternoons a week. Monday and Thursday. That only leaves the bodyguard to worry about."

"He'll probably have a pistol."

"So will I," Paul said.

Alina was leaning against a post by the porch rail, her arms folded. She stared past Paul at the beach stretching up the coast where the surf was only a flash of silver light. A shiver went through her, and Paul asked, "What's the matter?"

"Nothing," she murmured. "The feeling of being locked up, that's all."

But that was only a facile reply to cover some deeper anxiety that was more complex in its chemistry than she cared to acknowledge. Already he was aware of some slow downward spiral in her mood swings toward an interior dislocation where the emotions were depressed into a flat range of fear that was disconnected and free-floating.

"You're supposed to be in Buenos Aires," he said. "It wouldn't do to be seen."

"It's dark enough now. Can't we go for a walk?"

They followed a footpath down to the beach and walked along the white wall of breakers booming against the wet, shining carpets of sand.

"Do you ever wonder what we're doing here?" Alina asked. "It was all a bad nightmare, Hitler and the camps, but the world woke up from it. Now, it's as if you and I are still caught in the dream."

"So are Liesl and Ernst," Paul said, "and your father. They'll sleep forever."

"I wonder if the hate we feel for the Nazis isn't just an extension of the same hate they felt for us? It grows in the soul until one day it takes control and there's no other feeling left."

"I don't mind giving up my soul," Paul said, "to get the people who murdered my sister and brother. It would be a cheap price to pay."

Later, Paul took Alina's arm and pointed. They stopped walking. Farther up in the sand, a couple were making love under a blanket. Between the crash of breakers, the breathless sobs from the woman's throat carried across the darkness. Alina gazed at the shadowy movement, then turned away. They strolled back toward the lights set like gems on the dark slumping hills to the south. It was a while before Paul noticed the shine of tears in Alina's eyes. He stopped again and asked, "What is it?"

Her head was bent, and he lifted her chin with his curled fingers until she was looking up at him, the cool gusts of wind off the water stirring the hair across her cheek.

"I was only wondering if we'll ever have a normal life like other people. . . ."

The clouds along the horizon behind her head were white in the blaze of the moon, and the light touched his fingers in her hair as he bent toward her and their mouths clung together in a long kiss.

The night breeze unfurled itself on the lace of the curtain in the bedroom of the bungalow, and Alina lay staring at the shadow it made on the wall. The same shadow rippled across her bare back like a consoling touch, and Paul put his own hand there too in a loving caress and could feel the slight tremor of grief come back through her warm skin into his fingers.

The disappointment raging in her nerves was more intense for having gotten closer to some threshold of pleasure before the undertow of failure had dragged her away from it. Tonight, he had sensed something different in the quick desperate heat of her mouth on his, and the haste of her legs opening to him. Her straining body seemed to be in flight from the specter that would invade the glands and flesh with its cold memory. Even as she had tried to slip past it, her eyes tightly shut on the self-deception of her own aroused purpose, it had overtaken her, and Paul had become aware of the panic in her that suddenly blocked the way, turning the race into a retreat. Now she wept under the consoling touch of his hand, and he could feel the unrelieved sexual tension in her body ebbing into despair instead of the tranquil release of afterlove.

At last she grew quiet, as if she had passed beyond tears into a larger sadness. All the while she gazed at the wall where the windblown lace from the window unfurled its patterns of shadow on glittering spangles of moonlight. After what seemed an interminable time, she murmured, "It's all so absurd."

The words had a dispassionate calm, as if she were making a clinical judgment about a patient. The curve of her bare shoulder was erected like a barrier of cold privacy. He kept his hand there, but it was an unconscious gesture of affection, for his own mind was already locked into the problem of gaining access to the Hesse villa.

FOUR

On Monday afternoon the therapist, whose name was Berger, came punctually out the side door of the medical clinic into the covered drive and climbed into the panel truck to make his house call. A scent of lilac water clung to the blond Aryan face with its sun-bleached hair and eyebrows, and a dab of styptic plaster covered a razor nick on his dimpled chin.

He drove out along the Avenida Beira Mar past the Mount of the Widow, the bay shining off to the right beyond the promenade and sea wall. It was always a pleasant drive from the clinic to the villa of Senhor Rocca, whom he had attended since the older man's release from the hospital. Senhor Rocca was not Brazilian, but a German, like Berger himself. The difference lay in the fact that Rocca was an assumed name, and Berger was not.

From the start, Berger was convinced that Senhor Rocca was on the run, probably another SS man fleeing prosecution. It was also clear from his use of medical terms and insight into his own condition that he was a physician. Beyond that, Berger knew little about his patient. Then, of course, there was the wife. He had caught a glimpse of Senhora Rocca only once, from a distance, pruning roses in the garden. Yet he was sure she must be German too. The arrogant force came across in all her movements, in the cringing respect of the dogs to her presence, in the way she held herself, erect and domineering. Even the dyed hair had an element of defiance in its flame-red color.

The bodyguard, who escorted Berger from the gate and always stayed near, was sullen and uncommunicative and had the stiff bearing of a Prussian NCO. His name was Maurice, and probably he was SS as well, but from the ranks.

In any case, Berger thought, it was none of his business who they were. His own employer, Herr Fromm, was an expatriate Austrian whose clinic served more than one ex-Nazi in Rio. Ordinarily he assigned Berger to these cases, not only for the reason that it solved the language problem, but also because Berger was German, thus assuring his discretion.

Now he swung left, away from the bay, toward the green hills of Santa Tereza. He began to hum a carioca tune, but all at once it caught in his throat. The pistol pressed behind his ear did not seem half so deadly as the voice of the man who was holding it.

"Keep your eyes on the road. Reach up with your right hand and twist the rearview mirror away from you."

Berger did so and caught a glimpse of a uniform sleeve, chalk white like his own. The man had been behind the high seat and under a tarp stretched over equipment and supplies.

The steering wheel was suddenly slick under Berger's hands, which had begun to sweat.

"You're going to kill me," he said.

"Only if you try something stupid." The tone had a cold indifference to homicide.

"I have no money."

"Shut up and keep driving."

They drove through the quarter, past the stone arches of the viaduct, and the road climbed into Santa Tereza.

"Turn into that drive," the voice said.

Berger geared down and swung into the drive. It was a vacant property, the windows of the house shuttered, the grounds untended and overgrown.

"There's no one here," the therapist murmured.

"Just do what I tell you. . . ." The pressure of the pistol increased ever so slightly behind Berger's ear.

Fifteen minutes later the panel truck, with Paul behind the wheel, pulled up at the gates of the Hesse villa. It was his first close-up view of the bodyguard, Maurice, who gripped one iron spear of the gate with a hand the size of a ham.

"Where is Berger?" The high voice surprised Paul, who had imagined it would be deep and gutteral.

"Sick," Paul replied. "Food poisoning. Dr. Fromm said he'd call and tell you I was coming. Didn't he telephone?"

"No one called," Maurice said. "You're late, besides."

"I had trouble with the address."

The two Alsatians bounded up, snarling. The bodyguard silenced them and leaned down to look in the window. In the back, the tarpaulin was folded beside the boxes of supplies.

"You're not Brazilian," he said.

"No," Paul said. "German."

"How did you come to Brazil?"

"I was a medical orderly on a ship that was sunk. I spent the last year of the war as a prisoner."

"Where?"

"A camp in Texas. A month before the war ended I escaped and slipped across the border into Mexico. In Tampico I was able to get aboard a ship. By the time she steamed into Rio the war was over. There was nothing left for me in the Fatherland, so I stayed here."

"Senhor Rocca has had a stroke. Are you familiar with his treatment?"

"I know what to do," Paul said.

Maurice locked the gates. The running board sagged under his weight as he climbed into the panel truck beside Paul. They circled up through the trees to the villa, the dogs trailing at a lope in the sideview mirror.

In front of the house, both men got out. The bodyguard was not quite as tall as Paul, but twice as wide. The stocky legs and massive torso belonged on a wrestler, and his neck went straight up on a smooth dome of a head where only stubble grew. Probably he shaved his head because of the heat. Even now his face shone under a film of perspiration.

"That way." He wagged a thick hand.

Paul grasped his medical bag and mounted the steps ahead of Maurice.

"Down the hall. Second door on your right."

Close behind Paul were the bodyguard's footsteps, hollow and heavy, the floorboards creaking under their weight. From the other side of the door came the sound of a Victrola playing Schubert. Paul turned the knob.

The door opened onto a large, windowless study. Bookcases covered a wall. To the right, a table lamp burned dimly at a writing desk. In the center of the room a branched ceiling fixture hung, unlit, above a round conference table ringed with chairs.

It was a moment before he picked out Stefan Hesse in the shadows at the other end of the room. Hesse sat motionless in his wheelchair beside a table with the Victrola and a stack of record albums. It was as if, like some nocturnal animal, he preferred the darkness. The former SS doctor managed to turn his head slightly, and the lines above the bridge of his glasses crimped together in a scowl that fell just short of recognition. The Schubert ended, and the needle on the coiled neck of the tone arm hissed in the dead groove of the phonograph record.

"You . . ." he whispered. "I know you. . . ."

The medical bag was open and Paul was turning with the pistol. The lunging spring of Maurice left no time to aim the shot, and he fired point-blank at the massive shape as it slammed into him. He thought he had missed, for the quickness and power of the other man seemed unaffected. Maurice's shoulder rammed into Paul's chest, driving him backward into the Victrola and the stack of record albums, which went over with a crash. The blunt fingers clamping down on his wrist had the inert force of a steel press. In one sweeping motion they smashed his hand against the edge of the table, and the pistol flew from his grasp. A chopping blow caught the side of his neck above the collarbone, sending him to the floor in a heap, and for a moment he had no feeling in his shoulder and arm.

Maurice stepped in to finish him, and Paul saw the first wince of pain on the stony features, and the wet shine of blood on the white shirt below the right pectoral muscle. Maurice's hand went to the stain, and his expression changed from pain to mild annoyance as he gazed at the blood on his palm. Paul scrambled to his feet and caught Maurice with a short combination of clean, hard punches that had good leverage and should have knocked the bodyguard down. They did no more than stop him in his tracks. The look of annoyed surprise came back onto his face, which might have been registering irritation over an insect sting. Paul swung again, and Maurice blocked the punch with a forearm and caught Paul's wrist, twisting it, and suddenly Paul was flying across the room. He landed on the conference table, and the back of his head banged against a chair.

Maurice lumbered forward, his hand once more exploring his side where the stain had spread on his shirt. Paul rolled off the table, putting it between them. The two men moved this way and that, like children in a game of tag. Finally Maurice grunted and overturned the table as if it were a piece of toy furniture. Paul snatched up a chair and caught him coming in. One wooden leg broke with a splintering crunch against Maurice's burly forearm, which he had raised to protect his head. But part of the seat still cracked against his skull, and he dropped to one knee, stunned. Twice more, Paul swung the chair. The second time, the frame came apart in his hands.

Maurice lay with his mouth open on the floorboards. He had absorbed punishment that would surely have killed an ordinary man, yet there he was, like an ox, still breathing. Paul decided to take no chances. He pulled a roll of heavy-duty electrical tape from the medical bag and bound the bodyguard's thick wrists together behind his back. The side of Maurice's shirt was blood-soaked all the way down into his trousers.

From the wheelchair, Stefan Hesse watched, his pupils rounded in hate and helplessness. Paul recovered the pistol from the debris of shattered phonograph disks. The ex-SS doctor, his head partially craned, was staring at the prone figure of the bodyguard.

"You have probably split his skull," he said in a slurred whisper. A gob of spittle dribbled down his chin. "If he doesn't get help, he'll bleed to death."

"That's up to him," Paul said. "As long as he does it quietly."

"Is murder so easy for you?"

"Was it easy for you," Paul asked, "at Auschwitz?"

Recognition finally flashed across the other man's gaze, followed by fear.

"Now I remember you," he breathed. "But it's not possible."

"To rise from the dead?"

After a long silence, Hesse sighed and murmured, "So he had a twin. . . ."

"I'll give you a chance," Paul said, "a better one than you gave my brother."

"For what?"

"A clean death. One bullet. Painless. Quick. As soon as you tell me what I want to know."

"The police will be after you for this."

"Not the Gestapo?" Paul asked. "I'm disappointed."

"What information do I have that could possibly interest you?"

"At the end of the war, you carried a large amount of medicine, gold, and stolen art out of the Reich by U-boat. Two others were involved. Their names were Viertel and von Stroelin. Where are they?"

"Dead." Hesse frowned. "Killed in the raids."

"Have you ever seen a corpse turned to rocks? That's what they found when the grave of Sturmbannführer Viertel was exhumed. It's a biological mystery, but you can solve it. For the last time, where are they?"

"You can't surely expect me to know that. The survivors scattered after the war. Argentina. Uruguay. Brazil. . . . They could be anywhere."

The term *survivor* drew a smile from Paul. For a moment it fit both of them. But now Hesse was a condemned man. The only question remaining was the method of execution, and whether it was to be quick or prolonged.

"This side of your body is paralyzed," Paul said, pointing a finger. "In theory, you shouldn't feel a thing. Suppose we put that premise to a test!

Think of yourself as the subject of an experiment that will add knowledge to the body of science."

Paul lowered the pistol with its silencing tube to within an inch of Hesse's kneecap and fired.

The invalid jerked and let out a high scream—a sound of terror rather than pain. His knee was suddenly a draining mash of cartilage and splintered bone in the bloodied silk of the pajama leg.

"Don't tell me you felt pain," Paul said. "That comes next time. The question is still the same. Where are they?"

Hesse's mouth worked silently, except for the corner where the muscles were slack, and the spittle shone on his chin.

"In the name of humanity," he gasped.

"Humanity," Paul said. "You're confusing me with my brother. He had the humanity. For instance, he couldn't have hurt a helpless man in a wheelchair. But it doesn't bother me a bit. I left my humanity back in the camps. It was my passive contribution, like the gold your Sonderkommandos knocked out of Jewish teeth with pliers. I see you don't believe me."

He had leveled the pistol inches from the other knee, and once more the weapon coughed. This time, the scream from Hesse was long and agonized. Afterward his mouth hung open, and he stared down in horrified disbelief at the shattered kneecap already pouring blood down his leg into his slipper.

"My knee," he groaned.

"Where are they?"

Hesse raised his head slowly. The drooping eyelid gave his stare a baleful quality.

"I couldn't betray old comrades."

"You'll be surprised how easy it is when the pain gets unbearable. I could put one in the foot next time, or would you prefer an elbow?"

"Please," he begged hoarsely. "No more. Please. . . ."

"You can stop it," Paul said.

Tears were streaming down Hesse's cheeks, and a slime of mucus glistened on the scruff of the Hitlerian mustache.

"The men you want are somewhere in the north. Where, exactly, I can't say. Nobody knows that much about the next fellow. It's a matter of security."

"The submarine put you and von Stroelin onto a riverboat near Belém. Where did you go from there?"

"We only went into Belém, and scattered."

"Then how do you know von Stroelin stayed in the north?"

"I don't. I assumed from our last talk. . . ."

"Your mission was to set up a safe house for ODESSA," Paul said.

"I don't know about any ODESSA."

"That's why the U-boat was carrying gold and medicine."

"There is no such thing as ODESSA," Hesse whispered painfully. "You've been misinformed."

Paul waved the pistol and said, "Did we decide where the next bullet would go? How about the shoulder that isn't paralyzed? It would give us a chance to observe the effect of a shell on the trapezius muscle."

"In God's name," Hesse implored.

"How many Jews said that to you before you operated on them?"

The terror twisting across the physician's face seemed to pass suddenly beyond the capacity of the nerves to absorb it. His body stiffened in the wheelchair, his eyes rolled, and his head fell forward. The hand clutching the armrest let go and dangled next to the spoked wheel.

Paul pulled the other man's head upright. Hesse's mouth hung open. Even as Paul watched, he could see the life go from the pupils in two slow, concentric dilations, as if stones had been dropped into them. Already, the skin had a blue tinge of cyanosis. The head fell of its own weight as Paul let go of it. He touched the carotid, but no pulse beat back into his fingers.

Paul swore softly. He hadn't counted on a second stroke. The threat of a third bullet had broken Hesse, but now it was too late. Paul felt cheated. Hate for the man who had killed his brother was still blocked up inside him. Hesse had escaped execution—not so different from a Jew throwing himself onto the electrified wire on the way to the gas chamber.

Maurice still lay with his mouth open on the floor, his thick wrists bound behind him. There was a discolored lump of extravasated blood at his temple, but the flow from the wound in his side had slowed to a drip.

Paul calculated how much time he had before Frau Hesse would return. He slipped out of the study and made a quick search of the villa. Nothing looked out of place except for a sanitary pad, with an odor of menstrual blood, crumpled on the tiled floor of the bathroom. Evidently Frau Hesse was in her cycle. Another bit of bad luck, he thought. Would she sleep with her lover today, or cut short the appointment? He hurried back to the study.

It took another thirty minutes to sift through the papers crammed into the compartments and drawers of the writing desk. In the end he had before him a small map of the north country on which one location had been circled in red, and three letters dating from 1945 to mid-1946. Each envelope bore the postmark of Manaus, sixteen hundred kilometers up the Amazon from the coast. All were addressed to "Max B." at a post office box in Rio, and written in code that used only first names.

> Dieter arrived today with the seaplane and had no problem with the lake, which affords ample distance for takeoff and landing. Conflict with local authorities has been resolved. Uncle Manfred was paid in gold and will cooperate.

The second piece of correspondence, dated in February of 1946, dealt with a visit.

> Nephew Konrad will be in Rio on or about the 2d of March. We know you will make him comfortable and show him the sights.

Apart from the name and date, the third letter was identical to the second. All were signed "Felix."

Paul thrust them into the medical bag and glanced at his watch. The search had taken too much time. Where was Frau Hesse?

He groped in Maurice's pocket for the key to the gate. The bodyguard's respirations were shallow and labored, and the blood had formed a thick soupy pool on the hardwood boards below the wound in his side. Paul drew the pistol and pressed the silencing tube against the mastoid bone behind Maurice's ear. The bodyguard could identify him. Still, it struck him as improbable that they would go to the Brazilian police. The police would ask questions and dig into Senhor Rocca's past. ODESSA wanted no publicity. The logic served to reprieve Maurice from execution.

Paul slipped the handgun into the medical bag and started down the hall. He was still a dozen feet from the door when it opened. There stood Frau Hesse, the dogs on either side of her. Her mouth fell open, and one clenched fist flew to it in disbelief.

"Ernst!" she gasped.

Paul reached for the pistol, but he was a second too late. The snarling animals hit him, taking him off his feet. Greta Hesse was gone from the empty doorway.

On the floor, Paul struggled to get the wall against his back. The jaws of one Alsatian were clamped onto the forearm of the hand clutching the medical bag. The dog's forelegs were braced, his eyes raging above the snout that jerked powerfully from side to side like a shark tearing meat from a carcass. Paul had ducked his head to protect his throat, and the second animal ripped at his side. He was conscious only of the snarling and the slash of fangs and searing pain. All the while, he groped methodically for the weapon, and finally his fingers closed on the pistol grip.

He fired point-blank into the Alsatian tearing at his side. The animal gave a shrill yelp and jackknifed into the air. It collapsed halfway to the door, the frantic squeal dying to a whimper, one hindquarter jerking convulsively in some last reflex of flight.

The other dog still had Paul's forearm in a mauling attack, a red froth of saliva and blood gleaming on its bared fangs and snout. Paul fired and saw one of the raging eyes explode in a pulp of bloody sclera around the socket. The jaws let go, like the release of tension from a bear trap. The dog backed off a pace, barking savagely, its one good eye staring hatefully. It was clear, from the flexed stance, that it meant to spring once more, and Paul fired a second shot.

The animal lay on its side on the floor. Paul's breath came in hoarse gasps, and sweat poured from his face. He was shaking, and his white uniform was blood-soaked and shredded. He staggered to the door and looked out. There was no sign of Greta Hesse. Would she call the police, or had she gone somewhere for help? Either way, he had to get out now. Someone would be after him.

FIVE

Paul left in the panel truck and followed the looping road downhill as far as the church. At this hour the lane behind the rectory was drenched in shade. He parked next to the wall, climbed into the back of the vehicle, and stripped off the medical jacket and white trousers. A little fresh blood welled from his side into the T-shirt, spreading the rose-red stain on the cotton. He put on slacks, a loose windbreaker made from parachute cloth, and dark sunglasses, and wadded the bloodied garments into a bundle. It would not do to leave them behind in the truck. He took the medical bag from the front seat, wiped the steering wheel and gearshift free of fingerprints, and fled on foot. Stone steps took him down the last hillside terrace to a tram stop on the tracks above the viaduct. He stuffed the uniform into a trash barrel and swung aboard the first *bonde* grinding down out of the district.

By the time he reached the bungalow in Leblon, dusk lay across the sky, bonding to darkness. Alina drew him inside, and he winced when she touched his side.

"You've been hurt."

Paul eased into a chair at the dining table and asked, "Is there any brandy left?"

Alina was already moving to the larder. In a moment she was back with cognac and a glass.

"Take off your jacket," she said.

The T-shirt was blood-soaked from the armpit to the waistband, the fabric congealed to the wounds. On his forearm, the punctured flesh was inflamed and raw, but the flow of blood had slaked. Serous fluid oozed from the crusts, and there was pain when he flexed his fingers.

"Those need cleaning," Alina said. "I'll have to go out to the *farmácia*. Don't take your shirt off until I come back."

After she had gone, Paul poured another brandy and drank it. He took the pistol from the medical bag, extracted the half-spent magazine, and inserted a full one. From now on they would have to live with a loaded weapon at hand. Greta Hesse had identified him. ODESSA would send its own execution squad after her husband's killer. He laid the handgun on the table by the lamp and waited for Alina.

In a short while she was back with gauze, a roll of cotton, and a chemist's mixture of disinfectant. She used scissors to cut away the shirt then swabbed the wounds, and Paul told her what had happened.

"Have you ever heard of a place called Manaus?" he said.

"Manaus? Didn't it have something to do with the rubber boom at the turn of the century?"

Paul unfolded the map he had taken from Hesse's study. It depicted the state of Amazonas in the north.

"I found this among his papers." He tapped a spot with his finger. "There's Manaus, where the Rio Negro joins the Amazon, and north of that . . ." His finger moved to the mark made with the red pencil. "Something else. . . ."

"The map only shows it as rain forest." Alina frowned.

"And marsh," Paul said. "Manaus sits all by itself sixteen hundred kilometers up the Amazon. A nice place to hide from the world."

"The letters were mailed from there?"

Paul nodded. "One of them talks about landing a seaplane on a lake."

"I don't see any lake on the map. Do you?"

"Most of that country hasn't been explored yet. On a map it's just green paper once you get away from the river."

"And you think it's connected to ODESSA?"

"What else could it be?" Paul asked. "It fits with what Major Ward had to say. Hesse admitted that von Stroelin and Georg were in the north. It was all I could get out of him before the stroke hit."

"Are you sure he was dead?"

"I'm sure."

"God pity him," Alina said, "for his crimes."

"God damn him to hell," Paul said.

"But the bodyguard was alive, and Frau Hesse. What if they identify you to the police?"

"They can't identify me without identifying themselves."

"That won't stop the therapist."

"He never got a look at me. The injection worked on him the way you said it would. He ought to be waking up about this time." He gazed at her and shook his head. "It's not the police we have to worry about. It's

ODESSA. They're probably looking for me now. The quicker we get out of Rio, the better."

She finished cleaning the puncture wounds on his forearm, applied a salve, and tied on a bandage. Finally she raised her head in the lamplight and asked, "Could you have killed Greta Hesse?"

"With pleasure," Paul said.

SIX

They had flown north to Belém on the coast and booked passage on the river steamer *Camille,* bound for Iquitos by way of Manaus, and they were now two days out on the Amazon that streamed, mud-brown and smooth, between walls of jungle lifting off the banks. Patches of rust spotted the hull of the steamer like scale, and the white paint on the woodwork below the windows of the saloon was blistered and flaking.

The captain was a fat Hollander with a heavy-jowled face like a basset, and his neck bulged over the collar of his wrinkled whites that sported cheap gold braid. He had spent most of the day in the wheelhouse, which lay forward of the smokestack above the two covered promenade decks, but now, as the afternoon went to pieces in the equatorial heat, he came down the companionway ladder into the saloon and stopped to chat with Paul and Alina.

"Will you have something to drink?" Paul asked.

"Tea." The captain took a seat under the ceiling fan that dispersed the sluggish air above the tables and short bar. "How is your cabin? Satisfactory, I hope."

"Fine," Alina said.

"Hot as hell," Paul said at the same time, and the three of them smiled.

"I am afraid the heat and mosquitoes are beyond my control. Ask the purser for citronella. A rag soaked in it and hung above your hammocks will keep the insects away while you sleep. You are leaving us at Manaus?"

"Yes." Paul glanced sharply at the slack-jowled face where the drooping eyes were drawn permanently into slits from squinting at the river.

"Tourists are rare in Manaus these days," the captain said, and Paul wondered if he only imagined the touch of suspicion in his tone.

"My wife and I are journalists," he replied. "We're doing a series about the region."

"Really?" The captain seemed impressed. "In the old days, they called it the Babylon of Brazil. At the height of the rubber boom, five thousand people a day were swarming in. They built a racecourse and bullring— even an opera house—and the grandest hotel on the continent. The big rubber barons used Italian marble for the floors of their mansions and had furniture shipped in from London. Girls would bathe naked in *cordon rouge* at parties that went on for two or three days. It was a Babylon, all right. Alas, Babylon, eh?"

"What happened to it?" Paul frowned.

"Nineteen ten was the last big year on the river. Overnight, the whole thing went bust. They found that rubber could be produced more cheaply in Asia. The market collapsed. The rubber barons were ruined. The foreign money interests pulled out. The opera house closed. Abandoned mansions were turned into pens for cattle. Even the streetlights went out. The city was too poor to pay for electricity."

"What's it like now?" Alina asked.

The captain shrugged. "A memory, that's all. There's a stink of decay about the town. The old opera house sits up on the hill like a relic from a lost civilization. Someday the jungle will take it all back. You can feel the remains of it rotting in the heat, like everything else on the river."

"You don't like the river?" Paul asked.

"The river is like a prostitute, full of tricks. In time, she steals your soul, but you grow used to her. It's the truth. Anyway, I've been with her too long to give her up now."

Later, Paul and Alina went on deck and stood at the rail near the bow and watched the twilight spill onto the river in drowning gleams. On the banks, the jungle was dark against the dusk, which still held the heat of the day.

"It's like the middle of nowhere," Alina murmured.

"That's why they chose it," Paul said.

"I've never been afraid of the dark." She shivered. "Suddenly I am. It's as if something were closing in on us. A sense of the past, I suppose. We seem to be going back to it instead of away from it."

"We *are* the past," he said. "They're the ones trying to run from it. I'll follow them into hell, too."

"Maybe we're there already," Alina said.

"Listen," Paul said quickly. "All this happened because we were Jews. Do you think Liesl knew what a Jew was? I never wore a skullcap or set foot in a synagogue. But suddenly, I'm one of them, locked up for something I don't know anything about, and marched off to be shot. They're going to be sorry they made a Jew out of me."

Alina smiled sadly, gazing at the river and the last coagulations of twilight. She asked, "Are you so ashamed of being a Jew?"

On the last day out, the captain joined them again, this time on the stern deck, where the river trailed off in a khaki band. To the starboard lay a streak of black water.

"See that?" The captain pointed. "It means we're close to Manaus. The Rio Negro is black. Even the Amazon won't have anything to do with her."

"How far?" Alina asked.

"Once we reach the confluence, Manaus is only a few kilometers upstream. Do you have a place to stay?"

"Not yet."

"You won't find much in the way of hotels. Try the Estrela. Tell them I sent you, and you'll get a better room. If you're looking for someone who knows the area, ask for Jeff Blackmore."

"Blackmore," Paul said. "Britisher?"

"Hardly." The captain smiled. "I suppose you'd call him a *caboclo*. One of the river people. He traps jacaré for a living. The hides bring a better price than rubber these days."

"Where would I find him?"

"Ask anyone on the docks. They'll be able to tell you."

"How long will the *Camille* be tied up in Manaus?" Alina asked.

"No longer than it takes to offload cargo. The crew doesn't like the town any more than I do." The captain gazed at her. "I think it's a place haunted by dreams. . . ."

SEVEN

Later, the *Camille* tied up at the floating dock of Manaus. The town lifted away on a low hill, and from the rail of the steamer Paul could see the spire of a cathedral and the massive dome of the opera house squatting on the sky against a dark swirl of twilight.

A deckhand carried their bags down onto the wharf where dockworkers were unloading cargo amid the creak of winches. In the side street off the quay, Paul found a horse-cab. The driver was lighting the brass lamps. Paul handed up the bags and helped Alina into the seat under the canopy where the upholstery smelled of fodder and sweat.

The Hotel Estrela lay at the end of a narrow street on the hill below the plaza. There was still a touch of opulence in the marble columns of the lobby and the worn red carpet that bled down the grand staircase across the main floor. But the once-elegant furniture had lost its finish, and the elevator had a sign on the cage that read AVARIADO—"out of order." Even the clerk behind the desk seemed outworn, like an artifact from another time. His white linen suit had lost its press in the damp heat, and a glaze of perspiration covered his gaunt face below a poorly matched hairpiece.

"And how long will Senhor and Senhora Neumann be staying with us?"

"Two weeks," Paul said.

"I shall need your passports until tomorrow. It is a police requirement."

Paul handed them over. The clerk lifted a hand and snapped his fingers.

A dark-skinned boy hurried across to collect their bags and the key. They followed him upstairs and down the hall to one of the grand parlors. The room gave up an odor of musty rot, and the gilt was peeling from the cornices. The houseboy lit the lamp and opened the windows, and Paul tipped him.

Evening had come quickly. They stood at the windows and looked out over the roofs dropping away in the dusk to the glimmer of flare-lit wharves on the river. The *Camille* was putting out from the dock, its stack trailing smoke. They watched it slide downstream on the current, the lights melting until they were only a far-off glow on the black water. The town seemed barely alive in the humid darkness, as if the river were hooked to it intravenously.

"What did he call it?" Alina murmured. "A place haunted by dreams?"

"Dreams can't hurt you," Paul said.

"There was a time when you believed they could," she replied.

"I was somebody else then."

"I know," Alina said. "You were trying to find your memory. I was trying to escape from mine. You succeeded. I didn't."

"Why don't you just let go of it?"

"Because it's impossible," she said, "and being here makes it more impossible."

"You sound as if you want to give up on the whole thing," he said coldly.

"Sometimes I do."

"You're ready to forgive them, is that it?"

"How could I forgive them?" she replied sadly. "I can't even forgive myself."

"That's different." His tone had an edge of impatience. "You did what you had to do."

"Did I really?" She smiled bitterly. "Is it that simple?"

"Unless you want to complicate it."

Alina gazed once more at the *Camille,* no more now than a drowning ember of light. She might have been watching her own escape drift out of reach.

"I'm sorry," she murmured. "You're right. It's too late to change anything. I suppose the way I feel has something to do with the isolation of this place." She shook her head. "It's as if we were trapped here."

"So are they," Paul said.

When Alina woke in the morning, it was late and Paul was already gone. The sedative had given her sleep, but no rest from the anxiety that had spilled over into dreams of fear and flight. There was a note from Paul saying that he had gone out to look for Blackmore. The name puzzled her. Then she remembered that Blackmore was the trapper mentioned by the captain aboard the *Camille.*

She had to force herself past some odd inertia to dress and brush her hair in front of the mirror, and then she went downstairs to the dining room. The clerk who had been on duty the evening before was behind the desk, but he did not look up. The dining room had only one waiter assigned. It was as if the hotel had cut its staff for an off-season that would never end.

She ordered fresh fruit, a roll, and a *café sem acúcar,* but even a decision about the menu required some major effort.The lassitude was part of a paralyzing anxiety blocked up in her nerves. It had less to do with ODESSA than some chemistry of depression that she could recognize in a detached moment of clinical insight. But she could do nothing to change it. Her anger over Auschwitz had been deflected inward on a cutting edge of self-incrimination. *You are an accessory to unspeakable crimes,* a voice— her own—kept repeating. The loss of control, the slow breakdown of her nervous system, the sense of panic were all an acknowledgment of guilt.

She had no appetite, hardly touching the fruit and leaving half the pas-try on her plate. Her fingers trembled badly enough to spill coffee on her dress, and the same queer lethargy prevented her from reaching for the napkin to dab the stain.

There was a policeman at the desk in the lobby when she came out of the dining room.

"Senhora Neumann," the clerk said in his broken English. "The Civil Police are here with a car. A *delgado* at the headquarters wishes to speak with you and your husband."

"My husband went out this morning."

The clerk and the uniformed man spoke to each other in Portuguese.

"When do you expect him back?" the clerk translated.

"He'll probably be gone most of the day."

The two men conferred again. The clerk turned back to Alina.

"He wishes you to go now with him to the headquarters."

"I don't understand." She frowned in confusion.

The quick, feverish eyes of the clerk darted away as if he feared guilt by association.

"Here in Amazonas it is best to do as the Civil Police say and not ask questions."

"Yes," Alina said, and could remember the two Gestapo standing in the foyer at midnight, the rain dripping from their coats onto the floor.

"One suitcase is allowed. Be quick."

In his office at the police headquarters, the *delgado* sat stiffly at his desk under the creak of a ceiling fan that barely shaved the heavy air. Flies buzzed beneath the blades and lit on stale crumbs of pastry amid the clutter of papers. The officer was short and wiry, and his head looked as if it belonged on a larger man. The thin mouth in the pitted, swarthy face had no humor at all. Beneath a receding pompadour slicked back with grease, his gaze was brown and bright, and she thought he was a man who would use his position to gain a sexual advantage over women.

"You have come from Rio de Janeiro," he said in passable German.

"We booked passage out of Belém, actually."

"Why Belém?"

"It was convenient."

"Convenient for what?"

Alina tried to meet the heated stare and said, "Can you tell me, please, why I've been brought here for questioning? Surely it isn't routine for foreign visitors—"

"Not many foreigners come to Manaus," the officer said. "Those who do are checked closely. There is a problem on the river with smuggling. Where is your husband?"

"Looking for a guide."

"The hotel could have found one for you."

"Finding one yourself is usually less expensive."

"You are Swiss tourists," he said with an inflection that seemed contemptuous, as if he were repeating a lie.

"My husband is a journalist. He came to collect material for an article about the region."

"What has he published?"

"Before the war, he wrote a travel guide for Greece. Of course, it's out of print now."

Behind the officer, mold from the wet season spotted the wall. A roach crawled over the cracked plaster. The brown sheathing flashed in the light, and its antennae quivered each time it stopped.

"How long were you in Rio? Where did you stay?"

"Three weeks," Alina replied and gave the address in Leblon.

The glaring stare of the officer would not let go of hers. His knowledge of German made it more difficult to avoid the truth.

"Did you spend much time in Santa Tereza?" he asked.

One suitcase is allowed. Be quick.

"Santa Tereza?" Fear soured her ability to think. "I don't recall that we spent any time there."

"You don't recall," the *delgado* said.

On the wall, the roach crawled behind a picture of General Dutra. At least the insect could find cover.

"I shall have to hold your passports for another day," the officer said as if delivering a verdict.

"Surely there can't be any question about them?"

"A routine check through the Swiss embassy in Rio, that's all. When it's done, they'll be returned to your hotel. One of my men will drive you back there now."

The lanky policeman who had brought her to the headquarters escorted her outside to the car. Her mind was badly disorganized, and she did not try to communicate with him. It was several minutes before she realized they were driving in the wrong direction.

"This isn't the way to the hotel," she protested, but did not understand his reply in Portuguese.

The narrow street twisted down through a crush of tenements to the river, where empty warehouses loomed, their corrugated roofs glinting in the sun. A dirt lane ran behind them in the shade of a high wall. As they turned into it, she caught sight of a sedan blocking their way just ahead. She glanced back in alarm through the rear glass and saw a second car coming up fast out of the trailing dust, and it was then that she lost all hope.

EIGHT

On the wharf, Paul followed the boy through the crowd at the fish market. A slick of pink blood and slime shone on the marble slabs where fresh eels were coiled beside catfish and piranha, and the waste troughs of milt and offal were redolent in the sun. He had inquired in a dozen shops about Jeff Blackmore, and at last found a vendor who said he knew the trapper. They haggled in the shade of the stall among the chickens and Muscovy ducks that were slung, live, from poles, and finally the man called out to his son. Now, the boy led Paul down to the docks where hundreds of small boats were clumped together on the black water, a floating market of fresh fruit, cacao, and smoked rubber.

They slipped downriver in a canoe to a settlement along the jungled bank. The clapboard houses, on stilts, stood high above the water. The boy tied up at one and motioned Paul to follow. They climbed a ladder of skinned logs to the ramshackle porch.

A young mulatto woman holding a baby to her bare breast came to the doorway of the hut. In the shadow of the thatched overhang, Paul could make out little more than the whites of her eyes below the purple scarf that bound her hair. The boy spoke with her, then turned back to Paul.

"*Nao aqui*," he said.

"Not here?"

"We go him," the boy replied.

Later, on the floating dock above the market, they stopped beside a tavern shed, and the boy pointed to a man at one of the plank tables under the tin roof.

"Blackmore," he said.

After he had paid the boy, Paul went over to the man, who wore a wide-brimmed safari hat darkly stained with perspiration above the cloth band tied around the crown. He could not see Blackmore's face, only the bare forearms that were thickly muscled and burnt brown in the short-sleeved khaki shirt. They rested flat on the table, and the heavy fingers were curled around a glass of gin.

"Do you mind if I sit down?" Paul asked.

The brim of the hat came up slowly to reveal a seamed sunburnt face and a crooked nose that had been broken more than once over the years. The eyes were bloodshot, and one socket was puffed and discolored from a recent brawl.

"Not a bit," he growled, "as long as you do it at some other table."

Paul said, "I've suddenly grown fond of this one."

"I could break your bloody jaw for you," Blackmore said, "if that would make the choice of a different one easier."

"You've already got one eye closed." Paul smiled. "Why put the other one at risk?" He drew out a chair and sat down. "Besides, it would be stupid to break the jaw of someone who wants to hire you."

"*You*," Blackmore said, pointing a finger at Paul, then a thumb at himself, "want to hire *me*? What the devil for?"

"Something that pays better than alligator hides."

The stare was still dangerous, but now it had a touch of curiosity.

"Who sent you?"

"The captain of the *Camille* told me to look you up."

The truculence fell to a safe level in the eyes that were creased and weathered at the outer edges, and the trapper took a swallow of gin.

"What did you say your name was?"

"I didn't," Paul said. "It's Neumann."

"Neumann." Blackmore nodded. "Have you got any cruzeiros?"

"Yes."

"Loan me fifty."

"Why should I?"

"To prove that you're a man of means. Besides, it's bad form to discuss business over an empty glass."

Paul folded a cruzeiro note and handed it over. Blackmore called out to a dark-skinned serving girl who had a soiled apron pinned about her waist. She gave him a sullen look as she came over.

"Two gins." The trapper held up two fingers.

"I prefer a lager," Paul said.

"*Uma cerveja branca para este senhor*," Blackmore said to the girl.

She replied in broken English for Paul's benefit, "Meestair Toussaint—he say you no more drink until you pay monies you him owe for gins."

"Bloody hell." Blackmore sighed. He said to Paul, "Give me another fifty."

The girl was comely, in a slatternly fashion, and the sulky resentment in the stare she gave the trapper suggested there had been something between them at one time. Beads of perspiration shone above her full upper lip that curved into a line of sneering contempt.

Blackmore threw down the cruzeiro notes, but when the girl reached for them he gripped her wrist.

"Tell that black swine Toussaint if he ever doffs me again over a bill that's owed I'll give him a bashing." As if to make sure she understood the message, he roared it in Portuguese, and Paul saw a tiny ferret of a black man, whom he took to be the proprietor, glance nervously away from behind the bar.

The girl twisted her wrist free and turned, and Blackmore patted the curve of her backside where it swelled into her long skirt. She spun around, screaming obscenities, and he grinned and said something to her.

"Go to hell," she replied, even as her own mouth tried to bury a smile.

"What did she say?" Paul asked.

"She called me a tavern lout and a brawler, among other unspeakable things."

"What did you say to her?"

"I told her it was true, but that I was a lover who had given her pleasure and deserved her gratitude, not her wrath."

After a minute, the girl was back with their drinks. As she bent forward, Paul caught a faint ripe odor from the damp armpits of her long-sleeved blouse. Blackmore had taken off his hat and laid it on the table. His copper-brown hair was matted against his forehead, and only a touch of gray showed at the sideburns. The smile was still unbroken in his mouth, and his eyes had the cool flicker of an invitation in their unflinching stare.

"Did you tell that little swine that I may break his neck? I may, too, if this is the usual swill and not the Bombay gin the little black bugger keeps under the bar for his pals. Go tell him that."

The girl said nothing, but this time the slow roll of her hips as she went away seemed less antagonistic.

Still watching her, Blackmore said to Paul, "What's this business about?"

Paul unfolded the small map he had taken from the Hesse villa and tapped the area marked in red pencil.

"There's a lake up here somewhere. It doesn't show on the map."

"Those lines off the river are tidal creeks," Blackmore said. "In the wet season the Rio Negro rises thirty to forty feet. The lakes come and go."

"You've been in there," Paul said.

"Not lately."

"When I talked to the captain aboard the *Camille*, he said he thought there were a few Indian villages scattered through the region. He said you'd trapped with the Indians and could speak a bit of the language."

"That's true."

"Could you take me in there?" Paul asked.

"Why would you want to go in the first place?"

"Research."

"What kind of research?"

"Human." Paul smiled. "I'm interested in a disappearing species."

"You won't find many Indians in that area anymore. When the hunting goes bad, they move somewhere else."

"Is the hunting bad?"

"It depends on what you're after."

"What made it go bad?"

"Who knows?" Blackmore shrugged. "There isn't always an answer for everything."

"It depends how hard you want to look."

"If I were you, I'd pick another spot for research. That one isn't safe to go into."

"Because of Indians who aren't there anymore?"

"Other things."

"What other things?" Paul pressed him.

"Unknown hazards," Blackmore said.

Paul took a swallow of the lager that tasted cool and malty in the bottle beaded with moisture.

"Like Germans?" he asked.

Blackmore had been staring off at the river in the sun. Now his gaze came slowly back to Paul's and held fast.

"Who are you?" He frowned.

"There are Germans in that back country—from the war—aren't there?"

"It's no bloody business of mine," Blackmore said. "So I don't stick my nose into it."

"You don't have to," Paul said. "I'm asking you to take me in there. That's all."

"How the devil do you suppose you'll get out?"

"That's my worry."

"You want to go in and you don't care if you come out. Is that the drill?"

"More or less."

"What rot," Blackmore scoffed. "I don't believe you."

"Believe what you want." Paul shrugged. "Will you do it?"

The trapper shook his head in a puzzled way.

"You're an odd bloody fellow. Do you know it?"

"Does it make any difference as long as you're paid?"

"It won't be cheap, either."

"Nothing is," Paul said.

"Well," Blackmore said. "You're no researcher. That's clear enough. When do you want to go in?"

"Anytime."

"Give me a couple of days, then."

"Is there any surcharge for keeping your mouth shut?"

"I'll throw that in for nothing," the trapper said. He leaned back from the table and called out to the serving girl, who came over from the bar, her hips swinging lazily. "Bring another gin and cold lager, and tell that little black weasel you work for to put it on tick, or I'll kick his arse all the way to Venezuela."

While they were waiting for the drinks, they heard the drone of a plane slipping off the distance. Paul caught sight of it, a small amphibian with twin engines mounted on the high wing above the cockpit. It circled in low on the sky beyond the tin roof and touched down in a slow glide onto the river, the curved bow lifting a slash of white water as the engines reversed power. The ship taxied in toward a floating dock to tie up.

Blackmore said, "What day is it?"

"Tuesday," Paul said.

"That's odd." The trapper frowned. "She usually comes in on Thursday."

"Commercial or private?"

"Don't you know?"

"I can't make out the markings."

The smile pulling at Blackmore's mouth had a cryptic mirth that fell just short of mockery.

"It belongs to your German friends," he replied.

NINE

Only two men were aboard the cabin cruiser as it roared away from the deserted dock, dragging its wake out into the broad channel. One was at the wheel on the flying bridge. The other, who had a flat, Teutonic face scarred in the war, was below deck with Alina. He sat opposite her on a bunk, his shoulder blocking the porthole so that she could not see what part of the river they were on.

After a short time, the craft throttled down to slow speed. The man got up from the bunk, stepped into the companionway, and called up to the bridge. Through the porthole, Alina had a glimpse of the bank angling toward them. It climbed high on the glass as it slid near, and a turn-of-the-century mansion showed in the stranglehold of jungle growth that rose a hundred feet high on the hillside.

They tied up beside a motor launch at the bank. Stone steps, crumbling from neglect, went up steeply through the thick vegetation shot with sunlight and shade and the vivid hue of jungle flowers.

The house took shape slowly in the leaves as they climbed toward it. Three stories tall, it could have been a summer palace from czarist Russia, spires rising from onion-shaped domes on the sky. The paint had peeled from the wood exterior, the gilding was gone from the swollen domes, and the slats of the shutters were smashed or missing. Only at the very top was a set intact. There was glass, too, at the French windows, and looking up from the stone steps as she mounted them Alina could make out a man's bullish form behind the pane. He was only half perceived, like a tower guard at Auschwitz, and the image touched some long-buried feeling of dread and resignation.

Inside, broken glass and chalky debris crunched underfoot, and she had a glimpse of a large parlor strewn with fallen plaster and the hulk of a grand piano, legless and disemboweled. A billiard table squatted nearby,

its felt cover rotted and its wood warped by rain that had blown in the
empty gap of a window where curtains still hung in a few brown shreds of
disintegrating lace.

They climbed two flights of stairs to the top floor, and the hall was suddenly clean and maintained. The man with the bullet-scarred face gestured toward a door that hung open on what must once have been an
upstairs sitting room for the family. Now it had the look of a military billet. Two folding cots were made up, the blankets taut. The man she had
sighted from the steps stood beside a table with two wooden chairs. He
ground out a cigarette in a dish beside the kerosene lamp, and she knew
him at once from his early photographs. The shock of recognition passed
through her in a silent, numbing coldness, as if Death were already
breathing on her.

Von Stroelin smiled and bowed his head in a courtly fashion of old-
world manners. They might have been guests at a social gathering. He
stepped over to her, and the back of his hand cracked hard against her
cheek. The hair flew across her face as it jerked sideways, and afterward
there was blood in her mouth.

"That is so we understand each other from the start," he said.

Alina said nothing. The war had never ended, she thought. It was only
a dream that she had awakened from. Now she was back at Auschwitz—
condemned to spend the rest of her life there in some desolate state of
surreal memory that would melt across eternity.

Von Stroelin dragged out a chair and sat down, crossing his legs. He
laid a cigarette case on the table, but did not open it.

"The other thing you should know," he said, "is that we are quite isolated here. This place is no longer accessible by road, only by water, and no
one comes around anyway. It was built by a Russian count named Panov.
He shot himself after the rubber market collapsed. They say his ghost
inhabits the house and still plays billiards. So, you see, we're quite alone,
unless you believe in spirits."

Alina swallowed blood from the cuts inside her mouth. The man who
had brought her upstairs was standing by the French windows. Now, in
the sunlight, she saw that the scar ran in a deep furrow from his mouth,
across his cheek, to his ear. The bullet had taken out part of his cheekbone, leaving a concave hollow in the flesh.

Von Stroelin said, "Your name is Vicki Linz Neumann, and you are a
Swiss national?"

"Yes," Alina said. "Of course."

"And your husband?"

"The same."

"Does he have a profession?"

"Journalist."

"And I suppose he has come here to write an article about the region? Is that what brings you to Manaus?"

"Yes," Alina said, and thought how absurd it sounded, after all.

The smile dragging at the corner of von Stroelin's mouth was like a tic that came and went, distracting attention from whatever mood lay behind it.

"You are lying, Frau Neumann. Do you know what happens to liars?"

In her mind she could see clearly the inspecting SS officer at the barrack and hear his voice: *You are lying. Do you know what happens to liars?* On that day, the search had been for contraband. Now the only contraband, the most difficult of all to conceal, was the truth.

"I've told you the truth," she lied.

Von Stroelin stared at her, the smile still pulling at his mouth with some intermittent contempt. At last he drew two passports from his coat pocket, dropped one on the table, and opened the other, tapping Paul's photograph.

"But, you see, I happen to be acquainted with your husband. His name is Krenek, in case you're interested. Why are you traveling under forged passports? Who got them for you?"

"My husband's legal name is Josef Neumann. He suffered a head wound at the end of the war. It left him with amnesia. He has no memory of his past."

Above the smile, von Stroelin's gaze showed a flicker of clinical interest.

"Really?" he murmured, as if he half believed in the possibility.

"It's true."

"Except that Switzerland was neutral."

"I was in Munich with the International Red Cross just after the war. I met my husband while he was recovering in a rest camp, and we were married. That's how he obtained Swiss citizenship."

"Your husband is a Jew. He was shot in the back of the head at Dachau. Apparently he survived. Probably you're a Jew yourself."

She could remember standing with Paul on the deck of the river steamer at twilight and saying: *Are you so ashamed of being a Jew?*

"That's absurd," she replied.

"It might explain why you're here. An act of personal revenge. Were you in a camp, too?"

"I was in Switzerland. How would I know anything about your camps?"

. . . *The phenol is to be injected directly into the heart muscle, Fräulein Doktor. It is your responsibility to calm the patient so the procedure can be*

*carried out without resistance. Just tell them it is medicine to cure their infec-
tion. . . .*

"You are wearing long sleeves." He smiled. "Don't you find it impracti-
cal in this climate?"

"They give protection from the sun."

"Show me your left forearm."

"I have a scar, if that's what you're looking for. But it's from an accident
that required stitches."

The camps, she thought, were like an actor's school where one learned
the stagecraft of lying and applied it in a theater of improvisation. One
lied first to the SS staff, then to the other inmates, and finally to oneself.

Von Stroelin said, "Your husband is a murderer. A week ago, in Rio, he
killed two men. One was a former German officer. Your husband knew
that. Either he went on his own, or was sent as an assassin, in which case
his task was to force information from his victim before liquidating him."

"How can you call us murderers?" Alina said, and at once saw the
infant boy, his blue eyes widening as she pinched the nostrils shut, her
palm over his mouth. The vigorous movement under her hand had lasted
no more than a dozen seconds.

Von Stroelin rose unhurriedly from his chair and stood before Alina.
He said quietly, "Who sent you here? British Intelligence? American?
How did you know where to come? I suppose you just threw a dart into a
map of the world and it struck Manaus. Is that what you want us to
believe?"

"You can believe whatever you choose," Alina said.

Once more his hand swept out of nowhere. This time the heel of his
palm broke her nose, knocking her backward onto a cot. There she
remained, her back pressed to the wall, both hands over her face.

"That's a cure for Jewish insolence," he said in a conversational tone.
"If it doesn't work, I can prescribe something stronger. Look at me when I
speak to you."

Alina raised her head. She had no control of the tears sliding down her
cheeks. They flowed from some dark interior recess of shame and compromise and self-degradation that had opened suddenly. The psychological
pain was far more intense than that of the broken nose where only a thin
rivulet of blood shone below one nostril.

"I don't believe your answers," von Stroelin went on. "But we have
chemical agents to treat memory impairment, more reliable than a fist in
getting at the truth. Your husband is being picked up now. We'll have a
chat as soon as he gets here. When that's over, he'll be executed, along
with his accomplice, for the murder of a German officer."

He turned back to the table, and she heard the click of the cigarette case opening. The man with the disfiguring facial wound moved with a subordinate's instinctive reflex to offer a light.

Through her own tears, she could still see clearly the blue eyes of the infant filling with panic during the convulsive struggle for life.

"You are guilty of infanticide," she told herself, "and you are sentenced to die...."

She bolted past the two men before either could react. Von Stroelin's shout was lost in the loud shattering of glass as she flung herself through the French windows into a rushing blur of leaves and sun and stone that snapped all at once like a film on a movie reel, leaving only a white brilliance of light where the images had been.

Von Stroelin was the first to reach her. Behind him raced the man with the concave cheek. The man who had stayed with the boat was hurrying up the steps from the dock.

Alina lay in an awkward, broken posture. Her face and arms were badly cut, and she was bleeding from the ears. Von Stroelin knelt beside her and groped for a pulse. He thought he felt a weak flutter, like a startled bird taking flight from a great distance, and then it was gone. He pinched open an eyelid and saw that the pupil was dilated and fixed in its gray, expressionless retreat.

"Crazy Jew bitch," he murmured, but not without a certain cold admiration.

The man bolting up from the dock reached them, his chest heaving. A look of disgust twisted across his face, and he glanced away.

Von Stroelin stood up. There was nothing to do now but wait for Paul. His frustration over the woman's suicide was already receding in anticipation of forcing the truth from Paul. He almost hoped it would be difficult.

"Take her down to the launch," he said. "Wait until dark, then let the fishes have her."

TEN

The sun was dropping below the horizon when Paul got back to the hotel. Long shadows embalmed the lobby in a quiet gloom, and he caught a furtive look from the desk clerk, who pretended at once to be busy. At the stairs Paul glanced back and saw him lifting the phone at the switchboard.

Alina was not in the room. A maid had been in to make up the bed and lay out towels. He thought Alina might have gone out for a walk, though it seemed unlikely she would go without leaving a note. He went to the window and looked down at the narrow street, bathed in shade, where a few shops were still open. There was no sign of her.

He waited ten minutes and went downstairs to the desk.

"Did you see my wife go out?"

The clerk smoothed his hairpiece, and the quick eyes, like those of a small, nervous animal, seemed to cast about for an escape.

"The senhora left earlier."

"Alone?"

The clerk slid his hands back and forth along the marble desk while his gaze continued to dart out of reach. All at once he straightened, staring past Paul with clear relief at the policeman who had come in from the street.

"The senhora went with this inspector to the headquarters of the Civil Police. There was some question about your passports."

"Our passports are in order," Paul said.

The clerk had lost his nervousness.

"Naturally," he replied. "It is probably some silly technicality. A missing stamp. It happens, you know." The smile twisting off his mouth had a touch of malice, as if he hoped for the worst. "It is my understanding that one of the senior *delgados* wishes to speak with you and your wife together."

The policeman, who was from the lower ranks and was called an inspector, wore no cap, and the heavy curls of oily black hair and the swarthy skin gave him the look of a Sardinian fisherman.

Paul said, "You can telephone the headquarters and see if she's there, can't you?"

The clerk spoke in Portuguese to the inspector, who gave a curt shake of his head and a short response.

"He says the senhora is waiting and a call will not be necessary." The clerk's eyes broke contact once more, unable to hold the lie, and Paul smiled.

"Of course," he said. "Tell him I'll be with him as soon as I use the lavatory."

Paul crossed the lobby to the men's room and went into a stall. He lifted his trouser leg, peeled back the tape that secured the pistol below the bulge of his calf muscle, and climbed onto the commode seat. It was a turn-of-the-century toilet with a long chain attached to a high flush bowl, and he left the pistol and silencing tube and box of cartridges out of sight atop the lid. There was always a chance the police would search him, and he did not want to take the risk. He pulled the chain, flushing the toilet, and went out.

The police sedan was parked on the street in the shade. They climbed into the front seat, and Paul saw that the inner handle was missing from the door on the passenger side. There would be no chance to jump when the vehicle made a stop.

They drove uphill, circling the Praca São Sebastião, where the columns and immense dome of the opera house pressed against a sky inflamed by twilight. The streets narrowed into tributaries of shadow that dropped through the old quarter to the river and the galvanized roofs of warehouses. The inspector did not say a word as he drove, and Paul saw that he carried a Colt .45 pistol in a service holster embossed with "U.S." on the flap.

Halfway down the hill, Paul caught sight of a second vehicle trailing in the side mirror. The car slipped on and off the glass, sometimes falling behind, then closing, but never breaking contact.

There was no sign of a police headquarters, only the line of warehouses flying toward them on the chrome hood ornament of the sedan. A woman bearing a basket of limes stared at them as they went by. After that, Paul saw no one. The twilight had burned itself out and the shades of dusk lay across the road, but the inspector had not switched on his lights.

They turned down a dirt lane bordered by a stone wall behind the warehouses. Most of the buildings stood abandoned, their windows broken out, doorways gaping. Paul saw that the trailing vehicle had dropped back from the plume of dust lifted by the police sedan. The speedometer needle hung on thirty as a loading dock coasted up on the windshield. The other man was staring straight ahead, his jaw tensed under a film of perspiration. Twisting, Paul wrenched the wheel to the left. He had only an instant to brace against the impact that slammed both of them across the seat. From the smashed front end, a horn blared. Neither man had been seriously hurt, and the inspector was clawing at the flap of his holster.

Paul's fingers clamped onto the oily ringlets of hair, and he drove the heel of his other hand against the jaw and smashed the man's head twice into the window frame. He heard the skull crack against the steel and felt the struggle go out of the man even as he let go and jerked the handle of the door. One shove left the policeman sprawled half out of the sedan, his head and shoulders on the ground below the running board. Paul scrambled over the limp figure and raced for the door cut like a mouse hole in the side of the warehouse. The car behind them had come up fast, skidding to a stop, and the men springing from it were engulfed in a billowing cloud of dust. It flowed over them like a conjurer's smoke to make them vanish, and Paul was through the gap into the shell of the warehouse.

The ground sloped away in darkness, and he plunged into it, slipping away from the strident horn that still blared in the lane above, as if the car were a wounded beast waiting to be put out of its misery. He glanced over his shoulder at the slot he had come through and saw a dark shape drop across the dusky light. Somewhere outside, a running man shouted orders in German.

The floor of the warehouse was gone, and Paul circled a pile of stony rubble and a shallow crater where machinery had been taken up. A section of railing above a low drop-off came at him out of the dark. He paused, straining to pick out objects in the flood of shadow below, and heard the scrape of a shoe against chalky mortar somewhere behind him. Ducking under the rail, he dropped to the next level and sank ankle-deep into a wet pulp of plasterboard scraps. The silence was suddenly drum tight. Paul groped for a piece of the plasterboard and sailed it high into the darkness. It hit with a soft thud. Twice a pistol cracked, and he saw the red tongues of flame from the muzzle flash no more than thirty feet away.

He flattened himself on the ground below the parapet and heard the man moving along the rail above him. The soft tread of feet went on past.

Paul crawled on his elbows and knees into the deeper lesions of shadow. A wall came up where criblike offices had been, and his hands found the gap of a door.

Inside, he got to his feet and felt his way gingerly along the slotted partitions that ran like a maze in the dark. A portal had collapsed, and he squirmed past it into a larger room where the rusted iron of a massive scale caught the evening light from a row of smashed windows. A receiving dock ran past the windows on the outside, and there was a spur of abandoned track where a conveyer railroad had once shunted the fifty-pound balls of rubber to the cargo holds of steamers and square-riggers in port. Beyond the track bed lay the tin roofs of sheds and the gleam of the river.

Paul climbed out a window onto the concrete platform. Almost at the same moment, a figure came around the corner of the warehouse. Paul saw the pistol come up and dove from the dock as the shot rang out. The ricochet left its whine in his nerves even as he rolled to his feet in a patch of weeds and bolted across the track bed. There were shouts in the dark behind him, and he ran with his head low, plunging down between two sheds to the floating dock. The planks were warped and weathered, resting on frames lashed to pontoons. There was nowhere to go except into the water, and he dropped to his belly and let himself down over the edge feetfirst. The current pushed sluggishly against his chest, and he took a breath, dove under the float, and surfaced beneath the dock, water streaming down his face. The shouts were very close now, and the hollow pounding of feet drew near. Overhead, a little light seeped down through the gaps between the planks, dimming briefly as a man ran past. A thick scum coated the water under the dock where the pontoons blocked the current, and he heard a splash and caught sight of a rat, its fur glistening and oil-matted, swimming out from a support beam.

For a while the night was silent except for the slap of the river against the hollow drums. He thought of Alina, and a sick worry knotted itself into the pit of his stomach. The worst part was that he could do nothing about her as long as the men hunted him in the dark above.

Later, he heard voices, and this time two men moved along the dock. One shone a flashlight down through the gaps in the planks. Paul gripped the support beam and ducked away from the shavings of light. The creaking of the boards under the weight of the men slowly faded out, along with the low murmur of their voices.

Once more the night fell silent. After a bit, he heard a car drive off. He thought they might have left an armed man behind, and he stayed where he was, clinging to the support timber. Overhead, the cracks between the planks had darkened, and he could make out the glimmer of stars. He worked his way along the timber to a spot between the floating drums that gave him a view of the river. Half a kilometer downstream, the lamps of small boats were ablaze on the black water, and a few tiny figures moved in the glow of charcoal cookers.

He waited another ten minutes until the darkness was complete, then slipped between the pontoons and let the current take him along the shore toward the cluster of boats.

ELEVEN

From the thwart of the canoe Paul could see candles burning in doorways as the settlement of shacks drifted up on the current. He paddled in toward Blackmore's, and the prow bumped against a stilt of the porch. There was no sound above, and no candle burned to ward off evil spirits—or even fugitives in stolen canoes. Paul tied a line to one of the piles in the dark. He climbed onto the ladder and froze as Blackmore's voice, in Portuguese, delivered a curt warning.

"It's Neumann." Paul craned his head back and saw the dull shine of a rifle in the hands of the trapper, who loomed above.

"I said two days. You're early."

"There's been a change of plans. Can you put me up? I'll pay you for your trouble."

The trapper cradled the rifle in the crook of his arm.

"You're alone?"

"Yes."

"All right. Come up."

Paul climbed the ladder to the porch. His clothes were wetly plastered to his body and he was hungry.

"Been for a swim, have you?"

"Not by choice."

Blackmore's gaze raked the river.

"Did you steal the canoe?"

"You could say I borrowed it without the owner's permission."

"Go back down and cut it loose. It won't be good for you if it's spotted here in the morning."

After he had shoved the boat out into the current he scaled the ladder once more to the porch. Inside, Blackmore had lit the oil lamp, and Paul saw the young mulatto female bent over a wicker crib where the baby slept. Her breasts, heavy with milk, spilled forward into the cotton blouse that was tight at her waist where her belly still curved in new maternity, and her brown skin glowed in the light.

"She doesn't speak English," Blackmore said. "Who's been after you?"

"If I had to guess, I'd say whoever was on that seaplane when it landed this morning. I spent most of the afternoon watching it, but no one came back."

"Why would they have an interest in you?" Blackmore asked. "Or should I turn the question around?"

The woman sat down on the floor beside the crib, her back straight, her legs crossed beneath her in solid curves of bronzed flesh. A little milk had leaked from her engorged breasts into the cotton fabric of her pullover blouse, and a brooding curiosity was at large in her eyes as they fastened silently on Paul.

"I'm German, not Swiss," he said, "and half Jew in the bargain. The bastards who killed my family came here after the war to hide. That's what brought me here." He glanced at the woman, who looked fiercely protective beside the crib. "I think you ought to know that the police are probably after me, too."

"Naturally," Blackmore said. "They've been bribed at the top."

"They took my wife in today. It had to do with our passports. She never came back to the hotel. Now I'm wondering if she ever reached the police headquarters."

Blackmore gazed at him. "You could use a dry set of togs. Come along to the back."

Paul followed him down a cramped hall. The acrid smell of sulfur hung on the heavy air as the trapper struck a wooden match and lit a rush candle. The light flexed across a thatched ceiling that sloped above poles from which three jacaré hides had been hung to dry. Piled on a shelf were a dozen books with broken bindings and an odor of moldy rot, and several old photographs, cloudy about the edges, like daguerreotypes. Paul stared at one of a towering figure in a white tropical suit. The heavy hand at his side clutched a Panama hat by its broad brim, and in the heat one tip of a wide handlebar mustache had begun to droop. He was standing on the floating dock at Manaus in front of a paddlewheel steamer taking on a load of wood.

"My father," Blackmore murmured.

"A Britisher?"

"What gave you that idea?"

"You speak like one."

"He was a Confederate exile. Quite a few of them fled to South America after the war. He had a better reason than most. When he was seventeen, he killed a Yankee carpetbagger in a fight. The military government would have hanged him, but he got out of Savannah on a square-rigger and ended up prospecting for gold in the Mato Grosso. By the time he drifted north, the rubber boom was under way. He was able to put together a life that wasn't so different from the one he'd been born to. It operated on slave labor at a huge profit." The trapper smiled reflectively. "I never really knew him. My mother was an Irish chambermaid at the Grande. They lived together, as the saying goes, without benefit of clergy. But give the sod his due. He took care of me after she ran out on us."

"What were things like in those days?"

"Those days. . . ." Blackmore stared at the photograph. "Try to imagine planters like him lighting their cigars with banknotes worth a hundred pounds sterling. Families sent their laundry off to Lisbon and their children to the best schools in Europe. Opera companies were brought in from Italy, and people drove to see them in gold coaches and Deutz automobiles. Then came the bust. Planters were ruined overnight. The opera house closed. The public transport shut down. The electricity got turned off. People just packed it in and left."

"Your father, too?"

"I was at boarding school in England when a solicitor brought the news that he was dead. He'd set fire to the house and burned himself up in it. No gentleman's accounting for him. He had syphilis from the gold fields, and in the last stage he'd got to raving a bit. Maybe he thought Sherman was marching in. Sherman's men had burned the family plantation when he was sixteen. Now I was sixteen, back home to a burnt mansion and no money—not even enough to see him properly stiffed out."

"What did you do?"

"I got work emptying and polishing spittoons at the Grand Palace Saloon. I was a big lad by then and could use my fists, and I went from shining brass to bouncing drunks and finally to dealing cards. Someone called me out as a cheat. He was right, of course, but I couldn't let the bugger get off with my reputation as an honest gambler. We went to it in the street and I hit him too bloody hard. Like father, like son, eh? The police were after me for manslaughter. I wasn't keen on rotting in a cell. I had a young Indian pal who'd inherited my spittoon-polishing job. He took me upriver and into the back country to his tribe. I stayed in a *caboclo* shack near the village for almost five years. The Indians taught me to trap and fish, and I learned their language, and a few other dialects.

When I finally came back downriver, no one remembered me. The grand saloons weren't there anymore. The city was half deserted, rotting in the jungle. What few police were left didn't take any notice of me. I'd grown a beard and was using a different name. The gambler who'd killed a man in a fight over cards was forgotten—part of a life that didn't exist anymore."

Paul had shed his wet clothing and put on a pair of whipcord trousers and a tan pullover shirt stitched from chamois skin. He said, "I seem to be in the same boat."

"You want to scrub the trip upriver?"

"That's the last thing I want to do."

"It's your bloody hide." Blackmore shrugged. "Not mine."

"You're the only one I can count on," Paul said. "Is there some way you could make a few inquiries about my wife? Maybe she got back to the hotel, after all."

"I'll see what I can do."

"There's another problem. I had to leave a pistol on top of a flush bowl in the men's room at the Estrela. It has a silencer taped to the grip, and a box of cartridges. It's a Walther. I've got to have it back."

"Shouldn't be difficult," Blackmore said. "What about my pay?"

"I've got some cruzeiro bills that need drying out. If those aren't enough, I'll write out a promissory note. You can collect it from my bank if I shouldn't come back."

"It took me five years to get back," Blackmore said. "You'll be lucky to get back at all."

"That doesn't bother me."

Blackmore gave a low chuckle and put a hand on one of the books, a musty copy of *Plato's Works*.

"Plato would say that our real knowledge of things consists of our ideas of them, not of the things themselves. On the other hand, he never spent any time in a rain forest, did he?"

TWELVE

For most of the day they had chugged upriver in Blackmore's twelve-horsepower boat, which had a canvas tarp for shelter from rain and sun, and now they swung wide out of the channel toward the shade of a tributary where the branches of the rain forest joined high above the water. Paul glanced back to make sure the canoe, towed on a line secured to a stern cleat, did not yaw in the crosscurrent. At the mouth of the creek the leafy shade of the forest swallowed them silently, and the sun faded to a few drowning embers on the surface.

"How much farther to the village?" Paul asked.

"A few kilometers."

"I saw an adventure film once about headhunters. They were Mexican actors with paint and feathers."

"This lot is part of the Yanomamö tribe that migrated south from the Padauari. They don't take heads, but they can be nasty if you cross them."

The canopy of jungle drifted slowly overhead, and the tiny flashes of sun fell across Paul's stare like the beaded sparkle of a hypnotist's chain, pulling thoughts of Alina from some recess of denial. Her disappearance was a worry that he now had to live with, like a migraine that would not go away. But the possibility that she might not be alive was one he still refused to face.

Later, the village spilled into view on high ground, and Paul saw the *tapiris*, made from thatched palm fronds, clustered in the forest. The light was going from the tops of the trees, and there was no activity.

"Odd," Blackmore murmured. He had cut the engine, and they were idling into the bank, where only two dugouts were overturned. "There ought to be women and children about, and smoke from cooking fires."

As the bow nudged the bank, the trapper vaulted the gunwale and secured a line.

"Toss me that bit of dunnage."

Paul handed down a canvas bundle. Blackmore carried it up into the trees, drew his knife, and slit the cords. He unrolled the canvas on two cloth bags of salt, tobacco, and a pair of new machetes. Stepping back, he crossed his arms on his chest—the sign for talk.

Nothing stirred in the shadows that were iron-hard, as if they had been smelted over the ground, and Paul said, "There's no one here."

Blackmore climbed to a patch of high ground where the rain forest was half hidden in the sinewy grip of vines and leafy cascades of foliage. The trapper ducked through the ligaments and leaves and began to scale a tree into which footholds had been cut. Hand over hand, he went all the way up to the thatch, gripping the coils of liana with both hands as he made a reconnaissance of the village. Then he was back on the ground.

"What did you see?" Paul said.

The trapper did not reply, but moved out of the thicket to a nearby grove of saplings. He ran his hand along one that bore the marks of a machete, then bent down to lick a laceration in the smooth bark.

"It's a fresh cut," he said. "Somebody's home, but they aren't answering the door."

They strolled out among the huts. The ash beds of cooking fires lay sunken and cold in their rings of blackened stone, and the prints on the dirt floors did not look fresh.

In a large *tapiri* they found charms dangling from a pole and slivers of bamboo smeared at the tips with black tar that had hardened.

"Shaman's hut," Blackmore said. "The charms were left behind to prevent bad spirits from following the tribe. Mind you don't scratch yourself on one of those shafts."

"Curare?" Paul frowned.

"The shamans prepare it. They boil the bark of lianas and bush rope, and mix it with God knows what else, then evaporate it over a fire until it turns thick. Once any bit of it enters the bloodstream, you're finished. The facial muscles go first. Lips and tongue, so you can't swallow. Then the extremities. The odd thing is that the poison only attacks the voluntary muscles. The heart goes on beating. The mind stays alert. But you can't move. Finally the blood carries the poison to the muscles of respiration. They quit, and you suffocate." The smile on Blackmore's mouth had an air of grim appreciation. "The Indians call it 'flying death.' It's silent, and there's no antidote."

Paul raised his head and stiffened. Beyond a slit in the palm fronds, a painted face stared at them.

"I know," Blackmore said softly. "He's been with us for the last five minutes. He's only a boy. I expect they left him behind for a reason."

The eyes were almond shaped in the broad, flat-lipped face that was smooth and impassive like a Tiki carving.

"Can you talk to him?"

The trapper made another sign with his hands, then spoke to the Indian in dialect. Afterward, he said to Paul, "Come along."

Outside, the boy had retreated into the shadow of the next *tapiri*. The stripes of purple dye smeared across his face and body were like the camouflage markings of a jungle animal. He did not move a muscle, grasping the long hollow tube of his blowgun, the plaited quiver of darts slung at his side from a thong.

Paul watched the trapper talking and gesturing. Finally Blackmore motioned to him. They followed the boy through the leafy gloom to another hut where an old man leaned on a crutch-pole in the entryway.

"The boy's name is Nyashu," Blackmore said. "When the tribe moved away, he stayed behind to look after the old man. Probably a relative. He's crippled and can't see anymore to hunt."

"Did he say why the others left?"

"The first Germans who came in after the war settled on a deserted rubber plantation east of here. The main house was still standing, and so were the shacks of the *seringueiros*—the rubber gatherers. But the jungle had grown back, and the Germans needed a labor force to clear the tract. They took young men from this village and put them to work. Nyashu says the workers were treated like slaves. The first time they ran off, they were shackled in a stockade for punishment. If a man ran off a second time, the Germans cut an Achilles' tendon to cripple him." Blackmore glanced at the old man, whose face was wrinkled like the skin of a prune. "The tribal elders held a meeting. Some wanted to go in and kill the Germans. Others were afraid of the rifles and dogs. The council took a vote and decided to move the village far away so that even the iron bird of the Germans couldn't find them."

Later, they sat crosslegged on the floor of a *tapiri* and picked scraps of dried peccary meat from a communal gourd, and Nyashu passed a bowl of purplish liquid.

"*Masato*," Blackmore said to Paul. "They chew manioc root until it's broken down with saliva, then mix it with yams to ferment. Careful you don't drink too much or you'll have a head tomorrow."

After they had finished the meal, Blackmore spoke for a long time with the old man, who replied occasionally in a toothless rasp. The boy, who looked to be about fifteen, sat impassively, the firelight gleaming on his skin.

Finally, the trapper said to Paul, "It's all arranged. Tomorrow you'll go in with Nyashu."

"Nyashu?" Paul gave him a surprised look.

"This is as far as we can bring the boat. The water's still too low. It'll be another fortnight before anything bigger than a canoe can navigate in to those marsh lakes. You'll have one carry overland, but it's not difficult."

"How many Germans are in there?"

"The old man thinks about forty or fifty. He says they come and go in iron birds. They have a boat, but it can't get out while the river's low."

Paul glanced at Nyashu in the firelight. The face of the young Indian was flat and wooden, as if all expression had been carved from it.

"Don't worry," Blackmore said. "You can trust him. He hates the Germans as much as you. The men of the village have all sworn revenge. Even the old man. But he thinks you're a fool to go in alone. He says the Germans will kill you. I think he's not so bloody wrong about that. . . ."

THIRTEEN

When Paul woke the next morning the hut was empty. He crawled from his bedroll and ducked outside. A sheen of dew beaded the jungle ferns in the haze of light. He tramped down to the creek. The boat was gone. Evidently Blackmore had slipped away before daybreak. The small canoe with the supply pack in the stern was tied to a sapling on the bank.

He walked uphill and saw Nyashu in the clearing outside the *tapiri*. The young Indian pointed to a bowl of papaya and wild berries and made a sign for Paul to eat.

By the time they set off, the sun had climbed higher and the rain forest had begun to swelter. Nyashu paddled ahead in a dugout and Paul trailed in the canoe. A hundred feet overhead monkeys scrambled in the thatch, and a few birds slanted across the light. Animal trails drifted past in the leaves along the bank, and Paul could see tracks in the soft loam where ocelot, deer, and peccary had come down to drink.

Before noon they came to a fin-shaped ridge where the stream angled north along a range of low hills. Nyashu beached the dugout and stepped into the shallows to drag the bow of the canoe onto the bank. The Indian pointed to the ridge, and Paul nodded.

The canoe was not heavy, even with the bedroll and paddle lashed to the thwart, but the steepness of the climb along the looping trail in the heat took the breath from his lungs and drove sweat from his pores. Twice he had to stop to catch his second wind. Ahead, Nyashu kept on climbing, the dugout canted over his shoulders like a shell.

At the top of the ridge, Paul gazed at the country spread out below. Half a kilometer from them, the stream forked and ran north in two shining arteries around a wide tract of rain forest. In a few weeks, when the rivers rose, the island would become a massive wetland in the trees.

They picked their way down the ridge to a sandy spot above the fork and refloated the two craft. Paul slipped off his backpack and stowed it astern. His shirt was soaked with sweat where the weight of the pack had rested and where the harness straps had chafed into him.

Later, the stream flowed through a mangrove swamp. Pads of water lilies brushed against the hull of the canoe as it glided among the parcels of sunlight. Needlefish darted between clumps of floating vegetation, and a few herons stalked the shallows.

Beyond a thicket of bramble the swamp narrowed again to a slithering channel of black water under the canopy of rain forest. Everywhere the trees were caught in the constricting stranglehold of liana vines that twisted upward to migrate in the thatch.

Around four o'clock, they reached the lake. There were breaks in the rain forest where patches of sky drifted among the leaves, and the stream widened across islands of marsh grass. Nyashu left the dugout afloat among the reeds in a backwater pool, then helped Paul drag the canoe up into the grass that was bent and tall enough to conceal the shell.

They crept to high ground, and suddenly, the lake slid into view. It had the shape of an arrowhead, about four hundred meters at its widest, and there was a dock on the far shore and three floating sheds with tin roofs. A raised-deck cruiser was tied up under one, a second stall lay empty, and in the shadow of the third was the twin-engined amphibian he had seen in Manaus.

A long warehouse squatted above the dock. Half a century ago it would have been used to stockpile rubber in the dry season until the rivers rose and barges could get in to haul the cargo out. Now it served as a storehouse for supplies and petrol. Some distance behind it, in the center of a cleared tract, soared a guard tower, like a toy made from matchsticks and glue.

Nyashu gazed at him as if to say, "This is the place you are looking for."

Paul lifted the binoculars that he had taken from the pocket of the supply pack, and the floating sheds along the lakefront jumped into the lenses. The cowling was off an engine on the high wing of the amphibian, and a mechanic, stripped to the waist, worked on the bare assembly. Paul could see the grease on the backs of his hands in the shade under the tin roof.

A few figures moved inside the warehouse where the sliding doors had been left open for ventilation, but it was too dark to distinguish them clearly.

He lowered the binoculars and saw that Nyashu had slipped away without a sound. The Indian was already in the dugout, paddling out of the reeds.

A small plane droned in the distance. Immediately, Paul burrowed deeper into the marsh grass where he could not be spotted from the air. The craft circled in from the east and caught the glint of the sun. It was a single-engine monoplane, the wing fixed above the cabin cockpit, the underside of the fuselage fitted with two pontoons.

The plane skimmed in low over the treetops, flaps down to cut air speed, and landed on the lake, lifting a slash of white water behind it. The pilot taxied to the dock, cut the motor, and climbed down onto a pontoon, tossing a line to the mechanic, who had come along the pier from the tin shed.

A passenger dropped down from the cabin onto the pontoon and stood grasping a strut. Even before Paul lifted the glasses he knew who it was, and a tiny thrill of homicidal pleasure flashed through his nerves at the same time that the lenses seized and held the features of Fritz von Stroelin.

FOURTEEN

Paul worried that the dugout might have been spotted from the air, though it seemed likely the plane would have made a pass over the marsh for a closer look. The men on the dock did not appear in any hurry, and he watched von Stroelin and the pilot walk away from the tethered aircraft and climb toward the warehouse.

As soon as they were out of sight, he slipped back through the tall grass to the canoe, lifted the pack and bedroll from the stern, and crept higher up into the rain forest. In a dry swale hidden from the air he stretched the canvas shelter-half and mosquito net, and thrust the bedroll inside. He had not eaten since morning and opened a tin of sardines packed in a tart sauce, and he washed the last morsel down with a long swallow of water from the canteen.

There would be another hour or more of light on the lake, and he wanted to slip in for a closer look at the compound before dark. He snugged the Walther into his belt, looped the binoculars around his neck, and set out.

It took half an hour to skirt the lower shore of the lake and climb once more to high ground in the timber. Below, ringed by palms, stood the main house, its upper galleries steeped in the shades of the dying day. A screened veranda ran along the side of the house overlooking the lake.

The dock sheds and warehouse were blocked from view, but not the guard tower. It rose on stilt legs set in concrete. Halfway between the tower and the main house, a lone Quonset squatted in a grove of jacaranda. The faint hum of a gasoline generator faded in and out on the silence, and Paul thought if the hut had power that it must be an infirmary.

Fifty meters of open ground separated the Quonset from the nearest patch of jungle where clearing operations had been suspended for the day. A bulldozer was parked beside an uprooted tree and pile of brush.

Off to the right lay a dozen tin-roofed shacks. They were the huts where the *seringueiros* had once lived. Snaking into the jungle behind them were the *estradas*—trails that circled for miles into the rain forest. Twice a day the *seringueiros* would have trekked over them to the rubber trees scattered in the wild, first to bleed the latex into cups, then to col-lect it.

Now the huts were occupied by support personnel—cooks, mechanics, and security. Paul trained the field glasses on the site and spotted several naked figures in a makeshift shower. They stood on wooden slats under a water tower, open on top to collect rain, and passed a bar of soap among themselves. In a dusty clearing nearby, another group scuffled for posses-sion of a soccer ball. A dog barked faintly, and Paul shifted the glasses to a lone figure on a bench outside a hut. The man was teasing the animal by pretending to throw a stick. Finally he let it go. The dog raced to snatch it.

For a while Paul lay watching the house, his chin on his arm. Dining tables ran across the marble floor of the veranda, and at one of them two men were in conversation. He lifted the glasses and saw that the heavier figure was von Stroelin. The other had no distinct features, his face taped across the nose and cheeks with strips of adhesive. A third man, in a white jacket, served dinner from a dumbwaiter.

The men who had been kicking the soccer ball were at the shower, soaping down. The bench where the man had teased the dog was empty. Smoke rose from a vent on the tin roof of the mess, and the smudge hung on the air.

From time to time Paul trained the binoculars on the veranda. The two men had finished their meal. The sun was down, and twilight bled across the lake. The server in the white jacket had lit candles at the tables.

A sentry gripping a rifle and a bandolier crossed the compound and climbed the ladder into the guard tower. His head and shoulders made a dark silhouette on the high platform under the thatched roof.

On the veranda, von Stroelin lit a cigarette. He smoked while the twi-light burned itself out on the water. The sky paled to a blue dusk, the jun-gle dark against it.

All at once, the two men got up from the table and came down the steps of the veranda. In the binoculars Paul had his clearest view yet of the familiar features, the mouth shaped to a fine arrogance, the eyes lit with quick humor that ran too easily to contempt. The folds of a silk scarf were tucked into a shirt, unbuttoned at the throat, and the tan riding trousers were flared above high boots. He had paused at the foot of the steps to strip his cigarette—like a target fixed for a moment in the cross hairs of a telescopic sight—and Paul could easily have killed him with a rifle shot. But a death out of nowhere was too impersonal—an unfair exchange for Liesl and Ernst.

The two men passed out of sight behind the house and came back into view again walking toward the Quonset. They crossed the open ground beyond the bulldozer and brush pile, disappeared in the shadow under the jacarandas, and a moment later the lights flashed on in the hut.

Already, Paul's nerves were alive to the opportunity, von Stroelin all but alone in an isolated part of the compound. Except for the tower guard, no one was about. Two shots from a silenced pistol—would they be heard by the sentry? Not likely, he thought, over the racket of the gasoline generator. The odds of slipping in and out undetected were perhaps a bit less than even. The whole thing was a game of improvisation, but he had already decided to play it.

He screwed the silencing tube onto the barrel of the Walther and slipped downhill in the trees. The oil lamps from the house made a far-off glimmer in the leaves, and he kept them at a distance as he worked his way through the snarl of dark foliage.

A few minutes later he crouched in the shadow of the bulldozer beside the mountainous pile of brush. Beyond the dull gleam of the blade lay the stretch of open ground to the Quonset. Paul stared at the guard tower. The sentry under the thatched cover was lighting a cigarette, his face profiled toward the lake. Paul gathered himself and sprinted across the clearing, his head and shoulders bent low on the dusk.

The German who had teased the dog outside the mess was named Dietrich, and he was a specialist in aircraft engine maintenance. His big hands were usually dark with oil stains that soap would not take off, and he did not bother to scrape clean at knifepoint the black grit that had been driven up under the blunt fingernails.

After a meal of stewed rabbit and vegetables, he had left the mess and walked out to the field latrine in the trees that bordered the clearing. The enclosure was empty, and he dropped his pants and sat down on one of the holes cut into the long wooden frame above the waste pits. It was dark under the roof of thatched palm fronds, and for a while he stared absently through the trees at the clearing and the lake, which had the look of slate in the settling dusk.

Evening for Dietrich was the loneliest time. There were books to read, and the shortwave set for music, and within the last year, an occasional trip to the brothel in Manaus. Still, it was a lonely life, cut off from the world. It required an unflinching commitment to the ethics of duty and German honor, and these were the values that held him to his assignment.

Now, something passed across his stare, jarring it out of its vacant absorption. He blinked and rubbed a hand across his eyes. Surely he had seen a figure break across the open beyond the trees where the gray slack of dusk still hung above the lake. In the dark, fumbling with his trousers, he ducked past the serrated fringe of palm leaves and saw again the racing silhouette. It faded across the lights of the Quonset and vanished in the shadow of the jacarandas.

Paul hesitated only a moment in the trees, then pressed forward to the curved shell of corrugated metal and peered through a window. The Quonset housed a dispensary and small operating room. There was a stainless steel table under a lamp in the shape of a kettledrum and a sink for scrubbing down. Beyond a folding screen, two beds served as a recovery bay.

Von Stroelin was using a pair of blunt-tipped surgical scissors to cut the adhesive bandage from the face of his patient. He snipped the tape and peeled back the Vaselined gauze from the splinted nose. A little bloodied packing extruded from each nostril, and the purple bruises under both eyes gave the impression of a burglar's mask. The man's lips were swollen to twice their size, the vermilion unnaturally moist under a film of saliva. Yet, for all the postsurgical trauma, he looked oddly familiar, like a minor celebrity whose name would not come to mind.

Paul slipped below the window to the door and opened it softly. The man with the splinted nose saw him first, and his eyes widened in alarm. Von Stroelin froze, then turned slowly, holding the surgical scissors.

"So you've finally come," he said, as if the visit were no surprise.

"I felt an obligation," Paul said.

"I suppose I should have put it down on my calendar of appointments."

"It was on mine."

"Then we have a conflict of schedules."

"I brought a pistol to resolve it," Paul said. "A bullet is a reliable arbitrator. Ask the SS if you don't believe me."

The man with the packing in his nostrils was breathing through his open mouth. It exaggerated his look of panic. Again Paul had a troubling flash of recognition that would not quite come together in an identity.

Von Stroelin said, "Is that what you told Stefan Hesse when you shot him?"

"He betrayed you," Paul said. "It didn't take much to make him do it. For an SS superman, he wasn't very tough. Himmler would have been mortified."

"A cripple in a wheelchair. It must have taken all your courage."

"No more than injecting iodine into a child."

"So you are prosecutor, judge, and high executioner. On behalf of all Jews?"

"On behalf of myself." Paul looked for a sign of fear in the other man, but could find no trace. It was almost as if he were being cheated of interest on the account he had come to collect.

"You've got the pistol." Von Stroelin shrugged. "If you're going to use it, go ahead."

Paul smiled coldly. He admired the show of nerve, though it changed nothing.

"I just wanted you to know," he said, "who it was from."

Something slammed into him from behind, taking his arm down. The dull *thump* of the pistol came an instant too late, the bullet shattering a glass cabinet. The floor crashed into him, and it was von Stroelin who kicked the pistol from his grasp before he could fire again. Even as he struggled to break from the grip of the arms clamped around him, something blunt cracked against his skull, and a bolt of light behind his eyes seemed to disconnect him from the moment.

FIFTEEN

Paul raised his head, blinking into the light. A few feet away, von Stroelin pointed the Walther. The man with the splinted nose clutched a paperweight.

Von Stroelin said, "Let him up, Dietrich. Go back to the barracks and turn out every man. I want a search of the compound."

The leverage on Paul's arm eased all at once as the man who had him pinned to the floor got to his feet and bolted off into the darkness.

Paul sat up. He ran a hand behind his head and felt the lump from the paperweight. Already the ache from the blow had begun to throb. He stared up at von Stroelin, whose face seemed more slackly heavy after seven years, though the force and self-confidence were unchanged in it. The yellow hair came now from a commercial rinse, and the result was unnatural, like a chameleon whose chemistry has malfunctioned so the deceits of color blend to the wrong shades.

Without taking his gaze from Paul, he turned his head slightly and said to the other man, "Please go back to the house and alert everyone there. No one is to be out while the men are searching the grounds."

The man nodded, his mouth open, and circled away from Paul to the door.

"We knew you were in Manaus," von Stroelin said. "I didn't think you'd have the nerve to come out here. I should have known better. You always had nerve."

"If I don't get you," Paul said, "someone else will."

"Who?" The other seemed amused.

"Probably a Jew. One who slipped through the system."

"Fortunately," von Stroelin said, "not too many did."

"It only takes one," Paul said.

Some slight heat of impatience passed across von Stroelin's stare above the loose smile.

"Get up," he said quietly.

Paul rose to his feet, wondering if he could get close enough to make a lunge for the pistol. But von Stroelin was careful to keep a distance between them. He motioned Paul out the door.

"Clasp your hands behind your neck. If you try to run, I'll put a bullet in you."

As they crossed the clearing, Paul could hear shouting from the huts. A few flashlights bobbed in the darkness beyond the scrub. The heavy tread of von Stroelin's boots lagged a few feet behind. Ahead, the lights of the main house drifted toward them.

A dozen figures waited in the palms below the veranda. They had the look of a jury that had already delivered a verdict of guilt—a jury of former SS, on the run, without the power to acquit.

From the steps of the veranda, a woman with both hands on the railing peered out into the darkness. The candles flickered on the other side of the screen behind her, and Paul saw that it was Leni. The sight of her stopped him in his tracks, and he dropped his hands from the back of his neck. He wasn't sure what emotions twisted across her face, for they burned up too quickly in the atmosphere of her own disbelief and confusion.

"Paul," she gasped.

His gaze held fast to hers as she came slowly down the steps onto the turf under the palms. Beneath the cropped hair, short as a boy's and combed straight back, the lines of dissipation and neglect were prematurely etched into her face, which had no trace of the joy and animation that he remembered, but only a resentful sadness. Her waist had thickened, and the youthfully sleek body had become more rounded and full-blown in its contours. Her hands rested against his chest, as if the fingers needed contact to dispel her doubt, and then tears suddenly shone across a dry edge of embittered feeling.

"They told me you were dead," she murmured. "They said you were killed trying to get across the frontier with Liesl. All these years . . ."

"And you," he said. "I thought you were in a grave in Berlin. It seems we were both wrong."

She glanced past him and saw the pistol in von Stroelin's grip.

"What in God's name do you think you're doing?"

"Taking a murderer to task," von Stroelin replied, "for his crimes."

"You're not going to shoot him!" She shook her head in disbelief.

"There is a good possibility that I am."

"I won't let you," she cried.

"That is because you are upset, and your mind is not totally rational." Von Stroelin's manner had a touch of familiarity, like that of a lover who could risk a quarrel because he had been intimate on more than one occasion. "It would be best if you went to your room. I'll give you a pill to help you sleep."

"So this is why you brought me from Manaus," she said dispassionately. "He was there, and you were afraid I'd find out."

"I haven't time to argue," von Stroelin said curtly. "He may not have come alone. The men are searching the grounds. It is necessary for your own safety that you go to your quarters and stay there."

"I want your word," Leni insisted, "that he won't be harmed."

"Nothing will happen to him tonight. Now, please do as I ask, and stop making a fool of yourself."

"If you break your word . . ." she threatened.

"I'm not in the habit of breaking my word," von Stroelin said, and gazed at Paul, who could remember him in much the same mood the night of the party, years before, as the flush of anger mounted like a promise above the broken smile.

SIXTEEN

In the morning Paul woke as the first pale light spilled down through the crosshatched iron bars into the pit. His leg was shackled to a horizontal rod that ran the length of the cell, bare except for a slop bucket. There were three cells, side by side in the ground under cover of a long shed, and at the turn of the century they had been used as a punishment block for the slave laborers who worked the plantation.

He pushed away from the floor to a sitting position, his back against a wall, and stared up at the bars. They were encrusted with lime from pails that guards, standing on the catwalk above the cages, had overturned.

There was no possibility of escape, yet von Stroelin had posted a sentry through the night. Probably it stemmed from concern that he had not come alone and someone would try to free him.

Later, he heard the monoplane take off from the lake and circle to the west toward Manaus. The air in the cell was baking hot from the sun on the tin roof above the catwalk. All through the morning the bulldozer droned, and he could hear the crack of underbrush going down under the blade and the distant shouts of men at work. His mouth was parched, and he did not try to move in the heat.

At midafternoon, the soft ringing of boots on the catwalk pulled him out of a drowsy, half-conscious state. He raised his head and saw von Stroelin and the guard staring down at him through the corroded bars. Von Stroelin moved out of view, and Paul heard the scrape of feet in the passage outside the cell. The locking bolt slid from its cradle, and the plank door swung open.

Von Stroelin ducked inside and straightened, a fresh scarf knotted around his bull neck, and fumes of bay rum still clung to the clean-shaven face. In contrast, Paul sported a growth of black stubble, his clothes were dirty, caked with the salt of old perspiration, and insect bites covered his skin. He gazed at the canteen of water in the canvas jacket attached to the other man's belt.

"We found your camp this morning," von Stroelin said, "and the canoe."

Paul stood up. He wanted nothing more than to get within reach of the thickset figure, but the shackle and chain at his ankle restrained him. Von Stroelin saw the murder in Paul's face and seemed amused.

"You couldn't have got in here the first time on your own," he went on. "Who brought you?"

"I ran into someone in Manaus who knew you. One of his Achilles' tendons had been cut."

"What led you to Manaus?"

"Hesse kept notes that he should have destroyed."

"It's possible. But that raises a different issue. How did you track Hesse to Brazil?"

"He sold a painting in Rio. One that Ernst had made a copy of before you sent him off to Auschwitz."

"So Ernst broke his word and told you, after all."

"What did you expect?"

"Some degree of honor."

"From a half-Jew? That was stupid of you."

"Wasn't it?" von Stroelin agreed. "It makes me wonder if I can believe anything you tell me."

"Wonder all you want." Paul shrugged.

"For instance, traveling out of occupied Germany isn't so easy these days. You had a Swiss passport and false identity. How did you manage all of that?"

"It's not hard when you have money in a Swiss account."

"The silencer on the pistol we took from you was developed for the American OSS during the war. Who supplied you with it?"

"An arms dealer in Zurich."

"What was his name?"

"He forgot to tell me."

"And I suppose you didn't ask?"

"Why should I?"

Both men glanced up as they heard the plane coming in from the west.

"Ours," von Stroelin said. "I sent the plane in for Georg this morning. He'll take his wife back to Manaus. He practices medicine there. If you ever find yourself sick in Manaus, check the registry of physicians. Look for Paul Krenek. It should be an easy name for you to remember, Herr Neumann. But, I forgot, you won't ever be sick in Manaus."

"It must be dull work," Paul said, "with no Jews to experiment on."

Von Stroelin had unscrewed the cap of the canteen and poured a cup of water. He held it out to Paul, who knocked it out of his hand to the floor.

"You shouldn't have wasted it." The physician shook his head and picked up the cup. "In this climate the body dehydrates rapidly, and the effects can be quite painful."

He fitted the canteen into its canvas jacket and started to duck out. But in the doorway he stopped, looking back over his shoulder.

"The woman who came with you threw herself out of a third-story window. The fall killed her. Was she really your wife, or was it part of your cover?"

Paul said nothing. In the hot gloom of the cell, his muscles were swollen and taut, aching to get the other man within reach.

Von Stroelin was gone. Once more his boots rang on the catwalk overhead and faded into silence. Paul sat down, one knee upraised to support a clenched fist. He knew he should have been feeling grief. The odd thing was that he felt nothing. Hate was like a poison in the blood. It killed other emotions until finally nothing survived except its own toxic chemistry.

SEVENTEEN

The plump figure in the open doorway of the cell was hardly recognizable—a good seventy pounds heavier than Paul remembered, and much of the weight had gone to his hips. His hair was down to a few thin strands above the rounded face and puffed jowls, and a broomstick mustache made his mouth into a scraggy line. Even the wire-rimmed glasses were gone, replaced by plastic frames like a change of disguise.

"Congratulations," Paul said, "on your resurrection."

"And yours," Georg said quietly.

A silence fell between them, as if the gulf of years had left them nothing in common to talk about.

"I saw you on the hill that day," Paul said, "outside Dachau."

"It's true," Georg said.

"My being there was all your doing, wasn't it?"

"Yes." The whispered admission seemed almost painful.

The bitterness twisted away from Paul's mouth in a quick smile, and he said, "So you could have a Jew's serial number and his name?"

"No. It was more than that—something I knew. It happened the day I brought you back to the house and Leni told us the Gestapo had arrested Ernst. Remember when I went out to check the street for you? The fact is, I only pretended to go out. I saw what happened in the drawing room. It was obvious that you still had romantic feelings for each other. Of course, I knew it before that particular day. I knew all along. But I had to see it in order finally to acknowledge it." He gazed at Paul with what appeared to be genuine regret. "It wouldn't have mattered as long as you remained in a concentration camp. It was only when the war was lost that you became a problem. I was afraid if you got out alive you'd come back one day, and I'd lose her. She was the one thing in the world I couldn't bear to lose, you see. More important than friendship or loyalty or life itself."

"And Liesl?" Paul asked. "Was she a threat, too?"

"Her death was a mistake. I was sick about it. I found out too late what had happened. You can believe that or not, but it's true."

"Von Stroelin confirmed the order."

"I know. But she was in the Kinderhaus under a different name. Fritz told me himself, afterward, it was a mistake."

"He knew," Paul said. "Liesl died because she was a half-Jew, and the sister of a half-Jew who once embarrassed him at a party. Either crime was grounds for execution."

"I'll never believe it." Georg shook his head firmly.

"No, of course you won't. I suppose Ernst was another bureaucratic mistake?"

"Ernst is a different case altogether. He knew too much. It would have been too big a risk to let him survive. In time of war, sacrifices have to be made. You order men into battle knowing they'll be killed. The loss has to be considered part of a larger strategy."

"Whose body was it in Leni's grave? Another sacrifice to a larger strategy?"

"She was a secretary at the chancellery. Her flat had been bombed. She had no place to live. I'd already moved Leni to the outskirts of Potsdam, and I wasn't using the house much myself. I told the secretary to take the guest room. As it happened, she was blond, and about Leni's age. When the battle for Berlin started, the house took a direct hit on the first night raid. Her body was badly burned. She had no family, and so I identified her as my wife and had her buried. That was in the final days when there was mass confusion and everyone was trying to get out."

"And then the grieving husband committed suicide and was buried beside her. A corpse keeps its identity forever unless they open the grave. Have you still got my number tattooed on your forearm?"

"Yes." Georg nodded.

"How did you get out of the country?"

"I wandered into a refugee camp in Austria. For nearly a month, I'd been on a fast. Water and black bread. I went in half starved with a blue tattoo on my arm. I had no trouble answering questions. The authorities verified that I was Paul Krenek from Mauthausen and issued me identity papers. After that, it was simple to obtain a border permit to cross from Austria into Switzerland. Leni was waiting for me in Geneva. My passport had your name on it. We flew to South America. Fritz wanted me in Manaus. Physicians were in short supply, and not many questions were asked about your background if you happened to speak with a German accent."

"Do you always do what Fritz tells you?"

Georg pulled off his glasses and drew a handkerchief from his pocket.

"You never understood Fritz," he said, wiping the lenses. "You always disliked him."

"I understood him," Paul said contemptuously.

"No," Georg insisted. "You never had any sense of what he stood for. The simple truth is that we were ahead of the world in biogenic research by a quarter of a century. Germany could have engineered a new society by humanely eliminating the infirm and unfit and by controlling the reproduction of the species. Given time, that society might have triumphed over sickness and disease and human suffering. That, truly, is what it was about. The search for perfection. The victors in a war have the advantage of being able to point out only the evil nature of the defeated side. The virtues never pass into history. That's what brought us here."

The scorn in Paul's smile went unsuppressed.

"Saving your ass is what brought you here."

"Believe what you want," Georg said. "But a place had to be found where the important work of the Reich could be preserved. Science. Engineering. Biomedical research. Most of the data were brought here before the war ended. The next step was to bring out the best minds, the men who had conceived and carried out the programs. In occupied Germany, many would have eventually faced prosecution. An escape apparatus had to be formed, and that was done straightaway. Quite a few of the survivors passed through here. Some were well known, and it was necessary to alter their features. Does it strike you as so absurd—the sacrifice and effort to hold on to a noble idea? Whether you can appreciate it or not, it was an exalted concept of humanity, ahead of its time. . . ."

From somewhere above, a voice called out to Georg. The small cabin plane was ready for takeoff, but clouds were building and the flying weather might not hold.

"Is that what you came to tell me?" Paul asked.

"I'm not sure why I came," Georg said. "Maybe it was to say I'm sorry that it had to turn out this way. Sorry about Ernst. And Liesl. Maybe I wanted you to have an explanation of things. As it turns out, we're all at the mercy of forces we can't always control. If we could, it might be a perfect world."

"Too bad it isn't," Paul said.

"Yes." Georg nodded sadly. "Too bad for all of us."

EIGHTEEN

After Georg had left, Paul heard the sky rumbling. The first drops of rain fell like grapeshot against the tin roof, and the cell darkened. A flash of lightning sent a loud crack of thunder, and the rain came in a steely downpour.

In a little while the storm passed to the east, leaving the dim remains of the afternoon in the cell. Paul heard the whining crank of the monoplane at the dock and the crackling of the propeller. He wondered what they would tell Leni. Probably that he had been shot trying to escape. Fritz could give his word that it was true.

He listened to the plane taxi to the end of the lake. Twice the engine revved at high speed, and then the pitch changed as the craft raced at full throttle across the water. But all at once the pilot aborted his takeoff, cutting power before the ship was airborne. Paul could hear it taxiing back to the dock.

At dusk a guard brought a tin of rice and a ration of water. The rice was cold and congealed, and Paul ate the starchy clumps with his fingers and sipped the water.

As darkness fastened itself to the cell, he stretched out on the floor. He felt dead inside, and so the prospect of death held no fear for him. A bullet would only formalize the contractual arrangement. Fatigue pulled at his nerves, and he closed his eyes.

Asleep, he dreamed of Alina. They were on the beach again at Leblon. Hand in hand they walked beside the silver crush of waves under the starry darkness. Later, they stopped to kiss, only now they were both nude, their clinging bodies reflected in the wet gleam of sand that held the sheen of spent waves. They broke apart and Paul took her wrist, pulling her toward the surf. *No*, Alina cried over and over in the dream, *I cannot swim*. She tried to twist from his grip, but he drew her out into the foaming shallows. *I won't let anything happen to you*, he told her.

All at once they were in deep water beyond the breakers in the carved glitter of moonlight, and it was not Alina with him but Leni. She slipped her arms around his neck, and her laughing mouth on his was mocking and passionate at the same time. Suddenly she broke away and dove, and he saw the streaking glimmer of her arms and legs below him in the dark where unquenched stars, like incendiaries, burned away the blackness. He plunged down after her, but when he overtook her and snatched an ankle it was Alina who twisted toward him in panic, her mouth open in a silent scream, and then her terrified pupils rolled upward under her lids. A rip current swept her out of reach, and when he looked again there was no sign of her, only the trembling marine darkness below the star embers.

Now, in the dream, it was morning, and he was standing in the calm shallows of a tidal pool and staring down at her drowned form wreathed in seaweed. Fish had pecked out her eyes, and the hair floated in the water about her dead face. He glanced up the strand and caught sight of Georg and von Stroelin watching impassively from a distant hill in the stunning glare of cold sunlight. When he gazed down once more at Alina he saw that the blind sockets were fixed on him in an accusatory stare as if to say: *You are responsible. . . .*

The scream of a jaguar close to the camp wrenched Paul from the dream. He jerked up on an elbow and lay listening to the silences of the night. The big cat did not cry out again. Perhaps he had made his kill. Except for the occasional chatter of nocturnal monkeys, the quiet remained unbroken. Paul lay back on the stone floor, one hand behind his head. The dream had taken him outside the narrow obsession of his own hatred to a place in his mind where it was still possible to feel regret. The larger blame for Alina's death would always be his, just as the dream had made it out to be. The subconscious was a judiciary for guilt, not innocence, and in the prosecutions of sleep the evidence would be presented over and over. *You are responsible. . . .*

Much later, a shout woke him. He wasn't sure of its direction. The Amazon night was at its darkest. He strained to make out the luminous hands of his watch. A bit after three-thirty. . . .

More far-off cries answered the first one. They came from the lakefront. The thin seam of night below the eaves of the tin roof had an orange glow of movement. There was a sound overhead on the catwalk, and a figure paused above his cage. Leni's white face peered down in the dark above the crosshatched bars.

"Paul," she called out softly.

"Down here," he said, the leg chain scraping against the concrete as he rose from the shadows.

Moments later the locking bolt rattled and the door swung open. She slipped close to him, pressing a key into his hand.

"Use this on the shackle."

While he groped to fit the key into the padlock, he asked, "Why are they shouting?"

"I set a fire in the warehouse near the petrol stores. Hurry, you've only got a few minutes!"

"What about the guard?"

"Everyone's at the lake. Can't you hurry?"

The padlock snapped free, and he opened the shackle on its hinge.

Leni gripped his hand, and they climbed the stairs to the catwalk. Outside the long shed Paul glanced toward the warehouse. Yellow flames slid straight up into the darkness, lighting the lake and jungle.

Leni said, "Go that way," and pointed to the rain forest, black on the low ridge against the sky. "Once you get over that hill, there are dozens of foot trails into the jungle. Most of them run to the west for five or six kilometers before they circle back here. When the sun comes up, be sure you're moving away from it. If you keep to the west, you'll strike the Rio Negro. Take this with you. It's a land compass. You'll need it once you get off the trails." She slipped the closed case into his shirt pocket, then stooped down in the shadows near the door. "You'll need this, too," she said, and he saw the flash of a machete blade in the dark as she straightened.

"What about you?"

"That's my concern, not yours."

He gazed again at the flames on the night sky and said, "They're not above killing a woman for something like this."

"What difference would it make?" she asked tiredly. "Just go, will you?"

Paul started off, but it was no good. A psychological barrier came down like an invisible wall, shutting him into his own contradictions. He went slowly back. One woman dead in his conscience was enough.

"You're coming," he said, "or I don't go. You decide."

"Stop talking like a fool," she cried.

"We're wasting time."

"Oh, God. . . ." Her voice broke under the strain.

A fiery bubble swelled above the warehouse as the petrol stores exploded, and the concussion from the blast shook the night. Debris shot skyward, smoke from the flaming gouts trailing down in streamers like a
pyrotechnic display.

"Come on." Paul gripped her wrist. "You can't stay behind now."

They worked their way uphill through the trees, halting only once to
get their breath. Below, the warehouse and pier were ablaze on the water.

"They were going to interrogate you after Georg and I left," Leni said.
"Then they would have executed you."

"Why didn't you fly out?"

"An oil line broke. By the time repairs were made, it was too dark. We
would have flown out today." She gazed down at the burning dock, where
the running figures were tiny as ants. "They'll be after us at daybreak."

"That gives us about an hour."

They went over the low ridge and picked their way down the other
side, and Paul had a glimpse of the barracks, the tin roofs squatting in formation off to the left. Leni pointed down to a bare track in the scrub.

"There's one of the foot trails."

"I see it."

The *estrada* was overgrown and not easy to follow in the dark, and by
daybreak they had gone no more than two kilometers from the camp.
Now, as the first streaks of light impaled the umbrella of the rain forest,
Paul picked up the pace. For the next hour they made good time along the
path. Then Leni began to lag, and they stopped to rest, sitting a little
apart from each other on the ground strewn with the dead leaves of other
seasons.

"Last night Fritz told me about your wife," Leni said, her head bent.

"Did he tell you what happened to her?"

"That, too." She nodded, tracing the veined pattern of a decaying leaf
with her finger. "Only, he didn't believe you were married. He doesn't
think the two of you came here on your own. He's worried you might be
connected with the Allied commission tracking war criminals for prosecution."

"He *should* worry," Paul said.

"And the woman." She raised her head. "Were you married to her?"

He did not answer at once. Leni's face, in the morning light, was
stripped bare and defenseless. The skin lacked the honey sheen of its
youth, the golden gleam had faded from the cropped hair, and sadness had
been applied to the features like a wrong cosmetic that left the properties
of cynicism and bitterness unconcealed.

"We were married in Zurich," he said. "I loved her."

An emotion clouded her stare and went suddenly to pieces in a glaze of antagonistic tears.

"Then why did you bring her here?" she asked. "If you'd stayed in Zurich she wouldn't be dead. You're to blame!"

"Maybe I am," he said, and he could remember the look of shadowy betrayal in the drowned face in his dream.

"Why couldn't you just have gone on with your life after the war and let go of the past," she asked, "like everyone else?"

"Did they tell you how Liesl was murdered? She died in convulsions after an injection of iodine. In the end she was just a piece of data that passed across von Stroelin's desk. And Ernst. Did they tell you about him?"

"Stop." Leni pressed her hands to her ears. "I don't want to hear about it."

"Nobody wants to hear about it," Paul said. "You never loved Georg. Why did you stay with him?"

"I suppose it had to do with pity. Sometimes it's a more complex emotion than love. Pity has the virtue of being unselfish. Georg was alone, running for his life. I thought mine was over. It *was* over—the day he told me you were dead. Nothing mattered after that, except to kill the pain. Shall I tell you what I discovered about that kind of pain? You can mask it with alcohol and pills and sexual partners, but you can never kill it altogether, and the underlying therapeutic plan is self-destruction."

A curiosity nagged at Paul. It might as well have been a demon in possession. Only a question would exorcise it.

"Have you slept with von Stroelin?" he asked.

Beneath the film of tears, the edge of her mouth twisted down in an embittered smile that contained, beyond its stark unhappiness, some angry pleasure at the possibility of inflicting pain.

"Would it bother you?"

"What does that have to do with it?"

"I've slept with a lot of men," she said finally. "Including you. What do you want me to do? Make comparisons?"

They both heard the monoplane. It droned suddenly off the silence, and Paul sprang forward, pulling Leni with him to deeper cover. Distance took the sound, but then it came back, louder than before, and he caught sight of the craft banking low over the trees, wings canted into the sun. The pilot was circling to the north, flying a concentric search pattern over the stream Paul had followed in to the lake.

Leni asked, "Do you think he saw us?"

"No," Paul said. "But we'd better keep on the move. They can't be far behind us."

By midmorning they were well beyond the outer loop of the *estrada* and, with the lensatic compass, working their way west through the rain forest that sweltered beneath its sun-drenched canopy. The steamy heat pressed against them, and the green filtrations of light from the thatch did not reach down to the tangled gloom of the forest floor where the cries of birds and screech of monkeys fell like echoes in a chamber.

Later, they stopped to rest in a patch of *cipo de agua*, and Paul used the machete to cut one of the water-filled vines, holding it for Leni to drink. She closed her eyes wearily, and some of the water spilled down from her mouth and glistened on the skin above the cleavage of her breasts. He chopped through a second vine and held the severed coil so that the water trickled into his mouth. But all at once he clamped off the flow, turning his head sharply.

"Did you hear it?"

"What?" Leni frowned.

After a moment, the far-off barking of dogs drifted across the stillness.

"How many dogs did they keep at the lake?" Paul asked.

"Two, I think. They used them to track Indians who had run off."

"If we go due north we should strike water. It might throw them off the scent."

Paul opened the lid of the compass, set an azimuth, and for the next hour they moved quickly in the direction of the arrow on the magnetic dial. At last he spotted the first water marks on the trunks of the trees. The rings on the smooth bark were a foot off the ground. They rose gradually until they were over Paul's head. At the height of the wet season the whole region would lie underwater for several months. The trees were straight and smooth, like piles, with no lower branches. Ahead, javelin rays of sun fell through the thinning canopy of rain forest and picked up the shine of the mangrove swamp that Paul had crossed on the way in to the lake.

A spoonbill took flight as they splashed into the backwater, and a pair of white herons shied away on stilt legs. Paul gripped Leni's hand, and for another hour they slogged through the ankle-deep shallows among the twisted roots of mangroves and swamp flowers, the black surface gleaming and undisturbed except for the slithering thrust of an occasional snake, or the hooded stare of a jacaré half submerged like a dead log, and once they startled two swamp deer, which bounded off.

By midafternoon they had reached the tip of the swamp, clogged with hyacinth and floating lily pads and fed by the sluggish channel of the

stream. They climbed into the shady dappling above the bank and emptied the water from their shoes. Paul peeled off his wet socks, wrung them
dry, and put them on again.

"I know where we are now. With a bit of luck, we'll strike the Indian
village before dark. We can get a dugout there and make it downriver
tonight."

"Do you think they're still behind us?"

"If we've lost them, it won't be for long. We'd better keep moving."

At four o'clock they were halfway up the ridge when they heard the dogs
again. The leafy scrub of the hillside hid the lower terrain from view. Paul
picked a tree caught fast in liana vine, got a foothold in the climbing
plant, and pulled himself up to a break in the thatch.

Beyond the gap in the leaves lay the fork of the stream, its rivulet-thin
branches swinging wide from each other around the tract of rain forest.

On the sandy strip where Paul and Nyashu had refloated the canoe and
dugout, six figures were grouped. Two dogs on leashes barked excitedly.
Georg's bulky shape was easy to pick out, as was von Stroelin's, stocky and
erect, legs braced apart in a cocky stance. Above the flared trousers a car-
tridge belt with pistol and holster was looped about his waist. The other
men carried carbines.

The dogs strained to cross the narrows, and one of the handlers pointed to the bramble on the opposite bank. Paul knew they had spotted the
torn strip from Leni's blouse. He had impaled it carefully on a thorn, then
laid down a false trail for half a kilometer along the outer fork before
backtracking in the water. Afterward, they had waded the shallows of the
lower branch that ran close in to the ridge.

Now, as Paul watched the distant figures, they looked to be in a discussion. Finally the group divided. Three of them crossed the stream with
one of the dogs. Von Stroelin, Georg, and the remaining dog handler
moved in the direction of the ridge. Paul dropped back to the ground.

"What did you see?"

"Three of them. Coming this way."

"I don't think I can make it to the top." Leni gazed at the steep ascent
still above them in the trees.

"You can," he snapped.

They struggled higher, breathing hard, and Paul could feel his own legs
starting to cramp from the climb. Once, Leni cried out softly as a foothold
gave way and she slid downward, clutching at the twisted foliage. Paul
clamped a hand over her wrist and dragged her uphill. The ridge gave

itself up grudgingly, meter by meter, but finally he could feel the resistance go out of it.

At the top, Leni sank to her knees, and Paul leaned against a tree. A warm breeze blew from the west, bringing an odor of damp, rotting vegetation on its humid currents. A line of thunderclouds, boiling into the stratosphere, closed off the sky, and a black scrim of rain beneath the flat undersides obscured the jungle. Dagger thrusts of lightning flashed down, and the crackling of thunder raced toward the ridge.

Before they reached the foot of the slope, the forest had lost its light, and the first swollen raindrops spattered in the leaves. A blast of wind tore twigs and debris from the thatch. Now the artillery boom of thunder was directly overhead, and the downpour of rain was sudden and savage.

"We can't get anywhere in this," Leni cried.

"Over there." Paul pointed the machete at a hollow in the talon-shaped root of a dead tree that still towered aloft in the grip of liana vines. He snatched her hand, and they fled to its shelter.

For a quarter of an hour the storm raged. Beyond the cramped depression where they huddled, the sky was full of silver electric, and the steel flash of rain hid the jungle. Leni's blouse was drenched, her skin wetly glistening, and she was curled across Paul, her arms around his neck. He could feel the beat of her heart against his chest, and the tip of her breast was darkly indented into the damp fabric of her blouse. The contours of her body were more softly rounded than he remembered, the curves overripe in their maturity. All at once she lifted her head from the hollow of his shoulder, the fingers of one hand slid down to rest grazingly against his cheek, and she pressed her lips warmly and possessively against his mouth. He felt the blood flow of arousal, but his lips remained coldly rigid and unresponsive to hers, his body stiffly impassive in its sexual resistance. Her mouth slid away from his, and the hurt in her stare was bathed in a film of tears, though her smile was fatalistic in some calm dismissal of emotion.

"Is that really how it is?" she murmured. "Does it just come down to nothing?"

"Everything comes down to nothing," he said.

"Then what's the point of anything?"

"There isn't any point," Paul said.

As suddenly as it had struck, the cloudburst ended. The torrent of rain slackened and stopped as if a hand had closed a valve. The batteries overhead had been silenced as the storm retreated over the ridge, dragging the torn remnants of cloud down the sky like an army in rout.

They left the hollow shrinking out of view behind them. A little light spilled back into the forest, casting a sparkle over the beads of rain cling-ing to leaves and flowers, and the spiderwebs, anchored across space, looked to be diamond studded. But the glow did not last, the afternoon was too far gone, and the spent brilliance faded quickly underfoot as they fled across it. What dim light remained in the moving thatch overhead looked as if it had been scissored to bits and flung into the leaves, and soon it, too, melted away. Several times Paul had to swing the machete to chop a path through the snarl of vines blocking their way, and once Leni dropped to her knees and murmured, "You'll have to go on without me."

The tears streaking her face came now from the accumulation of exhaustion in her nerves, and her whole body was shaking from it. Paul could feel the same murderous fatigue in his own corded muscles, which were slowly giving out against the jungle, but the sight of Leni surrender-ing to it sent some anger-laced adrenaline into his blood.

"No," he said, dragging her once more to her feet and not letting go. "It's not much farther. You can do it."

All at once, they both heard the faint barking of the dog, muted by dis-tance, but still unmistakable.

"Come on!" he insisted.

In the deepening gloom, the stream was only an occasional black glint of water flashing past them in the trees. He could hear Leni's sobbing intakes of breath beside him, and his own lungs burned, as if they were drawing on empty cylinders of oxygen.

At last, the thatched huts of the village slid into view, dark and still against the incinerations of twilight. The intermittent barking sounded closer than it had been, and he was sure the men in pursuit could not be far behind. There was no sign of Nyashu or the old man.

"Hurry!" Paul had Leni's hand once more. They ran downhill among the *tapiris* to the bank where Blackmore had tied up beside the dugouts. The black water gleamed beyond the saplings, but there were no boats. The shock slammed through Paul and left him sick in the pit of his stom-ach. The barking of the dog was steady now, and he could hear the shouts of the men from the jungle on the far side of the village.

NINETEEN

Paul snatched Leni's hand and bolted uphill to the swell of jungled high ground flanking the village. They ducked low through the snarl of vines and leafy vegetation, and he groped for the footholds cut into the tall tree that had served as a lookout station for the Yanomamö.

The cluster of thatched huts fell away as he climbed, and there was a clear view of the jungle on the far side of the village, like a deserted film set. But now three figures came onto it, ready to play out their roles—von Stroelin, Georg, and the armed handler, who was down on one knee quieting the dog. They might have been actors at a script conference, except that the action was unscripted. The story lacked the architecture of an ending, or, for that matter, a beginning, unless a remark at a party could serve as one, or a bloodied nose in a schoolyard.

Von Stroelin's outstretched arm swept across a wide arc like that of a field commander imparting a strategy to his staff. Georg nodded and started downhill toward the stream. He was gripping the carbine with both hands like a recruit in training, his breasts jiggling as he moved at a jog trot. The man controlling the dog carried his carbine in one hand by the small of the stock, the leash taut in his other fist as the animal strained at its work collar. Paul watched them move into the village and disappear into a hut.

Von Stroelin had his pistol out and was striding to the upper edge of the settlement. He and Georg would take up static positions on the perimeter to block any escape while the man with the tracking dog went from hut to hut. Already the tactic was clear to Paul, and he let go of the vines and dropped quietly back to the ground.

"Up you go," he whispered to Leni. "All the way into the thatch, and don't move."

"What can you do against rifles?" she protested.

But Paul was already slipping away through the plunging streamers of vine and leaf. The jungle scrub broke off suddenly, leaving a gap of open ground floating across the dusk in front of him. Crouching, he glanced both ways, then sprinted across it, his body bent forward at the waist, and flattened himself against the nearest *tapiri*. It was the shaman's hut, and he crept to the opening in the palm thatch and ducked inside. The dangling charms confronted him like a curse alchemized into the dull shine of their own blunted surfaces. At once his nerves absorbed the shock of a figure asleep on a pallet beyond them. He stole across in the dark and peered down into the wrinkled face of the old Indian and saw that he was not asleep at all, but dead. His flesh felt cold and hard, the limbs had stiffened, and when Paul tried to place an arm of the corpse across its chest, a green gorge erupted from the side of the mouth. On the ground above the dead man's head, curare darts lay in some cryptic arrangement of poison-tipped defense against evil spirits. Paul wondered if Nyashu were nearby. He lifted two barbs from the pattern and slipped outside.

The shadows of evening were digesting the village. He dropped to the ground, crawling past a bamboo pen for small animals, and once more bolted across the ring of open terrain to the cover of jungle scrub.

He was sure that von Stroelin must be close, and he moved guardedly in the lead-colored leaves where the first darkness had been poured, touching the ground soundlessly with his toe and gingerly placing the weight of his foot until the heel made contact. Each dart was about ten inches in length, the shafts smooth, the tips sharply honed, and Paul gripped them carefully behind the tar-coated points as he might have gripped a venomous snake. The power of death concentrated there went all the way up his arm and shoulder into his head, where, now, only von Stroelin lived.

Then Paul saw the other man. He was suddenly just there, telescoped in the leaves, as if by an act of teleportation. The figure merged into the mental image that Paul carried, and for a moment they were as alike as twins. But then the impostor that was only a surrogate of hate in Paul's mind ceased to exist, and the survivor who was real remained, his pistol dangling at arm's length in the stance of a duelist at thirty paces. He was staring directly at Paul without seeing him in the slumping leaves, and then he turned his attention again toward the huts.

Paul sank slowly to his knees and stretched forward onto his hands. He inched through the coiled undergrowth, freezing instinctively in much the way that a stalking cat freezes with the slitted excitement of a kill buried in the yellow glare of its eyes. Von Stroelin was about fifteen feet beyond the scrub, below and to Paul's right. Paul opened his fingers and let one of the darts out of his grasp. He could see the gleam of perspiration on the back of von Stroelin's neck, and the damp saturation of sweat through the collar and at the small of his back where the shirt was plastered to his flesh. All the pleasure of homicide was backed up in Paul's nerves and swollen muscles, purpose and instinct nocked together in a taut and joyous breadth of feeling that was already balanced on an instant of release.

Suddenly von Stroelin moved away. The gap of open ground between them widened at the same time in Paul's nerves. The advantage of surprise went to pieces in his head, and the deprivation was a gorge of sour retreat in the hollow of his stomach behind the knotted muscles, and he could taste the bile of failure in his mouth. He swallowed it back and fought to keep his concentration from coming apart.

The universe lay outside the sphere of concentration, but now it was a clock of melting time, the hands and numbers part of a surreal eternity filled with the probabilities of failure and lost opportunity. The man and tracking dog making their search of the *tapiris* might well materialize on any of the moments wasting themselves in Paul's nerves, and then an attack would be impossible to mount.

But the flow of anxious uncertainty shut down once more as von Stroelin began to stroll back toward the rise of scrub. The leaves drifted blackly across his figure, which swelled to size in the recesses until it was no more than a dozen feet below Paul and positioned sideways, the face heavy as an image minted in relief on copper and impassive in its profile of arrested motion, as if it were alert to some unseen danger and puzzled by it. He had only to raise his head slightly to be staring directly at Paul on the fault line between opportunity and discovery where the outer leaves burst against their own massed gloom.

Somewhere in the village the dog began to bark. Von Stroelin jerked his head in the direction of the sound. Paul's body ached from tension held too long, the flexed muscles feeding on spent adrenaline and the racing molecules of excitement in the blood. He pushed up and drove hard with both feet in a flying rush at von Stroelin, who whirled and fired.

Paul's awareness was drawn down into a corner of his mind where there was nothing except the crashing impact of bodies, the physics of momentum and muscle. The two men were locked together, twirling on the ground like a pair of dancers gone mad in a reel that had Paul's left hand clamped over von Stroelin's right wrist, holding the pistol out at arm's length. Von Stroelin heaved upward, and the surge of power through the stocky frame nearly broke Paul's grip on the handgun. Instead, Paul gave up his leverage, and in the concession of that lost advantage, still locked together, they rolled back the other way until Paul tightened the pressure of his legs, scissored around the heavy thighs. Von Stroelin fought to kick free, and his left hand flew to Paul's eyes, trying to gouge them from the sockets. Paul twisted his face away from the attack, and the fingers clawed downward and fastened into his throat, closing off the windpipe. All the while he could feel the straining force in the other man coming together with the same force in himself so that the savage intakes of breath were as one, and the blood beating through the blocked chambers of the heart flowed out of a common source, as if mortality had overshadowed them both and could not make a choice. Then Paul's fingers, squeezing the dart, rammed the tip into the side of von Stroelin's neck.

The shock jolted all the way through the other man, and the shaft in Paul's grip acted like a conduit through which he could feel the short circuit of systems wired into the stunned nerves at the point of the barb. Von Stroelin's eyes widened in some delayed reflex of alarm, and even the shout of pained surprise and rage seemed to be exploited and slowed by a caprice of distorted time. The juice came back on, and he thrashed convulsively in a final frantic effort to throw Paul off, and then the resistance melted out of him. Paul could feel the systems of struggle shutting down, one by one, against the mortal overload at the tiny toxic point of the dart. The hand clamped into his windpipe no longer stemmed the flow of oxygen into his lungs. The fingers had no pressure. Now they dropped away of their own weight.

Paul eased back. A vein stood out in von Stroelin's neck. It might have been corded into the flesh as part of a second outcry, this one aborted before sound could be produced, and it only throbbed slowly where the dart was embedded in a trickle of bright blood. His eyes were wide, the stare fixed as if in astonishment at Death's trickery. His mouth opened twice, but only a whimper came from it.

The dog, Paul thought, had been barking before the pistol shot, and after it, too. But the sound had gone suddenly dead, and the disconnection had drifted off like a piece of puzzling silence absorbed into the night, which was now utterly still.

Paul took the pistol from the unresisting hand that had no power now over the trigger curving in its half smile against the whorled ridges of the index finger, as if the trigger itself were mocking its master. He said softly, "Do you know about curare, Fritz? It's not as quick as gas, or a syringe of iodine, but they tell me you can feel death crawling through you right up until the end. I hope you enjoy each other."

Already, von Stroelin's eyelids were starting to droop. Only the panic remained alive on the unblinking stare.

Paul left him on the ground and slipped into the village, the huts gliding about him in the darkness. Halfway downhill he came upon the handler and dog, sprawled in the open. The animal looked to be dead, lying on its side, tongue out, forelegs and hindquarters crossed in a relaxed attitude of pursuit.

The handler was alive, curled in a fetal posture with his knees drawn up. One hand gripped the shaft of a dart extruding from his abdomen, but that was as far as he had got in pulling it out. Paul knelt over him and saw that the facial muscles were wholly limp, the lids half shut over the dull stare.

He heard a rustle of fronds and turned his head sharply. In the opening of the nearest *tapiri* stood Nyashu. The Indian was grasping his long blowgun, the light, hollow tube taller than himself, the mouthpiece fused to the weapon by clay and snail nacre, and the plaited quiver of darts hung at his side from a thong.

From the stream, Georg called out twice to the handler. When there was no response, he called out Fritz's name. Paul moved into the shadow spilling off the *tapiri* and waited, the cocked pistol a comfortable weight in his hand, as if the solids of blued steel were eager to execute his will in this last uncollected debt.

The second time Georg shouted for Fritz, he was close to the *tapiri*, and Paul caught sight of the pear-shaped figure, striding uphill, still gripping the carbine tightly like an overgrown boy at his first hunt. He stayed in the open, as if afraid of the shadows, or perhaps, ultimately, he was simply confident that Fritz would survive and let nothing happen to him.

At the sight of the handler on the ground, Georg froze in his tracks and stared. Fright immobilized him as effectively as a curare dart. Paul stepped out of the shadows into the other man's line of vision so that Georg had only to raise his head slightly to confront him across a dozen meters of open ground where the years stretched down to a moment. The muzzle of the carbine pointed down and to the left. It could be swung easily into line and fired from the hip.

Paul said, "If you're going to use that, do it now. Just remember that I was always better than you with guns. If you don't want to try, then throw it down."

Georg hesitated, and some agony of indecision worked across his face and spilled all the way through him down into his hands and hardened like concrete. The stone-heavy fingers could neither raise the carbine nor let go of it.

"Either use it or throw it down," Paul said quietly. "You decide."

Something cracked in Georg, and the tiny dislocation of resolve was no more than a movement in his shoulders like a shrug of defeat. The carbine dropped at his feet as his fingers opened stiffly and remained opened as if posing a question.

The two men gazed at each other across the corruption of friendship, which was all that was left.

"Turn around," Paul said.

Georg's stare was full of questioning despair. But he obeyed wordlessly.

"I want you to know how it felt," Paul said, "that morning at the trench when you stood on the hill and watched."

Georg said nothing. But all at once his fatalistic acceptance broke, like a last psychological defense against hysteria, and the seismic tremor from its collapse went into his shoulders, wrenching them hard. A loud sob came out of him from some epicenter of dread, and he sank to his knees, not unlike the prisoner with the stink of incontinence in his striped pajamas who had been executed next to Paul at the trench.

"Paul." Leni's voice came out of the dark between the huts to his left.

Paul's face was iron-hard in the dusk, as if the expression on it would last forever, and the cold unsatisfied rage behind the uncompromising purpose fixed into the features was locked into the memory of the small unmarked grave in the glade outside the hospital grounds at Eglfing-Haar.

Leni had both hands on his arm. She did not speak, but the sad plea in her stare seemed to say, "You owe me a life. Let it be his."

The stifled sobs from the kneeling figure were being offered like a ransom. In the currency of pity, given the deflations of cowardice, it was still an exorbitant bribe. How many years, Paul thought, lay between the muzzle of the pistol and the boy who had sat in a corner of the schoolyard and wept with both hands over his face? Contempt could be measured in caliber size, pounds of chamber pressure, and the feet per second of muzzle velocity, but the ballistics of pity could not be reduced so simply to a set of statistics. Georg, he saw suddenly, was beyond both. Like the vision of the Third Reich, he could neither be pitied nor held in contempt.

Paul said, "Don't worry, I won't shoot him in the back of the head. That would be too quick. It would be like a mercy killing. No, I want him to live with the pain of his own fear. Other men are going to be hunting him. I want him to be on the run for the rest of his life. I want him to be afraid every time he goes to sleep."

The soft snick of metal against bare metal as Paul uncocked the pistol caused Georg to flinch slightly, as if his nerves had been anticipating the impact of a bullet and could not adjust. Paul stuffed the handgun into his waistband. He picked up the carbine, ejected the magazine from the receiver, and jacked the bolt to the rear, extracting the chambered round. Then, from behind, he tossed the weapon onto the ground in front of Georg, who was still kneeling.

"Don't turn around," Paul said. "Just pick that up and start walking out of here. If you try to come back, I'll let the boy kill you. It's an ugly death. Slow. You wouldn't have the patience for it."

Georg reached for the carbine and got shakily to his feet. For a moment, head bowed, he seemed unwilling to move. Then he stumbled downhill toward the stream, the shadows devouring all but the dark lurch of his head and shoulders.

Paul tramped back uphill, and Leni followed him. Nyashu trailed in the dark off to the left. At the sight of von Stroelin, Leni's eyes widened. Paul dropped to one knee and looked down at the other man.

The dart still dangled from von Stroelin's neck, like a parasite feeding on the vein. His lids were now half shut over the panic circumscribed into his fixed gaze, and a trickle of saliva had run down from the slack mouth where the paralyzed lips and tongue prevented swallowing. The curled fingers of one hand twitched weakly, as if they were the last part of him capable of begging help or expressing terror. It would only be a few minutes, Paul thought, before the poison reached the chest and diaphragm, and then the suffocating weight would descend in silence on the lungs in a last agonizing paroxysm.

From somewhere on the stream, a rifle shot cracked, its echo hammering into the forest. Paul rose, frowning. He glanced at Leni. But the sound, already absorbed on the darkness, needed no confirmation. This time it lacked the artifice of rocks in a coffin. The loss of Leni was real, and Georg had carried it as far as the stream.

"I thought you took the bullets from him," she sobbed.

"He wasn't wearing a bandolier." Paul shook his head. "He must have had extra rounds in his pocket."

"Oh, Paul . . ." she said quietly, and slowly buried her face in her hands. "*Why?*"

"Ask the dead that question," Paul said. "But don't be surprised if they can't hear you."

One brass-jacketed shell could serve as an accomplice to escape, an end to pain, an apology for evil, a compensation for cowardice. Death was endlessly cheap in its versatility.

Paul gazed down once more at von Stroelin. Three men were dead. He had thought his hate would go away. The odd thing was that it was still there. Now he realized it would always be there, internalized, beyond reach. Hate was the rich endowment of all survivors.

TWENTY

On a blue evening a little less than a fortnight later, Paul stood with Major Ward on the terrace of the villa that served as a residence for the U.S. consul in Belém. The intelligence officer and one of his subordinates had flown in from Europe to conduct personally the debriefings for Paul and Leni, which had now spanned three days. In the gray double-breasted suit with its wide, pointed lapels, the American had the look of an old-time Chicago mobster, lacking only a Tommy gun. Now he relaxed the tense, uneven planes of his face with a cigarette and said, "We've finished with her. I hope to God we got everything, and I hope to God everything we got was true. If it is, then we've struck a gold vein, pure and simple. All we have to do is mine it."

"Gold veins run out." Paul shrugged.

"So does luck," Major Ward replied. "She gave us some important names. Bormann, for one. We thought he might have got through Russian lines after he left Hitler's bunker, but no one was ever sure. Now it seems likely he may have got to Manaus for a new face. Nose broadened. Lips everted. Chin rebuilt. That would be quite a cosmetic change from his photographs."

"When I saw him he still had quite a lot of swelling and bruises. It's hard to say what he'll look like when the surgery heals. Von Stroelin was an artist, too. He created some important fakes."

"That's the one we'd most like to recover," the American said.

Below, the tiled roofs of the town sank across the equatorial dusk drowsing on the sky where the brown sea-mouth of the Amazon emptied onto the horizon. The lit docks gave up the clutter of ships and cranes like toys put away for the night, and street lamps drew a glow of faded pastel colors from the galleries and squares steeped in the descending darkness and the dry investitures of decay.

"Bormann." Paul smiled. "I almost killed him for you. I would have. He was in the way."

"And you almost got killed yourself," Major Ward said. "You should never have gone in there alone. What it comes down to is that you disobeyed orders. We had an understanding. ODESSA was supposed to be the target, not just the three men you killed. You broke your word."

"You got a piece of ODESSA," Paul said. "A big piece. It didn't cost you anything. Don't forget who picked up the check—for both of us."

"I'm sorry." Major Ward nodded. "She was a courageous lady. I had great admiration for her."

"So did I. In the end, it's not enough."

"It's all there is," Major Ward said.

They were quiet, watching the city clothe itself in the night as a long streamer of smoke from the officer's cigarette took the hushed stillness across the horizon like a sorcerer's trick.

"Frau Viertel asked to go back to Germany," he said. "I promised to help her."

"Recruit her, you mean?" Paul asked.

"The information she gave us was voluntary. No rewards were attached to it. But we owe her something. We can see she gets proper security and a decent means of support."

Paul wondered what inventory of jobs would be open to informers. Perhaps serving drinks at one of the American officers' clubs. But it wasn't his concern.

"By the way," Major Ward added, "she's in the garden. She wanted to talk to you. You can see her now, if you like."

They had been separated for the full three days of the debriefing sessions, and the week preceding their arrival in Belém was already fading like parts of a dream in which the flight from menacing forces seems never to end. It had begun in a dugout that had carried them downstream by night to Blackmore's shack, and the trapper had got them aboard a small *gaiola* bound downriver for Santarém. There, it had taken Paul two days to secure passage to Belém, and they had stayed out of sight in a seedy hotel with mold-flecked walls on the Avenida Adriano Pimental off the quay. The first night in the room's humid darkness Leni had come naked to his bed while he lay awake and murmured, "I can't sleep. I'm afraid. . . ."

But the tenseness in her body had nothing to do with fear, and he had felt the weight of her breasts, damp with perspiration, press heavily against his chest as she lay down next to him. There was a looseness of flesh now at her belly which before had been concave and hard, and her thighs were more rounded in their contours, though still solid in the long, harmonious lines that had a skier's strength shaped into them. His hand ran upward to the swell of the gluteus muscle, and in the hot room the rank heat of her desire came to him even before his two extended fingers slid deep into the love slick of that sexual estuary welling toward them.

Then, with no pretense of tenderness or love, he took her. The intercourse was savage and swift, an act of rage and cruel possession, as if she were the neutral object on which he could discharge all the accumulated hate and unsatisfied fury—hatred for Georg—hatred for himself—hatred for all. His mouth ground down on hers carnally, and the hardness of him that was in her drove against the wet flood of her own love like a reprisal of blows. Some dark contradiction of pleasure and pain rose in the rapture of an explosive climax that tore sobs from her throat even before the seed came loose in warm flowing shame from his anger, and the spent antagonisms of cold lust settled in him.

But he had wanted that unbearable pleasure to be wrenched from her, if only to make the retaliation complete, to put the hurt and humiliation beyond reach in that sexual recess he had touched, but which remained untouched by others.

And now she understood the complexities of it, or at least the sexual flash point of his rage. Understanding came like the sensations of withdrawal as she lay beside him, her body absolutely still, the shine of tears on her cheeks, unwilling to let her pain break the silence.

Waking in the morning, he had found her dressed, sitting in an attitude of chaste sorrow at the window where the grimy pane, open at a slant, gave back her reflection—the face fuller now above the broad unpainted mouth, the years carelessly flung across it in small uncaring lines of dissipation that were the prescriptions for sadness.

"I'm not pretty anymore," she said to the image, then turned her head slightly and gave Paul an indifferent smile. "Am I?"

Now, in the walled garden of the consulate, Paul found her standing in the windblown shadows of a large mango tree. An ascending moon struck half a dozen orchids clustered in a lower juncture of the tree and cast their burning whiteness on Leni's skin.

"Why are you going back to Berlin?" he asked. "It's nothing but rubble and people grubbing for food."

"Maybe I just want to close the circle," she replied.

"On what?"

"Something you wouldn't understand."

"You're right," Paul said. "I don't trust explanations anymore about life."

After a moment, Leni folded her arms and asked, "What about you? Don't you have any plans?"

"I've got some affairs to settle in Munich," he said.

"Your wife's?"

Paul nodded.

"And then what?" Leni pressed him.

"A trip to Auschwitz if it can be arranged."

"Auschwitz?" She gave him a startled look. "What on earth for?"

"To visit my brother's grave and say Kaddish for him."

"But there is no grave," she protested gently.

"His ashes are his grave."

"You never practiced the religion."

"Ernst did," Paul said. "Maybe I will."

The warm respirations of night air off the river drifted across the walled court, and the white flowers shivered at the touch.

"Oh, Paul," Leni said in a flat tone that lacked even the sad nuance of despair so that the words themselves were dead and hopeless. "Why couldn't it have been always for us the way it was that night on the Greek island? I know I'm not perfect. I was always selfish and self-centered and I had a stupid jealous temper, but I was perfect for you. Nobody could have loved you as I did, not even your wife. Nobody will ever give you what I could give you. I wish we could go back to that night in Greece and never leave it."

Paul gazed beyond her at the stars burning across the night, as if the promise of their youth were there to be reclaimed among the points of light in that untouched wilderness. But it was already past them, beyond reach in the bright brilliance of its own beginnings in the cloudy dust of unseen nebulae.

"That was another time," he replied, "in another place." He shook his head and added, "This is now."

A tear streaked down Leni's cheek as if it had fallen from her gaze like Liesl's star.

"You once asked me why I married Georg, why I stayed with him. When I came back from Greece I was pregnant with our child. That day on the beach at Molos, when you told me about yourself—you said it didn't matter if one were a half-Jew or quarter-Jew, that he was still a Jew under the Nuremberg Laws and subject to the same treatment. I married Georg to protect our child. It was the surest way to be certain that he would always be safe—as the son of an SS officer." She paused, and her tone took on the deeper sadness of memory. "Yes." She nodded softly. "It was a son. A little boy. I lost him. I lost the most precious thing we had together. The only thing. Sometimes I try to imagine what he would have looked like. I think he would have had the bluest eyes of anyone ever— like the reflections of that Greek sky on the water where he was conceived."

Paul asked thickly, "Why didn't you ever tell me?"

"Would it have made any difference? Knowing I'd lost our child? Does it make any difference now?"

"Everybody was lost. Liesl. Ernst. Alina and my father. Even my son. Everybody made a difference. They made it impossible to go back. The world can't ever go back. It's changed for all time. So are we. There's no love in me to give now. There's just hate."

"You should have left that back in the camps."

"Nobody who was ever in the camps will get out of them. The barbed wire is psychological, and the internment's for life. You go on hating your captors into eternity. Hate has eternal life. That's what I've got to offer. Is that what you want?"

"It doesn't stop me from loving you, if that's what you mean. You could try." She put her hand on his arm. "We could try, Paul. If it didn't work out, what would you have lost?"

He gazed past her once more at the starry blaze sweeping over the horizon. The tiniest moment, he thought, lay as stillborn and impassive as the silver of light-years.

"It's not too late." Leni's fingers tightened on his arm. She was pleading now for his sake, not her own.

"I think it was always too late," he said with a fatalistic contempt for that unseen force, neither human nor divine, that was the fault in the human heart. "The Paul you knew was shot dead in a ditch at Dachau. I'm not him."

"You are to me."

"That's what makes it impossible," he said, and he saw the tears brim again in her stare. It was as if tears were the last fragile retreat of hope in her. His own stare was dry. No tears would flow in the hate that burned back into the soul.

"I'd go with you to Auschwitz," she said. "I'd recite the prayer, too. You shouldn't go alone."

"I have to." He shook his head.

Pride forced a tiny smile into her mouth that struggled briefly against the sadness.

"I won't ask you if you'll come back to Berlin," she said. "But I'll wait for you. This time I'll wait. . . ."

An image came into his mind of a white beach at Molos and locks of dune grass sun-glazed above two lovers, and he thought of their dead child. Something unlocked inside, like a piece of contraband saved from the past, and he felt the first tenderness breach the anger in him.

"*We could try. . . .*" Leni murmured.

His fingers grazed her cheek, but he only half believed in the possibility.

ABOUT THE AUTHOR

MAYNARD ALLINGTON was born in Santa Cruz, California, and grew up in Redwood City. After high school he entered the air force. In 1957 he completed officer candidate school and was awarded the military honors for his class. He served two tours in Vietnam, first as operations officer with an experimental ranger-type unit and later as an adviser to the South Vietnamese on air base defense. His final field assignment was as director of security police for the U.S. Air Force Academy. He is the author of two previous novels, *The Grey Wolf* and *The Fox in the Field*, and lives on Merritt Island, Florida.